THE PITY OF IT ALL

THE PITY OF IT ALL:

Polarisation of Racial and Ethnic Relations

Leo Kuper

Duckworth

First published in 1977 by
Gerald Duckworth & Co. Ltd.
The Old Piano Factory, 43 Gloucester Crescent, London NW1

ISBN 0 7156 1114 3

Photoset by Specialised Offset Services Ltd., Liverpool
Printed by Unwin Brothers Ltd., Old Woking.

CONTENTS

Acknowledgments

I would like to thank René Lemarchand who generously made available to me basic documents relating to the massacres in Burundi, and whose own writings have been a source of inspiration to me. I would like to thank Pierre van den Berghe, Peter von Sivers and René Lemarchand for their comments on the manuscript of this book, Seamus Thompson for his help as my research assistant, the African Studies Center and the Senate Research Committee of the University of California, Los Angeles, for their support, and Hilda Kuper for her unfailing sympathy for my anguish in the writing of this study.

Leo Kuper

University of California, Los Angeles
June, 1976

INTRODUCTION

1

The Logic of an Infernal Machine

At a conference on Burundi, at which the sponsors hoped to initiate dialogue between Tutsi and Hutu, Professor René Lemarchand spoke of the internal logic in the events leading to the massacres of 1972, a certain rationality even in arbitrary action. It was a logic, he said, of an 'infernal machine', of a situation in which challenge provokes repression, terrorism, counter-terrorism, until there is no longer the possibility of compromise with the adversary.

It is this logic of the 'infernal machine', this process of polarisation of race and ethnic relations, by which members of the same society are ranged against each other in deadly enmity, that in this book I seek to analyse on a comparative basis. The state of polarisation, in its most extreme form, is indeed one in which there is no longer the possibility of understanding, of dialogue, of adjustment of interests. Evolutionary programs of reform have broken down, and there has been an elimination of the middle ground which might have offered a social basis for policies of reconciliation. Relationships across racial or ethnic divisions become tenuous, guarded, suspect, dangerous. There are no longer effective interracial or interethnic political associations. The *interlocuteurs valables*, the influential mediators, have disappeared from the scene. The society is now divided into two mutually exclusive hostile camps. There is a superimposition of cleavages and an accumulation of issues of conflict. Associated ideologies proclaim the irreconcilability of goals, the illusory nature of reforms, and the necessity and justice of violence.

Violence becomes endemic. It goes beyond the interrogations, the tortures, the isolated atrocities, the terrorism and counter-terrorism. There may have been a holocaust of violence, as in an admonitory massacre,[1] representing a point of no return in the conflict. Or the conflict may have reached the stage of the automatism of war.[2] Or the terrorism and counter-terrorism take the form of massacre and counter-massacre. Or a final solution is attempted or achieved by genocide.

The four case studies analysed here, of Algeria, Burundi, Rwanda, and Zanzibar, are all of plural societies,[3] constituted by the contact between indigenous and invading groups, and characterised by the continued salience of the original racial and ethnic divisions. They shared in common a conflict generated by the process of decolonisation, or developing as an aftermath to decolonisation. In each, a resident minority dominated the society so that two levels of decolonisation, internal and external, were involved. In each society too, the struggle took the form appreciably of racial conflict, and included genocidal massacre.

Beneath these gross similarities, however, there were marked differences in the structure of the societies and in the course of their conflicts. The somewhat fluid structure of Burundi society seemed to offer a promising basis for harmonious adjustment of ethnic and race relations. In many ways, Rwanda and Burundi, though of somewhat similar composition and history, represent polar opposites in the course taken by escalating violence and genocidal conflict, the dominant Tutsi minority being the luckless victims in one society, and the mass murderers in the

---

1. Phrase used by Sartre (1968: 39).
2. Courrière (1971: 161) gives this picture of the automatism of war. 'The warrant officer at the head of the column stopped a young girl, then a woman in her haïk, then a worker in patched jacket. Instinctively the man raised his arms: he already held his identity card in his left hand! A soldier rapidly frisked his body, then examined his papers ... Mechanical movements, automatism of the war. Arms raised, hands against the wall, the search. Your papers? All right! Carry on. The women themselves moved away the vegetables and fruits in their baskets of woven alfa to show that they hid neither arms nor grenades!'
3. For discussion of the concept of plural societies, see Kuper and Smith (1969), *Pluralism in Africa*, Ch. 14.

other. The more complex ethnic and racial structure of Zanzibar might perhaps have provided a social basis for evolutionary change, but a process of polarisation, during a largely constitutional struggle for power, was abruptly terminated by cataclysmic violence. In Algeria, a much more massive and greatly extended struggle reflected the larger scale of the society, the higher level of economic development, and the more powerful involvement of the metropolitan power. Thus, notwithstanding the selection of a single type of plural society, the diversity of social contexts offers many contrasted situations for the analysis of the processes of racial and ethnic polarisation. I think that the conflicts in these four societies are racial conflicts,[4] but I do not believe it is material whether they are described as racial or ethnic: the processes of polarisation do not seem to be significantly different for these two types of structure.

Part I introduces three case studies relevant to the process of polarisation. The first, Chapters 2 and 3, deals with the failure of attempts at reform, this being a common feature of polarising societies. The second is concerned with the problem of the 'point of no return', consequent upon events of dramatic and atrocious violence. Both these studies draw on Algerian materials. The third, based on Burundi, presents a situation of extreme polarization, in which the enemy groups are seemingly locked eternally in deadly embrace. These phenomena correspond to different levels of polarisation. Part II analyses the processes of polarisation in the four societies, with the attendant elimination of the middle ground, and the associated development of exclusive ideologies. Part III presents conclusions drawn directly from the case studies, and ends with more general reflections on problems of polarisation and genocidal massacre, and on the possibility of transforming oppressive social systems without resort to cataclysmic violence.

The study was stimulated by previous research into the relations between race, class and revolutionary change in plural societies, based on case studies of Algeria, Rwanda, South Africa

---

4. See my discussion of this point in *Race, Class and Power*, pp. 256-257.

and Zanzibar. But the structural base, whether primarily race or class, and the ideological perceptions of the structure, are part of a much broader phenomenon, the actual process of polarisation: and it is to this more inclusive problem that I now turn.

Part One

FROM REFORMISM TO GENOCIDE

2

The Failure of Reformism; or The Problem of Missed Opportunities

Episodes of cataclysmic violence are often analysed, somewhat nostalgically, from the perspective of 'missed opportunities'. *Les occasions manquées* or *les occasions perdues* is a common theme in French writing on the Algerian revolution. Ch.-André Julien devotes an entire chapter of his book *L'Afrique du nord en marche* to a discussion of the politics of lost opportunities. These are the theme too of the book *Nous algériens*, written by a former mayor of Algiers, Jacques Chevallier, in 1958, during the course of the revolution. Chevallier hoped to derive from the analysis of past opportunities missed the knowledge which would enable Algerians to take advantage of General de Gaulle's proposed reforms, which he thought might offer the last opportunity for constructive cooperation between settlers and indigenes in building a new Algeria.

The lost opportunities generally refer to reforms designed to initiate a process of evolutionary change. They imply an indeterminacy in the situation, a judgment that other possibilities of choice were available. Discussion of this problem in the literature proceeds within the context of different perspectives, and in relation to different objectives. The complexities of French constitutional law and policy and, perhaps one might add, sophistry, provided a wide range of alternatives between varied conceptions of assimilation, integration or association.

There was the goal of Algérie française, that is an Algeria fully assimilated or integrated into France, or the goal of Algeria associated with France, or federated to France, or of an Algeria endowed with various degrees of autonomy, or of a fully autonomous and fully independent Algeria: and then, quite apart from these alternatives defining the relations between the two countries, there were the perspectives and values regarding the means of political change. The present discussion of 'missed opportunities' in Algeria will be from the perspective of the possibilities of nonviolent change to equality between the indigenous peoples and the settlers. Was the revolutionary holocaust, with its death toll of hundreds of thousands of Algerians, and all the indescribable anguish and atrocity of civil war, inevitable? Or might equality and independence have been achieved by peaceful means?

'Les occasions manquées':
The Blum-Viollette project

Chevallier (1958: 62) refers to the failure of the Blum-Viollette constitutional reforms, proposed by the French Popular Front Government in 1936, as a *'magnifique occasion manquée'*.[1] These proposals for extending citizenship rights to some sections of the Muslim population are certainly the most acclaimed of the missed opportunities in the literature on the Algerian revolution.

The French had recently celebrated the centenary of their invasion of Algeria in pageantry which included a dramatic reenactment of the original landing in 1830 and a triumphal march through the streets of Algeria. Speech after speech proclaimed the glorious achievements of French colonisation, commemorated also in a monument to 'the colonising genius of France.'[2] Muslim notables, members of what Ferhat Abbas, first President of the Provisional Government of the Algerian

1. Phrase used by the Minister of the Interior during the debate on the Statute of Algeria.
2. See the account by Gordon, 1966: 18-20.

Republic, describes as the *mandarinat* (Abbas, 1962: 125), also played their part in the fanfares of adulation.

If this was an occasion for jubilation by the European settlers, there was little cause for rejoicing among the indigenous people of Algeria. Despoliation and discrimination had created vast inequalities between settlers and indigenes. Abbas (1962: 101) contrasts the two worlds of Algeria, a modern Algeria, for which the Arabs had paid by their taxes and by their sweat, and an Algeria of the illiterate masses, of the chronically undernourished, and of children in their millions without schools or bread: an Algeria of nauseating shanty-towns, of infinitely high rates of infant mortality and of tuberculosis, spreading out its monstrous tentacles in the midst of alien riches. Like leprosy, he writes, destitution to the condition of tramps (*clochardisation*) had become the general and characteristic malady of the country.

Increase in population from almost $4\frac{3}{4}$ million in 1911 to over $5\frac{1}{2}$ million in 1931 had added to the misery of an essentially rural population, driven by colonization into the more marginal areas, and discriminated against in the allocation of resources for agricultural development. A picture of overwhelming poverty among the peasants in the mountainous Kabyle area emerges from the moving series of articles contributed by Camus to *Alger republicain* in June 1939.[3]

By contrast, European agriculture had developed on the fertile coastal plains suited to commercial crops, including the highly profitable cultivation of vineyards. Murray and Wengraf (1963: 33), writing of the situation before the revolution, comment that the dichotomy between the two agrarian systems could not be fully perfected, but that there was a schematic truth in 'the conventional opposition of a "rich", export-oriented European agriculture, established in the fertile littoral plains and sub-littoral plateaux, confronting and dominating a wretchedly poor indigenous agriculture, mainly autosubsistent (60% of product in 1953-4), desperately attempting to maintain traditional extensive

---

3. See Camus' collection of essays, *Actuelles, III – Chroniques algériennes 1939-1958* (Paris: Gallimard, 1958). See also Berque, 1962: 353-356.

cereal-livestock cultivation patterns on wooded mountains and upland plateaux.' The contrast was by no means complete. A small Muslim rural elite had established itself in the European plains, and many European settlers farmed small holdings (see Aron, 1962: 230).

Inevitably, Algerian peasants were driven to seek other means of subsistence. They found employment on European farms as permanent workers, but mostly as casual agricultural labourers under wretched conditions of service.[4] They moved into the towns, as dockers, workers, servants, peddlers, and into a precarious existence of intermittent employment on the fringes of European society. At the same time, Europeans were beginning to leave the farms for the towns. There was great expansion in the tertiary sector of services, without real modification of the economic structure, a somewhat parasitic development, expressing the profound disequilibrium between a relatively prosperous European sector, and a marginal indigenous sector with many bottlenecks (Nouschi, 1962: 34).

Industrialisation might have provided employment for large numbers, but it was restrained in part by a convergence of interests between the major European growers, fearing a rise in agrarian salaries consequent on industrialisation, and French industry, apprehensive about, and actively sabotaging, the creation of possibly threatening subsidiaries in a cheap labour zone. The 'millionaires of colonial exploitation' *themselves directly intervened* in politics, as senators, deputies and counsellors in the French and, later, Algerian Assemblies to defend their interests and to act as a colonial lobby. They did not invest their huge profits in an industrialisation which would transform Algeria; they invested in politics to maintain the status quo' (Murray and Wengraf, 1963: 38, 36).

In consequence, at the time of the Blum-Viollette proposals, the industrial labour force numbered only some 90,000, of whom half were Algerians. Industries were small, often marginal and

4. See Nouschi (1962: 48-50 and generally ch. 3) for a discussion of the economic and social evolution of Algeria from 1919 to 1939.

tied to agriculture. They made no great demand for skill from the workers, whom they paid below the normal rates. Most Algerians laboured at manual work, while Europeans monopolised the supervisory and administrative posts. As a result of this discrimination, and the general racial inequality, European workers who might have provided the cadres for an efficient trade union movement, showed little interest in the plebeian Algerian work force (Nouschi, 1962: 52).

Migration overseas opened new avenues of employment. In the years immediately preceding the revolution, large numbers of Algerians worked in the industries of France. But this migration was already appreciable during the First World War, numbering some 76,000. Between the two world wars, in the period 1920 to 1938, notwithstanding a decline in the movement of workers as a result of the world economic depression in the early 1930s, the number of Algerian workers migrating to France reached the figure of 617,469, of whom 537,658 had returned to Algeria (Nouschi, 1962: 33, 50).

Education might have provided new openings, but this again was highly discriminatory. Educational policy is always a political issue, and it was partly shaped in Algeria by the political philosophies of the metropolitan government. These changed from time to time, and there were many fluctuations and conflicting tendencies in French educational policy. 'Assimilation', the official policy for many years under the Third Republic, implied the *francisation* (frenchification) of the Muslim population. It should have meant the opening up of schools on the French model and the realisation of the *mission civilatrice* by mass education in the French idiom and by insemination of French culture. But assimilation was never vigorously pursued in educational policy by the French government, and measures in this direction were also frustrated by political reactions within Algeria itself. For a time, Muslims themselves reacted with indifference or distrust toward an educational system introduced by the colonising power of a French Christian government, and subversive of their own traditional culture: and there was a great reluctance to send girls to the schools. But, above all, powerful settler interests were able to sabotage the effective extension of French education to the Muslims.

These influential settler groups were hostile to the general policy of assimilation. Or rather they desired it for themselves, though with additional powers and privileges over and above those enjoyed by the French in metropolitan France. But they were opposed to assimilation for the Muslims. They resented the demands which an extension of education would have made on the budget, over which they exercised appreciable control, and they feared the political consequences of education. They argued that French education would not civilise the indigenous peoples; it would merely create a stratum of the *déclassés*, enemies of France, ready to challenge French domination. And they were also hostile to education in Arabic and in the traditional schools, conceiving of these as undermining European influence in the colony, and as constituting foyers of fanaticism and of anti-French intrigue.[5]

Thus at the time of the centenary there was extreme inequality between Muslims and Europeans in educational opportunity. Between the years 1907 and 1928, the ratio of public expenditure for education on Europeans as compared with that on Muslims, was between 4:1 and 5:1. Given that the Muslim population was about six times the size of the European, the relative allocation of funds to Muslims hardly exceeded 4% of the European grant. In 1928, when the Muslim population was over 5 million and the European population about 850,000, some 66,475 French children as against 55,476 Muslim children attended primary school, and 6,428 French children as compared with 690 Muslim children attended secondary school (A.M., 1963: 631-632). The disparity in educational opportunity becomes even more marked at the higher levels of the educational system, and in 1930, the year of the centenary celebrations, there were 1,907 French

5. I am following closely a most excellent discussion by A.M., 'Regards sur l' enseignement des Musulmans en Algerie', published in *Confluent*, June and July 1963, pp. 596-645. See Heggoy (1975: 149-160) for a further discussion of French neglect of Arab education.

students and 93 Muslim students at the elite level of the *enseignement supérieur*.

Education in Arabic was totally inadequate for the needs of the Muslim population. The French had imposed their own language as the official language of the country, and as the language of instruction in the public schools, Arabic being relegated to the status of a foreign language. Three official *médersas*, in which instruction was given in Arabic, trained small numbers of students, primarily for positions as Muslim magistrates, religious officers and teachers. There were few primary schools in which students could learn written Arabic, and little opportunity for advanced education in Arabic and Arabic culture, comparable to that offered in Fès and Tunis.

Nevertheless, notwithstanding these formidable obstacles, a small intellectual elite had emerged, educated in Western culture or in Arabic culture. Members of this elite were in growing tension with the colonial system. French appreciation of Algerian support during the First World War, promised reforms by the government of Clemenceau in 1919, and transformation of the Arab world in the course of, and as a result of, the war, had encouraged high hopes for radical change in Algeria. But expectations that France would now vigorously pursue its *mission civilatrice*, at a time when there was an increasing demand among Muslims for French education, or that it would respond effectively to the aspirations of Algerian Muslims as a people, were frustrated in the years between the world wars. And the jubilations of the French over their hundred years of colonisation could only impose on the Muslim intellectuals the sombre accounting of their own misery (A.M., 1963: 626-628). Those oriented to Western culture in their campaign for the emancipation of their people, would be largely dependent on the French government and the Algerian administration. Their counterparts among the intellectual elite of Arab culture could fall back on traditional sources.

The systematic discrimination in the economy, in the allocation of resources, in education, was rooted in an extreme political inequality between the European settlers from France,

Spain, Italy and Malta, and the Muslim population. The former, that is to say Algerians *de souche européenne*, enjoyed the status of French citizens and exercised a quasi-monopoly of political power. As French citizens they were represented in the French Parliament. They held a greatly preponderant representation in the *Délégations Financieres*, which by 1930 exercised appreciable control over the Algerian budget: they elected three quarters of the general counsellors, and two-thirds of the municipal. In addition, numbers had entered the Algerian administration, where they occupied most of the important posts. In many respects they were the masters (Le Tourneau, 1962: 304).

By contrast, Muslims were relegated to the position of French subjects, and governed by the *code de l'indigénat*, which conferred powers of summary punishment for a whole series of offences, created by decree and specifically applicable to the *indigènes*, such as failure to report births and deaths, holding meetings without authorisation or demonstrations, and being in arrear with payment of taxes (Favrod, 1959: 46).[6] Local administration discriminated in civil rights between communes with appreciable European settlement, communes with a predominantly indigenous population, and the Saharan area under military regime.

Assimilation to France need not have implied the renunciation by Muslims of their laws and traditions. A distinction might have been drawn between the public and private domains, with differentiation readily accepted in the private domain, but this was not the conception which prevailed. Under a decree of 1865, full rights of citizenship could be granted to Muslim subjects on application, on the condition, however, that they renounced Muslim (Koranic) status for French civil status. This was hardly an avenue for an evolutionary process of political change. Muslims were reluctant to renounce their Muslim status, and government administrators were reluctant to admit them to

6. Ouzegane (1962: 215) argues that the *code de l'indigénat*, based on political, economic, cultural, religious and technological inequality resulted, under a brutal or hypocritic form, in the same racial segregation as Afrikaner apartheid.

political equality. By 1934, only some 2,500 Muslims had acquired citizenship under this decree (Julien, 1952: 31).

Somewhat similar results flowed from a law passed in 1919, in recognition of Algerian war service. This recognised the right to citizenship under specified conditions, again including renunciation of Koranic status. Nouschi (1962: 54) comments that the categories which could benefit from this law were, roughly speaking, decorated ex-servicemen, the more important landed proprietors and those who had attracted the attention of the administration by their pro-French attitudes: the law contained nothing which could challenge European political preponderance. Nevertheless, it provoked lively resistance by the settlers. The small number of Muslims acquiring citizenship under this law, only 7,817 by 1936 (Le Tourneau, 1962: 315), was hardly indicative of a great willingness by Muslims to renounce Islam for the benefits of French citizenship. More significant for political participation by Muslims was a decree enacted about the same time, which greatly increased the number of municipal electors, and enlarged the representation of the *indigènes* in local and communal assemblies and in the general councils. As a result of these reforms, there was an appreciable increase in the number of elected Muslims in the municipal councils, general councils and *délégations financières* (Le Tourneau, 1962: 303-304, 313).

The situation then at the time of the Blum-Viollette proposals was that European settlers were politically dominant in Algeria, and politically influential in France through their parliamentary representatives and their extra-parliamentary pressure groups. Muslims had no effective access to power; they were totally subordinate; but new political movements had started, based on the structural changes brought about in Algerian society as a result of colonisation.

Algerian migrant labourers in France constituted the social basis for the Etoile Nord-Africaine. Founded in 1926 among North African workers in France, it rapidly became an Algerian nationalist movement, dedicated to Algerian independence and injecting a revolutionary ideology into the political scene. It was from this movement that the men who launched the revolution in

1954 ultimately derived. Two other movements were based on the bourgeoisie, presumably for the most part the lesser bourgeoisie, of professionals, of a cultural elite in Arabic or French, and of the elected representatives in the various Algerian councils.

The *Association des Oulémas d'Algérie*, founded in 1931, drew its inspiration from traditional sources and its leaders from the Arab cultural elite. It sought to revive the purity and vigour of traditional Islam and to renew Arabic culture in Algeria. Le Tourneau (1962: 318-320) argues that though the movement disclaimed political involvement, its objectives could not but be political, the restoration of a Muslim power, and he quotes from its leader, Ben Badis, to show that in fact the goal was independence, not by violent revolution, but by means of a long process of peaceful evolution. Quandt (1969: 37) writes that the idea of Algerian independence only appeared later in its goals and that in the mid-1930s, the major political role of the Oulémas was that of articulating the themes of a distinct Algerian identity, as summarised in the slogan, 'Islam is my religion, Arabic is my language, Algeria is my fatherland.'

The second bourgeois movement, established in 1927 under the title of the *Fédération des élus indigènes d'Algérie* and reconstituted in the 1930s as Federations of Muslim Representatives, was committed to modernisation within the framework of French sovereignty. It represented the aspirations of a new bourgeoisie of Muslim educated elite, steeped in French culture, and of businessmen integrated in the modern economy, seeking political and administrative equality, but without renunciation of Koranic status.[7]

This was the general situation when the Popular Front

7. I have omitted reference to a segment of the Muslim bourgeoisie who became the willing servitors of French colonialism, the so-called *beni-oui-oui*. These included large landowners, whose interests depended on the exploitation of the peasants, and official candidates in the departmental or colonial assemblies, who responded to indications from the prefect or government commissar, charged with the duty of signalling either for applause, or with his paper-knife, the moment to raise hands in approval of motions bearing the government's stamp of approval. (See discussion by Julien, 1952: 102-105).

government of Socialists, Communists and Socialist Radicals came to power in France in May 1936. Ferhat Abbas (1962: 128) writes of the explosion of joy with which the victory of the Popular Front was received by the Algerian people: *'jamais le peuple algérien n'avait été aussi unanime dans ses espérances.'* Julien, who was politically involved in the Blum-Viollette proposals as Secretary-General of the High Mediterranean Committee attached to the Presidency of the Council of State, writes to similar effect (1952: 126) that the accession of the Popular Front to power was hailed by Muslims as the dawn of a new era.

The elected representatives, the Western educated elite, the Oulémas, the Etoile, and the communists participated in an Algerian Muslim Congress, which met in Algiers in June 1936. This Congress represents the beginning of concerted national political action. A charter of demands was formulated which included (1) the suppression of all laws of 'exception'; (2) the attachment of Algeria directly to France, without intervention of such special institutions as the Governor General, the Délégations Financières, and the *communes mixtes*; (3) maintenance of personal Muslim status; separation of the Muslim cult from the State; restitution of all religious buildings, freedom of instruction in Arabic and freedom of expression for the Arabic press; (4) compulsory education, projects for public assistance and unemployment benefits; (5) equal pay for equal work, equal rank for equal qualifications, economic aid commensurate with need and regardless of origin; creation of agricultural cooperatives and centers of education for the peasants; an end to expropriations, the distribution of vacant land; and (6) a single electoral college, universal suffrage and representation in the French Parliament (Le Tourneau, 1962: 326). This was a programme for integration of Muslim Algeria into the French system by a process of reform. It was in no way a programme for Algerian nationalism, and it was opposed by the leader of the Etoile, who stood for independence and an Algerian parliament elected by universal suffrage.

The Blum-Viollette proposals were very modest by comparison with the Congress Charter, but they introduced an important new principle, that of the separation of political rights from private status, whereby the rights of French citizenship could be fully exercised without renunciation of Muslim status. Provision was made for admission to citizenship of former officers and warrant officers, Muslims decorated for war service, holders of university diplomas, official representatives of commerce and agriculture, elected representatives, civil servants, some workers (*ouvriers titulaires de la médaille du travail*), and trade union secretaries of ten years' standing. About 20,000 Muslims (estimates vary), mostly members of the Algerian elite, would have been entitled to citizenship under this law. In addition, there would have been representation in the French Chamber of Deputies on the basis of one deputy per 20,000 electors or fraction thereof.

The proposed reforms, introducing an evolutionary process of political assimilation, seem very modest indeed. They were nevertheless received with great enthusiasm by the majority of Muslims. The Federation of Representatives, expressing the aspirations of the Western educated elite, spread the mystique of the Blum-Violette project among the masses. Looking back at the reactions a generation later during the Algerian revolution, Julien (1961: 23-24) writes that it is difficult to understand the enthusiasm for the project, and he suggests that an important factor was the contrast between an immediately preceding period of repression, permitting the worst abuses, and the sudden call to exercise the political rights of French citizenship without renunciation of Muslim status, this being a long-standing aspiration of the *évolués*.

Only the nationalists did not join in the support for the bill. Messali Hadj, leader of Etoile, denounced it as encouraging deviation from the commitment to nationalism and independence, and as a new instrument of colonialism, designed, in accordance with traditional French practice, to divide the Algerian people, by separating the elite from the masses. The Oulémas, even though the provisions of the bill were not consonant with their objectives, collaborated in supporting it, either from motives of opportunism or because they felt there were positive benefits to be derived from the Bill, and from the French connection generally.

The settlers were always hostile to political reform. The modest nature of the Blum-Viollette proposals, which opened the gates of the city of France to Muslim Algerians, but permitted only small numbers to enter, by no means allayed their furore. If there was no immediate danger to settler supremacy, there was an ultimate threat (Le Tourneau, 1962: 329ff). Settlers mobilised their forces, sending delegations to ministers, to parliamentary groups, to commissions. Their press raged against the threat to reduce them to the level of 'pariahs' by means of an 'anti-democratic' law which compromised not only the future of North Africa but also the Empire, while Muslim demands were only for bread (Julien, 1961: 26).

The Algerian administration supported the settlers in their opposition. Julien (1961: 26-27) writes that 'the permanent betrayal by colonial civil servants constitutes one of the fundamental elements in the drama of overseas (possessions). Nowhere did it take a more acute form than in Algeria. Recruited for the most part locally or rapidly converted by the milieu, the officials shared the prejudices of the settlers, and considered it a pious duty to prevent the application of measures they deemed contrary to the interests of the country ... No disinfection could ever completely cleanse of its putrescence the enormous white sepulchre of the governor-general's headquarters. The power of the Algerian French lies in their coalition against the tentative liberal initiatives of the Metropole. Administrators, officers, men of affairs, settlers, *petits blancs*, formed one bloc, uniting in solidarity the most miserable with the most fortunate.'

The opposition by settlers and administrators found considerable support among conservative elements in France. The government was preoccupied with domestic problems, it was uncertain of the strength of support it could muster for the Blum-Viollette proposals, it was unwilling to impose them by decree, and it was confronted by a strike of mayors (all European) in Algeria, which paralysed the administration. As a

result, the project was not submitted to the French parliament
during 1937, and it was eventually dismissed by the Senate in
September 1938.

Thus ended the parliamentary career of the Blum-Viollette
Bill, but its consequences extended far into the future. For the
settlers, their defeat of the bill and their triumph over a Popular
Front government, renewed a precedent for political pressure,
and they would use Algiers repeatedly in the future as a
launching pad against metropolitan initiatives for reform, and
indeed against the metropolitan government itself. As for the
Muslims, the high expectations of radical change raised by the
accession to power of the Popular Front Government, and the
Blum-Viollette   proposals   were   totally   frustrated.   The
effectiveness of settler resistance to even the most timid
metropolitan reforms 'was a political education in itself, a crucial
demystification for Algerian politicians who henceforth would
find it less and less possible to 'recourir a la France liberale' ...
The disclosure of the power realities, the weakness of the
metropolitan government when confronted by an alliance of the
largely self-governing colonate with the French right in defence
of colonial capitalism, inevitably led towards a radicalisation of
demands.   Disillusion   and   bitterness   was   extreme   among
francophile Algerian politicians, though not all of them
immediately turned to the outright nationalism of Messali ... the
logic was irresistible, as Viollette had foreseen in 1935: 'Take
care, the natives of Algeria, and through your own fault, still
have no country; they are looking for one. They ask us to let
them enter the French nation. Let them do so swiftly, for
otherwise they will create their own' (Murray and Wengraf,
1963: 49).

The nationalist movement, Etoile, suppressed by Government
decree, but reconstituted as a political party, now began to gain
ground among the workers of the Algerian cities. The Oulémas
returned to their own initiatives: they rejected collaboration in
the different assemblies until equality should be achieved, and
they intensified their efforts to advance Arabic Islamic culture,
thereby guarding against any attempt to undermine Muslim

status and promote assimilation (Aron, 1962: 76). The *évolués*, the elected representatives, were the most deeply affected. Out of their disarray emerged two movements; one, somewhat in the idiom of the Muslim Congress, and quite ephemeral; the other a political party, *L'Union Populaire Algérienne pour la Conquête des Droits de l'Homme et du Citoyen*, founded by Ferhat Abbas. This was a call for mass action, the failure to fulfil promises necessitating reliance on their own resources for emancipation from colonial imperialism. Policy was directed to political equality and freedom, to advancement of Arabic, to religious freedom and racial equality. There was rejection of assimilation, but not of integration with France.

This then was the lost opportunity of the Blum-Viollette reforms. Julien (1952: 36, 138) writes that the success of the project would have changed the course of North African history. As it was, the settlers had closed the road to the gradual integration of the natives into French citizenship, thereby promoting a nationalism which would rise up against them. Nouschi (1962: 96) comments that an opportunity, possibly the last opportunity, had been squandered. Aron (1962: 74) concludes that the best chance for France to initiate progressive evolution had vanished. Le Tourneau (1962: 331-332), on the other hand, questions whether the rejection of the bill really constituted a critical turning point in the evolution of Muslim opinion. He argues that there is no evidence to establish that the passing of the bill would have changed the course of events entirely, and he shows by quotation from Abbas, for example, that there was bitterness and disillusion, though not yet despair, but rather indication of a confidence ready to reemerge.

The Statute of Algeria, 1947

The second major '*occasion manquée*' was that constituted by the 1947 Statute of Algeria. The war years had intervened, with their humiliation of France by defeat and the destruction of the French fleet at Mers el-Kebir in 1940, and by the Anglo-American landings in Algeria in November 1942. This was a period during which Algerian Europeans had demonstrated enthusiasm for fascism in their political movements, in their press, in their collaboration with the Vichy government, and in their response to the persecution of Jews. Particularly significant in this latter connection was the abrogation of the Crémieux decree of 1870, which had accorded full French citizenship to the Jewish population of Algeria. A citizenship exercised for 70 years could thus be revoked suddenly by the whim of the very authority from which it derived, indicating to Ferhat Abbas (1962: 138-139) that the word of France, even when guaranteed by law, signified nothing, and that the controversy over renunciation of Muslim status as the prerequisite for citizenship was simply pretext. Abbas comments specially on the explosion of joy with which the French of Algeria greeted this unjust measure.

The Nationalist movement, the *Parti du Peuple Algérien*, had been suppressed shortly after the outbreak of war; the Oulémas, having withheld their support in a conflict which they felt did not concern them, were under surveillance: but the *évolués* had given full support. Le Tourneau (1962: 335) writes that they displayed a perfect loyalty, that no serious incident marred the mobilisation in Algeria, and that witnesses to the sombre period of the French defeat were all agreed that most Algerians seemed overwhelmed by, and refrained from exploiting, the calamity which had overtaken the French.[8] But the political mood changed rapidly under the negative impact of an increasing loss of confidence in France, of disillusionment with the Vichy government, of the spectacle of leading settlers fêting the armistice commission of German and Italian officers, and other such demonstrations of joy in fascism. More positively, the upheavals of the world war, the propaganda directed to the elites of Africa and Asia, the Atlantic Charter, and the Anglo-

8. Chevallier (1958: 33) writes to somewhat similar effect that 'in 1940, we were conquered, and everyone knows that in Islam territory to be conquered is to lose face. Without troops, without means, without possibility of rescue, worked on by enemy agents, the situation was ripe for liquidating us. But those who lived in Algeria during that period had never experienced from the Muslims more friendship and more sincere expression of solidarity in the misfortune of the fatherland.'

American landings in Algeria, raised high hopes for self-determination, stimulating more radical demands.

The profound change in political perspectives from the period of the abortive Blum-Viollette proposals is clearly documented in the *Manifesto of the Algerian People* drafted by Ferhat Abbas, and signed by some fifty Algerian leaders, representing a broad range of political participation. This was in February 1943, at a time when a call for the mobilisation of twelve Algerian divisions had provided Algerian leaders with an opportunity to press their demands. The Manifesto emphasised the assurance given by President Roosevelt in the name of the Allies, that in the organisation of the new world, the rights of all peoples, small and great, would be respected. It called for the condemnation and abolition of colonisation, for the application of the principle that all peoples should have the right to dispose of themselves, for an Algerian constitution, guaranteeing *inter alia*, the liberty and equality of all its inhabitants, without distinction of race or religion, and for immediate and effective participation in government. The supplement to the Manifesto, passed a few months later, urged the 'recognition of the political autonomy of Algeria as a sovereign nation, with a right of surveillance for France, and military assistance from the Allies in case of conflict' (Murray and Wengraf, 1963: 51). It sought the establishment at the end of the war of an Algerian state, which should be endowed with its own constitution, framed by an Algerian constituent assembly, elected by all its inhabitants on the basis of universal suffrage. The Manifesto thus provided a platform for a broad alignment of political forces, committed to Algerian nationalism. A nationalist front had now become possible. In a brief period of time, there had been a sharp movement away from the politics of assimilation and integration toward the goal of national independence.

The response of the French government was given in an Ordinance of March 1944. This affirmed the principle of equality between Muslim and non-Muslim French, it abolished the laws of exception (excluding, however, certain areas), it opened all civil and military positions to Muslims, it accorded immediate rights of French citizenship to specified elite categories, in all some 50,000 to 60,000, without requiring renunciation of Muslim status, it offered citizenship to the remainder of the Muslim population under conditions to be established by the forthcoming Constituent Assembly, but conferred on them immediately the right to vote for the local assemblies, where the Muslim proportion of representatives was increased to two-fifths.

In some ways, the Ordinance embodied important new principles. There had been frequent demands for the abolition of discriminatory measures, and these measures were now suppressed; the Blum-Viollette project had innovated in detaching citizenship from personal religious status, and its provisions were taken up again, with an increase in the numbers accorded the rights of French citizens, while the entry of all other Muslims into the city of France was envisaged within a short period of time. But only the moderates applauded. Ferhat Abbas, the Oulémas, the clandestine nationalist PPA, rejected the ordinance as an assimilationist measure entirely contrary to the principles of the Manifesto (see Le Tourneau, 1962: 345-346). Ferhat Abbas (1962: 149-150) commented on the revival of the Blum-Viollette project, that the reform was *dépassé*, and that it was categorically condemned by the people, rallying only those frightened representatives who were anxious above all to please the authorities so as to conserve their *mandarinat*.[9] His response was to establish the broadly based nationalist movement, the *Association des Amis du Manifeste* (later the *Association des Amis du Manifeste et de la Liberté*), propagating *inter alia*, the idea of an Algerian nation, and the desirability of an autonomous Algerian Republic federated to a renewed, anti-colonial, anti-imperialist French republic. In Le Tourneau's view, an ordinance which would have been acclaimed in 1939, and perhaps even in 1942, as heralding a new era, was received in 1944 as a derisory response to the aspirations of the Algerian people.

9. In assessing the response to the Ordinance, Le Tourneau (1962: 345) writes that the mass of the people remained indifferent. Nouschi (1962: 139) remarks that socialists and communists approved the measure.

The years which intervened between the ordinance and the Statute of Algeria were a time of troubles, of inflation, of food shortages, of famine. Above all there was the terrible repression which followed the riots at Sétif and Guelma, encouraging settler groups, somewhat muted for a time by their collaboration with fascism during the war, to raise their voices again in opposition to reform. But this did not deter the government from introducing reforms, relating to services for modernisation of traditional agriculture, Muslim participation in municipal administration, a programme for schooling, and plans for industrialisation (Le Tourneau, 1962: 355-356). At the level of political rights, an electoral law of August 1945, granted adult male non-citizen Muslims, constituted as a second college, the right to elect to the French parliament, the same number of representatives as the citizens of the first college. This reform, like the Ordinance in March 1944, appeared quite derisory to Ferhat Abbas. 'For an Algeria, deeply wounded, in which thousands of its people had perished, this reform was a drop of water in an ocean of bitterness and suffering' (1962: 159).

Unless one accepted the view Messali Hadj had expressed to Ferhat Abbas, at the time of the Manifesto movement, that France would give nothing, that it would yield only to force and that it would grant only what had been seized (Abbas, 1962: 151), it would have been reasonable for Algerians to anticipate radical change under the Statute of Algeria. This was all the more the case since France had experienced a foreign occupation, a resistance movement, and a national war of liberation.[10] But in fact, the Statute of Algeria was a compromise; and though it did introduce important innovations, these were quite remote from the demands of the main Algerian Muslim parties. None of the Muslim proposals was assimilationist: all envisaged the formation of an Algerian state (Le Tourneau, 1962: 361-362). The new

10. Ferhat Abbas writes (1962: 151) that he personally had confidence. 'A France, rising out of the Resistance, could not abandon us. In the eyes of many of my friends, it was inconceivable that the French, having experienced Hitlerian domination over four long years, would not recognise our legitimate aspirations. The occupation had prepared France to receive new ideas.'

party established by Ferhat Abbas, the *Union démocratique du Manifeste algérien*, in succession to the party dissolved by the Government, proposed an autonomous Algerian republic, in association with France, within the framework of the French Union. Messali's new party, the *Mouvement pour le triomphe des libertés démocratiques*, took the position that the French National Assembly had no right to frame a Statute of Algeria, but that this should be a matter for discussion between the delegates of a Constituent Algerian Assembly and representatives of the French Government. By contrast, the Statute maintained the institution of Governor-General, 'the colonial citadel, the Algerian Bastille'.[11]

On the one hand, the Statute defined Algeria as a group of departments endowed with civil personality, with financial autonomy, and with a distinctive organisation. It established an Algerian Assembly with competence to vote on the budget; and it envisaged special dispositions for the Muslim cult and for associating Muslims more closely in the administration of the country. The Statute thus accorded an independent juridical existence to Algeria and recognised its particularity. On the other hand, the Statute maintained 'Algeria within the French republic, by proclaiming the equality of rights and duties of the citizens, save as regards Muslim civil status, by continuing the institution of Government General, and by placing the decisions of the Algerian Assembly under the close control of the French Government' (Le Tourneau, 1962: 364). Moreover, the powers conferred on the Algerian Assembly were very limited, excluding military organisation and recruitment, the electoral system, the status of local assemblies, administrative organisation, judicial organisation and procedure, the determination of crimes, delicts and their punishment, the system of landed and immovable property, customs, amnesty, litigable administrative questions, and provisions in regard to French nationality (Nouschi, 1962: 151).

Again, on the one hand, the Statute confirmed the enjoyment

11. Phrase used by Abbas (1962: 159).

of citizenship rights by Muslims under a law of May 1946, and proclaimed the effective equality of all citizens. On the other hand, citizens were classified into two colleges, each returning 60 representatives to the Algerian Assembly, the first college consisting of citizens of French civil status as well as certain categories of French citizens retaining their personal Muslim status,[12] and the second college consisting of citizens of local status. Numerically, the first college would have 532,217 electors, 63,194 being Muslims of personal status, and a very small number Muslims of French civil status, while the second college would comprise 1,301,072 Muslim electors (Aron, 1962: 269). Clearly the system was heavily weighted in favour of the settlers, contrary to the declared principle of equality. Moreover, the decisions of the Algerian Assembly could be made conditional on a two-thirds majority vote upon the demand of the Governor General, the Commission of Finances or one quarter of the members of the Assembly. Finally, the Statute made provision for important changes in local government (suppression of the mixed communes, transformation of the administrative regime of the Saharan territories into departments), for the enfranchisement of Muslim women, for the separation of Mosque and State, and the promotion of Arabic. But the implementation of these provisions was left to the initiative of the Algerian Assembly.

Ferhat Abbas (1962: 178-179) protests that the Statute was never deliberated by the Algerian people, but only by the French, and that it was the result of a compromise between the Metropole and the Algerian French, between the 'legal' power

12. See the discussion by Jacques Lambert, *Manuel de législation algérienne*, p. 213ff. In the debate on the Statute, one of the controversies clashed round the issue of the homogeneity of the colleges, since the first college would include a small proportion of citizens of local status and thus affect the principle of parity between the colleges, i.e., between the two communities. A second problem was the fear that the first college might be swamped by Muslims, if open to further entrants as originally proposed, for example holders of certificates of primary studies, not already enrolled in the first college. An interesting aspect of the debate was the distinction between sociological identity and racial identity, in the argument that the issue was the inclusion of Muslims retaining their personal status, and not the inclusion of Muslims of French civil status. The distinction is clearly framed in terms of a political philosophy of assimilation.

still held by Parliament and the *de facto* power exercised by the
ultras in Algiers. Yet despite its compromises and its extreme
caution, the Statute did provide a basis for cooperation in
government between Muslims and Europeans and it did establish
institutions for evolutionary change. Moreover, though severely
criticised by both French and Muslims, no party decided to
boycott the elections; all the political formations contested seats
in the Algerian Assembly, proof that they saw possibilities in the
provisions of the Statute (Le Tourneau, 1962: 367). But these
possibilities were never realised. Systematic electoral fraud
eliminated the nationalist candidates and secured the election of
the administration's nominees. The phrase '*elections a l'algérienne*
became part of the universal political vocabulary of our times'
(Murray and Wengraf, 1963: 58). Soustelle, Governor-General
of Algeria in 1955, reported to his government, that the 'pseudo-
elected, now currently designated by the term the prefabricated,
installed in their seats by means of electoral fraud, mostly
illiterate and frequently dishonest, represent no one, they enjoy
no influence in their constituencies, and they do not even render
any service to the administration which has made them' (Abbas,
1962: 186). The changes outlined in the Statute, but left to the
initiative of the Assembly, remained a dead letter. By 1954 only
one had even reached the stage of committee discussion. 'The
others remained as testimony to the impotence of the Fourth
Republic to enforce its fundamental constitutional principles
against the will of the Algerian colonate' (Murray and Wengraf,
1963: 57). The *maquis de la procédure*, as Abbas wrote in another
connection (1962: 109), had robbed the Statute of Algeria of its
promise. It was as if settlers and administration had entered into
collusion to make a mockery of the possibility of evolutionary
change.

The miracle of May 1958

These then, the Blum-Viollette Bill and the Statute of Algeria,
are the main missed opportunities discussed in the literature, but
brief mention might also be made of the legislative elections in

Algeria, in November 1958. Chevallier (1958: 184) describes these as the last chance. They were part of a sequence of events, which included demonstrations by European settlers against the French government on 13 May in Algiers, the occupation of the headquarters of the Government-General, the assumption of power in Algiers by the army, the collapse of the Fourth Republic, the accession of General de Gaulle to the Presidency, and the new policies announced by him. It was a sequence of events in which the settlers, in association with military forces sharing their aspirations for an integrated Algeria, had played an important role in bringing about the downfall of the metropolitan government.

Chevallier (1958: 158) stresses the so-called miracle of spontaneous fraternisation on 16 May, when the European masses of Algeria reached out their hands to the Muslim masses converging on the Forum of Algiers, a fraternisation which swept aside the miasmas of the Algerian rebellion, rendered empty all the prejudices, banished the rancours, and made acceptable policies previously repugnant. Some of the other pronouncements on the fraternisation read even more strangely today, as for example, the call by General Salan for the revolutionary forces to surrender their arms: 'Unity has been achieved. 150,000 Frenchmen, Muslims and Christians, proclaimed it on 16 May in Algiers. Everywhere, the French, both Muslim and Christian, proclaim it in the towns and villages.' Or Jacques Soustelle's announcement from Radio-Algérie to the Metropolitan French: 'Ten million human beings, from the Mediterranean to the Sahara, have finally taken the historic resolution to be forever French, full members of a free community, effacing at one stroke, all the manoeuvres and hatreds of the past' (Chevallier, 1958: 161).

For some analysts, 16 May was no miracle of spontaneous fraternisation, but a masquerade. Courrière (1970: 346) states quite positively that the Muslim processions were entirely organised by the army, that they carried banners and shouted slogans devised by the army. Le Tourneau (1962: 428), on the contrary, takes the view that most of the Muslim participants had come of their own volition. Both agree however that there were extraordinary demonstrations of fraternisation. Courrière writes movingly of the spontaneous reaction to a call from the Forum: '*Voici nos frères musulmans … Faites une place à nos frères musulmans.*' He writes (1970: 346-347) of European hands extended, of chests embracing, of arms which protect and clasp. It is not possible, yet it happens. The crowd on the Forum, the crowd committed to a policy of NO to all reform, the crowd of the race pogrom, embraces heartily the crowd from the Casbah, the crowd of the terrorists, the crowd of the FLN, those who had planted bombs. Everything is forgotten, swept aside under a sky uniformly blue, in an immense merging, spontaneous and affectionate. A versatile crowd, a marvellous crowd. Capable of the worst and of the best. It all appears so impossible, so inconceivable, these hands extended, seized, gripped. These skins of 'French' and of 'ratons', that seek and find each other. There is weeping, laughter, crying. Is it possible to have no more fear, no terror for the FLN grenade, no trembling at the passage of paratroops? Is it finally the end of the nightmare? On the Forum, 16 May 1958, forty thousand Europeans and thirty thousand Muslims believe it all the more firmly because it seems impossible. There is no time to think, to reflect. Above all, one does not wish to think or reflect. One believes. One believes as at Lourdes or at Mecca. It is joyous exhilaration. It is peace found again. It is the grand parade of reconciliation.

There appears to have been a genuine fraternisation, whatever the role of the army in organising the Muslim processions. The demonstration certainly raised hopes of reconciliation, and this was strongly encouraged by the new policies of General de Gaulle. Almost immediately after his investiture as President on 1 June 1958, de Gaulle left for Algiers, where he made the following declaration:

From today and forever after, France considers that in all Algeria, there is only one category of inhabitants, that there are only full Frenchmen, with the same rights and the same duties. This means that there must be opened to many, the possibilities still closed to them. It means that the opportunity for a livelihood must be given to those who do not have it. It means that there must be recognition of the dignity of those to whom it has been denied. It means that a fatherland must be given to those who may have believed that they did not have one ... Frenchmen to the core, voting in the same single college – this we will prove within three months, on the solemn occasion when all the French, including the ten million French of Algeria, will have to decide their own destiny. For these ten million, their suffrage will have the same weight as the suffrage of all others. They will have to single out, to elect, *I will repeat in a single college*,[13] their representatives for public office, as will all other Frenchmen. With these elected representatives we will see how to accomplish the rest (Le Tourneau, 1962: 429-430).

He was received with delirious enthusiasm by a mixed crowd of Muslims and Europeans at the Forum. The settlers were now ready to accept reforms they had consistently and passionately rejected in the past.

In addition to these general constitutional principles for the government of the new Algeria, General de Gaulle announced, in October, a five-year plan for the social and economic evolution of Algeria. Its objectives included the creation of 400,000 new jobs; the recruitment of Muslims for employment in the public service up to a proportion which could reach 10% of the posts to be provided; equality of salary and conditions of employment with the Metropole; distribution of 250,000 hectares of arable land to Muslim peasants; the provision of schooling for two-thirds of the children of school-going age, and the building of 200,000 new lodgings (Le Tourneau, 1962: 432).

Events, however, did not follow the hoped-for pattern of reconciliation and reconstruction.[14] The Europeans of Algeria were largely committed to a policy, no longer of assimilation, but of integration – an integration of Algeria into France, an Algérie française. The revolutionary movement, on the contrary, sought national independence. It immediately reacted to General de Gaulle's declaration in June, as constituting a continuation of traditional French colonial policy, in no way responsive to the

13. My emphasis – but it appears to be General de Gaulle's.
14. I am relying on Le Tourneau's account (1962: 430ff).

struggle of the Algerian people for liberty and independence. The FLN (Front de Libération Nationale) exercised pressure to prevent candidates presenting themselves for election, while European candidates sought out fellow candidates among the Muslims, with the result that almost all the deputies sent to the National Assembly were partisans of the policy of integration. This had the effect of frustrating hopes of meaningful dialogue between the contending sections in a parliamentary setting. The Government vigorously implemented educational and housing programmes, and took effective measures to recruit Muslims into public employment. But the agrarian and industrial programmes were less successful. Private industry hesitated to make substantial investment in a situation of political insecurity; the FLN threatened peasants who accepted the land offered by the French administration; there were also few applicants for these lands. The reforms did not arrest the war, which continued its deadly course, ending in holocausts of mutual terrorism and atrocity.

3

Missed Opportunities and Revolutionary Violence

The frustration of expectations by constitutional reforms proposed, but not enacted, as in the case of the Blum-Viollette project, and by laws passed but sabotaged, as for example the Statute of Algeria, and more generally by the failure to respond to reasonable demands for reform, provided fuel for revolutionary challenge. The career of Ferhat Abbas is particularly illuminating on the relationship between missed opportunities and revolutionary violence, not only because he was one of the main leaders over the long struggle for political rights and independence, becoming the first President of the Algerian Provisional Government, but above all because he was the very embodiment of missed opportunities. Courrière (1968: 47) describes him as *'l'exemple parfait, le plus représentatif des occasions manquées en Algérie'*. Lacouture (1961: 266) writes of his having become the advocate of a bloody revolution, but only after a quarter century of struggle, dedicated to reformism and non-violence. In tracing the movement of Abbas' ideas from assimilation to independence, and from progressive non-violent evolutionary change to revolutionary violence, I shall follow appreciably his own autobiographical account, no doubt rationalised, as he gives it retrospectively in *La Nuit coloniale*, published in Paris in 1962.

The problem of missed opportunities is linked with the political philosophy of 'revolution by law' as Abbas describes it (p. 177). For Abbas, it was a philosophy equally applicable to the most varied goals, whether of assimilation, integration, association, federation or independence. It rested on a commitment to evolutionary change by constitutional means. Initially, Abbas thought very much along the lines of education as the qualification for citizenship. He writes (110) that his generation believed that the discipline of the intelligence ought to be the antechamber of liberty. His early campaigning was for equal rights. He argues (130) that the right to education, employment and work, the defence of Arabic culture, the fight against discrimination, could assist the people in their struggle, until they are in a position to choose their own destiny. 'Political activity is not only and necessarily the conquest of power. It is also the struggle for amelioration and regulation of human relations, for civic education of the masses and for promotion of social justice.'

In a celebrated passage in the journal *L'Entente*, in February 1936, Abbas had written that if he had been able to discover the existence of an Algerian nation, he would have been a nationalist. He was severely criticised by Muslim spokesmen for this denial of an Algerian fatherland, and later by the colonialist press, for the contradictions in his political commitments. In *La Nuit coloniale* he seems to be offering a defence of his political position at the time of his pronouncement on nationalism. 'The restoration of the Algerian state', he writes (130-131) 'could result as easily from an equality of rights between colonisers and colonised as from a denial of that equality.' And he adds that without doubt, the politics of equal rights and the social promotion of the masses, would not have arrested the process leading to Algerian independence. *'But the politics of equality would have had the advantage of drawing together all the inhabitants, of whatever origin, of interweaving their interests, of making them live in symbiosis. This could not have failed to create a community of interests, to weaken racism, and to speed up by peaceful means, the advent of a fraternal Algerian Republic.*'[1]

Consonant with these objectives, Abbas pursued a policy of

---

1. Ferhat Abbas' italics.

conciliation over many years. Muslim espousal of an autonomous Algerian republic could hardly commend itself to the great majority of European settlers, but in the charter of the *Association des Amis du Manifeste et de la Liberté,* the programme of action, phrased in a conciliatory way as embracing all groups, was directed, *inter alia,* to creating solidarity, equality and community among the entire population of Algeria, Jews, Christians and Muslims alike (150). One of the essential tasks of the movement, he explained, was to convince the settlers of the solidarity of their interests with those of the Muslim population (153).

On 8 May 1945, the day of the disturbances at Sétif in the Constantinois, Ferhat Abbas was arrested, though he had no knowledge of the events, and was in no way involved. Released after a year of interment, he formed a new party, since the Association of the Friends of the Manifesto had been dissolved as part of the repression which followed the events in the Constantinois. The new party, the *Union Démocratique du Manifeste Algérien,* submitted to the French Constituent Assembly a proposed constitution for Algeria, calling for recognition of Algerian autonomy in the form of an Algerian Republic, with the status of an associated member state of the French Union. Abbas (166) draws attention to the nature of the proposals, which re-affirm and make concrete the national aspirations of the Algerian people, but on a conciliatory basis, without any suggestion of xenophobia. A more obvious indication of the desire to conciliate is to be found in the acceptance of the procedure of the double college, which he saw as conflicting with any conception of an 'absolute democracy, which would imply a single electoral college, and the full application of the law of numbers, without distinction between categories of citizens' (176). This, and the acceptance of parity of representation, he justifies as an interim measure which would safeguard European interests, while leading the indigenes toward the full exercise of a civic franchise. Moreover, notwithstanding his opposition to the Statute of Algeria, he pressed on successive governor generals the demand that there should be, at the very least, a loyal application of its provisions (Lacouture, 1961: 305).

Given the desire to conciliate, it was to be expected that Abbas would reject the use of violence. He writes of his hatred of violence (109), and of his continuous and unsparing efforts, during the crucial period of 1943-1954, to offer counsel to the French, to warn them against the dangers of the course they were pursuing, to preach moderation to Muslim compatriots, to achieve peacefully and legally a revolution, which would guarantee the dignity, security and liberty of all Algerians, and which would both unite and liberate (144). In August 1954, barely two months before the Revolution, Abbas interviewed the French Minister of the Interior, President Mendès-France, various leaders, and the representatives of the communist and socialist parties, alerting them to the explosive situation in Algeria and to the need to respond to the legitimate aspirations of the Algerian people (188-189). And even in the press interview he gave in April 1956, when he joined the FLN leaders in Cairo, he showed concern for a peaceful solution (Lacouture, 1961: 316).

These commitments were maintained over a long period in which Abbas' political position became increasingly radical. His ideology in the period before the Second World War is usually described as 'assimilationist'. Julien (1952: 276) uses the term 'vigorously assimilationist'. There is much evidence for this view. A collection of his early writings, brought together under the title *Le Jeune Algérien* in 1930 bears the subtitle '*de la colonie vers la province*'. The opening article defends the right of Algerians to die for France. '… the *indigène* is called because he is French, and as such, must pay his dues in blood. I serve under the flag because I am French and for no other reason. The *indigène* is in the Ruhr as a Frenchman, he is in the Levant as a Frenchman, he is in Morocco as a Frenchman. Whether the people of *l'Afrique latine* wish it or not, we are Muslims and we are French. We are *Indigènes* and we are French' (24). At the time of the Blum-Viollette proposals, Ferhat Abbas, speaking in the name of the *Fédération des élus indigènes*, affirmed that the only course for the country was assimilation, fusion of the *indigène* into French society. Julien (1952: 124-125) adds that Abbas even went so far as to admit that, if necessary, the *évolués* would bow to the law, accepting citizenship with renunciation of Muslim status. At the outbreak of the Second World War he enlisted in the French army, calling on his friends to devote themselves entirely to the salvation of a nation on which their future depended. 'If a democratic France should cease to be powerful, our ideal of liberty would be buried for all time' (Lacouture, 1961: 277).

Yet there was nothing weakly conformist in his commitment to assimilation. He was vigorous in denunciation of colonialism, its defeat being a necessary basis for understanding between French and Muslims (Julien, 1952: 110). He refused to write an article for the celebration of the centenary. 'The century which has passed was a century of tears and of blood; it is particularly our people, we, the *indigènes*, who have shed their tears and spilt their blood. The Europeans in this country will refuse to hold out their hands as long as we remain in a precarious situation materially, and in ignorance, and in tatters. It is human nature to fraternise with a neighbour, only to the extent that the latter commands respect' (Lacouture, 1961: 270-271). And he was strongly committed to Muslim civilisation.[2] Lacouture (303) describes the ambivalence between the two loyalties, the Algerian and the French – in sentiment and passion Algerian, in reason and political commitment French, his espousal of federalism in 1946 representing a compromise between anger and necessity. It was toward the Algerian side of the ambivalence that the pressure of events moved Abbas from what Lacouture (278) describes as provincialist assimilation, through integration broadly conceived, to federalism, nationalism, and finally support of armed insurrection.

The picture of Abbas which emerges is that of a dedicated leader, totally opposed to racism and discrimination, courageously seeking to lay the foundations for reconciliation and harmonious relations. It is a picture of a leader deeply

2. One of the principles put forward in *Le Jeune Algérien* was the absolute respect for Islam, for Arabic and for Muslim civilisation. In *La Nuit coloniale* (1962: 121) Abbas writes: 'Islam is at home in Algeria. Fourteen centuries in this territory have established its rights. To combat it, is time wasted. It will survive all efforts at demolition.'

committed to the use of non-violent means in the struggle against colonialism and in the campaign for equal rights, rejecting force, but rejecting also base submission. It is a picture of a man who remains remarkably steadfast over many years of the frustration of his most reasonable and moderate aspirations. I have only dealt with some of the major frustrations of his career – more particularly the shattering of the hopes raised by the Blum-Viollette proposals, and the compromised response of the Statute of Algeria to the promises of the war years. But Abbas' autobiographical account overflows with episodes of humiliation, repression, chicanery, corruption, venality, and with anguish over the contempt and injustice repeatedly visited on his people. It is this history which drove him inexorably to the conviction that it was impossible to seek conciliation with colonialism and colonialists, or to achieve decolonisation by evolutionary means.

This view he crystalises in the title '*L'impossible "revolution" par la loi ou l'experience de ma génération*', which he gives to the chapter in *La Nuit coloniale* describing his political experiences as a progressive reformer. He writes (190) that his generation had fought for decades against hatred and sordid conservatism. With the law in their hands, and with all the altruism of youth, they had awakened the masses. They had spoken to them in simple terms, training them to resist arbitrary rule and arming them for the civic defense of their interests and their liberty. They had made it a rule to avoid violence and to spare the masses the blood-bath the colonialists had always promised them. Lenin had written somewhere that it is true that what had been established by force could only be destroyed by force, but that when propaganda profoundly penetrates the masses, it also constitutes a force. Why then, Abbas asks, had their campaigns of persuasion, explanation, and indoctrination arrived at an impasse? What had gone wrong? And he finds the answer in the nature of colonialism and colonialists (191ff).

For five centuries the colonies had been part of the normal life of the metropolitan powers. Consciously or unconsciously, the French themselves had become colonialists. The colonial virus had attacked the entire society. Even the left and the liberals were not truly anti-colonialist but paternalist, at best. For years, he had tried to win over to constructive political action leading French politicians, men his generation regarded as heirs to the French Revolution, but all to no avail. As to the French working class, the liberation of the colonies was quite a secondary matter. His generation had linked together, in solidarity, the struggle of the colonised peoples with the struggle for the emancipation of the European proletariat. But the French working class having conquered such rights as Social Security benefits, family allowances, now aspired to other conquests (the motor car, the refrigerator, the television, the washing machine). They had not raised up barricades, nor even staged a strike of solidarity, in protest against arbitrary rule in the colonies, the violation of law, racism and torture.

The most passionate denunciation, however, Abbas reserved for the European settlers, more particularly their leaders, the great landowners who controlled the budget. These were the men who had exercised power over the entire country, who had made and unmade governors, dislodged high civil servants, distributed prebends, named and supervised the cadres of indigenous functionaries, organised and developed the economy of Algeria, exploited a people subjected to racial laws, amassed scandalous fortunes and sabotaged French laws they judged contrary to their interests (197). These were the masters of Algeria, men correctly described as having only a digestive tube. It might be possible by extreme measures to cure a cancerous person of his cancer: one would never cure those colonialists of their colonialism (193).

The heart of the matter then, is that the establishment of normal relations between Europeans and non-Europeans, between French and Algerians, presupposes the end of the colonial regime. But the colonial regime is brother to the fascist regime, and these regimes can only persist through lies and violence. It is a waste of time to try to humanise them: the 'human' is alien to them (195).

Abbas continues that experience had shown the futility of negotiation, and of honest and sincere compromise, with such regimes. His generation had sought revolution through the law. This was a conception quite foreign to the way of thinking of those with whom they negotiated. Abbas quotes (225), with approval for its prophetic truth, a comment published in 1930.

Like all the oppressed, the indigenous Algerian cannot expect his salvation by evolution of the law. It is possible that under growing pressure, the French Parliament might accord over a long period some new rights, drop by drop. The French bourgeois does not directly exploit the *indigène*: he does not rejoice day by day in the pleasure of being the master, in the sensation of belonging to a superior caste ... But the Algerian (i.e. the French of Algeria) is there. For him, domination over the *indigène*, and the exploitation of the *indigène*, confer both pleasure and profit. He does not intend to be deprived of them. One may vote what one wishes in the French Parliament: one does not apply it in Algiers. A law is nothing in itself: everything depends on its application. Now it is not in Paris that the law will be applied, but in Algeria, by the Algerians ...'

Legal channels were barred; and quite obviously the problem of the colonial regime is not to be posed in juridical terms. When the imperialists do not even respect their own laws, which they themselves have elaborated to protect their profits, it was futile for the colonised, on their side, to establish themselves as a progressive party, respecting the laws (189-190). The experience of the years 1943-54 had finally persuaded even the most moderate Algerians that there was nothing more to be expected from the law (229). The only solution was violence. They had no more faith in the possibility of a peaceful solution. At the moment when 'the bomb' exploded on 1 November 1954, the divorce between their people and French law was consummated (227). The colonial regime is born of violence and arbitrary rule, and it relies on violence and arbitrary rule for its maintenance. It is in the nature of the colonial regime, that it will only yield to violence (190).

Given the flow of events, and the failure of reformism, it was almost inevitable that there should have been the resort to violence. The cynical manipulation of the Statute of Algeria seems to have been a particularly significant factor in the movement toward revolution. Nouschi (1962: 159-160) writes that at the congress of the nationalist party (*Mouvement pour le Triomphe des Libertés Démocratiques*), held in 1948, a plan for military action was presented by a small group, which included Ben Bella, the first president of independent Algeria, and Mohammed Khider, Minister of State in the Third Provisional Government; the recent elections had shown the manner in which the administration intended to apply the Statute of Algeria and they believed there was no possibility of a solution by legal means. However, it should be noted that the nationalist movement had already taken the decision to establish the paramilitary Organisation Spéciale in 1947, that is before the elections under the Statute.

Quandt, in a schematic analysis of the revolutionary leadership, draws a distinction between different generations of leaders, Liberals, Radicals, and Revolutionaries. He includes Ferhat Abbas, whose ideology I have discussed, among the Liberals. The Radical politicians, active in the leadership of the MTLD, represented a transitional group between the legalistic style of the Liberals and the violence of the Revolutionaries (Quandt, 1969: 43ff). Caught in a dilemma of alternatives, they were attached to legal political activity, though seeing no value in legality *per se*, yet at the same time, they were willing to investigate the possibilities of the resort to violence. 'But neither path was chosen with alacrity, for the 1948 elections were a warning for those who trusted the legal path just as the 1945 repression served as a grim reminder to the Radicals of the consequences of a precipitous use of violence' (61). As to the consequences of the electoral frauds, Quandt writes (54-55) that the elections of 1948 were certainly a major reason for the abandonment, particularly among the Radicals, of parliamentary methods which seemed relatively congenial to them, in favour of armed force. Courrière (1968: 61) sees the elections as an important victory for Grand Colonisation, but comments that without doubt the humiliation suffered would also plunge into revolutionary action men who, in their heart of hearts, had always hoped for a peaceful solution. Favrod (1959: 83-84) writes that the events of

1948 mark an important stage in the movement to the *cristallisation de la colère*, and he cites from an intervention by Ferhat Abbas in the Algerian Assembly after the outbreak of revolution which the President of the Assembly would not allow him to present. In this intervention, Ferhat Abbas argued that perhaps there would have been neither maquis nor maquisards, if the Statute of Algeria had been applied.

Apart from the assessment of commentators, there is the testimony of the Revolutionaries themselves. I have already referred to Ferhat Abbas' account of his own conversion to revolutionary violence. Amar Ouzegane, a former General Secretary of the Algerian Communist Party, expelled for nationalist deviation, devotes an entire chapter of his book *Le Meilleur Combat*, published in 1962, to a denunciation of national reformism ('*Le Palais-Bourbon, tombeau du national-réformisme*'). He is scathing in his comments on the sophistry and hypocrisy of colonialist strategy, which he demonstrates through the history surrounding the Statute of Algeria. The Ordinance of March 1944, conferring on French Muslims complete equality with the French of Algeria, was a daring action – on paper (109ff). In the past, Algerians were described pejoratively on their identity cards as *MA*, Muslim Algerian, *IM*, Indigenous Muslim, *IMNNF*, Indigenous Non-Naturalised French Muslim. These labels had been changed later by the revolution to *FM*, French Muslim, *FSNA*, French of North African stock, and *FAPE*, French All Parts Entirely (*à part entière*). Given the past history of deception and of inequality, and the mythical nature of equality in the frame-work of colonial society, was vigilant Muslim scepticism surprising? More than two centuries ago, Diderot had written that to have slaves was nothing: what was intolerable was to have slaves and to call them citizens.

Change by the Second Constituent Assembly of the numerical formula for electoral representation adopted by the First Constituent Assembly was a lesson in French Parliamentary versatility, as was also the juridical-ideological battle over the status of Algeria. By conferring on Algeria, under the Statute of 1947, the bastard status of 'a group of departments', imperialist

France had betrayed its own constitutional undertaking to end colonialism and had made a mockery of the aspirations of the majority of the Algerian people: it had confirmed, by its parliamentary '*filouterie*', the habitual criminal policies of slave-owning governments. This was an irreparable blunder. By inflicting a cruel humiliation on the deputies of the Algerian manifesto, French colonialism had dealt a mortal blow to the national-reformist ideology. It had rendered impossible all peaceful evolution in a country thirsting for liberty and independence. In violating a solemn constitutional undertaking, French colonialism, through its blindness and thirst for blood, had driven Algeria to armed strife.

Ouzegane argues that the failure of parliamentary action was a necessary experience, dispelling the illusion that a wolf might become a sheep, and destroying the idea so deeply rooted in the hearts of Algerian intellectuals, that there might be peaceful evolution within the colonial regime. Without this parliamentary experience, revolutionary ideology would not have been able to triumph over reformist ideology; and without the defeat of reformism, there could be no victorious revolution.

Presumably, the commitment to revolutionary violence pre-supposes the rejection of reformism. This rejection is quite explicit in the following extract from a letter addressed by the National Liberation Front to the people of France in May 1956. 'The history of the democratic dialogue which the Algerian people tried to establish with France within the actual framework of the institutions imposed by France itself is thus nothing but a long series of humiliating refusals and brutal repressions. You cannot conceive the sentiment stirred in the hearts of Algerians by the systematic faking of elections since 1948, the sentiment of dignity ridiculed. This parody of liberty was in many ways much more painful than simple privation. The gates of revolution open progressively when the aspirations of a people are not respected. It was only when all means of expressing its aspirations had been exhausted, that the Algerian people decided to take up arms' (Favrod, 1959: 175).

Interpretations

Three types of explanation are usually advanced for the failure of reformism in Algeria. The first two ascribe responsibility to the settlers, and to the metropolitan government and its administrators. Both assume that there was the possibility of radical change by progressive reform. The third explanation more or less totally rejects the conception that progressive reformism could ever have been effective, and takes the position that its failure was inherent in the system of colonial domination.

One of the distinguishing characteristics of settler politics was the resistance to reforms. Abbas (1962: 106) opens his chapter on the impossible revolution by the law with a quotation from Julien to the effect that in matters relating to the indigenous people, the settler was obstinately, biologically opposed to all reform. The great landowners and entrepreneurs in commerce and transport led this opposition, shaping settler opinion in Algeria and intervening directly in French politics. It is not difficult to understand why they should have acted in this way; they were able to advance effectively their own power over many years. But the small settlers, the *petits blancs*, were also committed to resistance to reform. Ouzegane (1962: 227) describes them as the most fanatical supporters of French colonialism, and Abbas (1962: 100) writes to similar effect that the *petits Européens* were generally more racist than the very large proprietors.[3]

The opposition to reforms was remarkably consistent. On the eve of the First World War, the settlers demanded the maintenance of the special disciplinary *code de l'indigénat*, on the ground that without this code, the security of Algeria would be

---

3. So, too, Nora (1961: 47-49) argues that the political comportment of the settlers was homogeneous, the small employee identifying his interests with those of the great landed proprietors, understandably since at lower social levels, Muslim competition becomes more formidable. In these circumstances, the maintenance of French sovereignty seemed to them the only guarantee against destitution. Thus the most deprived majority among the French served the political fortunes of a flamboyant colonialism. Race relations had crushed with all its weight the relations between classes.

compromised. They were opposed to the education of indigenous intellectuals, who, in their judgment, could not assimilate true culture, and would become embittered, importunate, *déclassés*: they raised protests against the conferring of citizenship: even the most liberal thought it inadmissable that a mayor should derive his powers from the vote of Muslim subjects: they rejected the conscription of Muslims not only for fear of possible insurrection, but because higher salaries would result from the incorporation of young Muslim soldiers (Julien, 1952: 107). The legislative reforms of 1919 had to be imposed upon the settlers, and they continued to resist them after their passage in the French parliament (Nouschi, 1962: 54-56). They mobilised effectively, in association with conservative opinion in metropolitan France, against the Blum-Viollette project. This would have admitted increasing numbers of Muslims to French citizenship over the years, thereby reducing and ultimately annihilating their supremacy. They were not able to defeat the Statute of 1947, but they campaigned effectively for compromise in its provisions; and in collaboration with the local administration, they sabotaged all prospect of implementing the legislative reforms in a way which might have contributed to evolutionary change.

This consistent opposition was ideologically justified in a form generally described as expressing the perennial fears of dominant minorities. There was resistance to any extension of citizenship for fear that it might ultimately swamp settler representation, and there was opposition to economic and social advancement which might challenge settler privilege. Justification was found in derogatory stereotypes of the colonised, in the rights and contribution of the colonisers, and in the presumed interests of metropolitan France, or of the Christian or non-communist world.

It is not quite accurate to write of consistent opposition to reform. The large crowds gathered on the Forum of Algiers accepted with enthusiasm de Gaulle's declaration of equal citizenship rights exercised through a single electoral college, a policy they had passionately rejected in the past. But this was in

June 1958, after almost four years of revolutionary struggle, and
in the belief that de Gaulle was pledging support for the policy of
Algérie française.

In interpreting the political behaviour of the settlers, it seems
most plausible to assume that it was shaped by the dynamic of
their interests (or presumed interests) in a domination which
conferred on them many privileges, and that it was moulded by
the history of their past actions and policies, which forged rigid
commitment to a few guiding principles, and which
institutionalised routines of political action, in a rapidly changing
social situation. There is also, however, a very appreciable
literature dealing with the personality of the '*colon*' or of the
settlers generally, as a significant factor in their political
commitments. Presumably one can agree that there may be some
elements of a basic personality shaped by somewhat similar
experiences of racial domination, but I am not at ease with these
interpretations, being very conscious of the wide range of
personality in the settler societies I have known, and of the
variety of personality types in any political movement. There is
something quite stereotypical in these accounts, which seem to
'parade' literary elegance and subtlety of psychological insight.
Jean Cohen writes in *Les Temps modernes* (November 1955, 580-
581) that colonialism is first of all an economic fact, but that it is
also a fact of psychology and of daily routine, the understanding
of which is to be attained through the analysis of anecdote and of
common language, and the amassing of small facts and petty
actions, insignificant individually but in their combination
constituting the profound aspect of colonialism, its spiritual
murder. But what am I to make of the solidity and political
significance of such characterisations of the Algerian *colon* as
neither hating nor cruel, but cordial, *bon enfant*, loving laughter
and ease of living?

I have myself restricted comment to the political aspects of
settler behaviour, but my comments also have a stereotypical
quality, ignoring the range of variation between settlers.
Ouzegane is at pains to show that the revolutionary movement
was aware of, and responsive to, these differences in political

commitment. In the chapter on the European minority (1962: 210-244), he refers to the support, refuge and solicitude extended by the priests, and to the role of the Catholic Church in breaking with the colonialist past and the compromising *rapprochement* of the Cross and the bayonet.[4] He comments that not all the settlers had the congenital ferocity of the French colonial monster. 'Outside of the colonial fascists, the indifferent, the egoists and the racists, there was the floating mass of the disoriented, the ignorant, the wavering, the neutral, the charitable, the humanists dissatisfied with a predatory humanity' (232). He writes of the first Federation of Liberals, associated with the appeal in 1956 for a civil truce, and reports that the FLN saw in this movement the opportunity to rescue European democrats from their disarray, their immobilism and their voluntary isolation (232). Fanon, in an extended analysis of Algeria's European Minority (1967: 147-162), discusses sympathetically the role of European democrats and pays tribute to the large numbers of non-Arab Algerians who identified with the Algerian cause and collaborated actively in the struggle, or actually fought in the ranks of the Algerian Revolution (153).

In French writing a distinction is usually drawn between the *colons*, established on the land, and other colonists. My own use of the word settlers for the entire European population rather blurs this distinction. There is often reference to the differences between settlers of French origin and settlers of other European provenance. Above all, a distinction is almost invariably drawn between the small people (the petty farmers, clerks, workers) and the agrarian capitalists. Responsibility for the failure of reforms is often laid upon the great landowners, shippers, financiers, who are said to have manipulated the ordinary people for the enhancement of their own domains, and to have misled them as to the nature of their true interests, whether of class or of

4. Georges Hourdin (1962: 66-84), in a discussion of the Christian contribution, distinguishes between the two categories of clergy in Algeria, the clergy of the established church, increasingly recruited locally, and the missionaries, such as the White Fathers and Sisters of Notre-Dame d'Afrique. A section of the clergy, he writes, were marked by Algeria and by the influence of their original social milieu.

common humanity. Any discussion of the settlers' role in the failure of reforms would need to take account of different strata and of varied political perspectives.

The significance of the liberal, or democratic, commitment is a matter of controversy, as is also the relative responsibility of Algerian settlers as against the metropolitan power. These issues emerge in an exchange of articles between Yacono (1970: 121-134) and Ageron (1970: 355-365), relating to an earlier period. In a review of Ageron's study (*Les Algériens musulmans et la France, 1871-1919*), Yacono places the responsibility for the course of events primarily on the prodigious indifference of France, its weakness, parsimony and exploitation, and argues further that the Algerian French never constituted a bloc, but that there was always a very small liberal and reformist group, active in all periods and in almost all domains. The real battle, he writes, was waged by a liberal minority (including some Algerian French) confronting a very dynamic small Algerian group (with numerous allies in the metropole), in the presence of a mass of people, conservative (particularly in Algeria) or indifferent (essentially in the metropole).

To this Ageron replies that during the course of Algerian history two camps have ceaselessly emerged, which may be described as that of *Algérie française*, to which Yacono belongs, and his own camp of *Conscience française*. He declares that the themes of French parsimony, exploitation, indifference are well-known to those who have lived in Algeria, but for his part, he can only say that during the period studied and in the course of fifteen years of research he had never come across a group of active liberals. Perhaps one may find some old French settlers in Algeria favourable to Muslim demands, but what liberal group? And he quotes from de Tocqueville: 'One may set up individual cases against my argument: but I speak of classes. It is only with classes that history should concern itself.'

Camus (1958: 141-142), writing in the second year of the revolution, reverts to the same theme of French responsibility. 'Who, in effect, over the last thirty years, has wrecked all projects for reform, if not the Parliament elected by the French?

Who closed their ears to the cries of Arab misery? Who, if not the immense majority of the French press, allowed the repression of 1945 to pass with indifference? And who finally, if not France, waited with nauseating good conscience, until Algeria should bleed for having finally discovered that she exists? And if the Algerian French cultivated their prejudices, was it not with the blessing of the metropole?'

These mutual recriminations or attributions of responsibility express the ambiguity in the status of Algeria. There is the ambiguity of the different policies of assimilation or association or integration pursued or advocated over the years. Thus assimilation could mean an assimilation by fusion of Muslims who renounce their personal status, or it might mean an assimilation of the settlers or an administrative assimilation, Algeria being divided into departments of the same status as the departments of metropolitan France. The ambiguity can be seen in the changing policies with reference to the institution of Governor-General, and in conceptions of the constitutional status of Algeria (see Lambert, 1952: Chapter 2). It is quite evident in the Statute of Algeria of 1947, which defines Algeria as consisting of departments, thereby implying a policy of assimilation, while at the same time specifically declaring it to be a *group* of departments, endowed with a civil personality, a financial autonomy and a distinctive organisation. But whatever the theory of assimilation, it was quite illusory in practice: there never was effective assimilation of Muslims on the same basis as the settlers. Sahli (1955: 592) indeed argues that the growth of the settler population gave rise to a need for an administrative system sufficiently supple and varied to maintain domination over the Algerian people, while endowing the settlers with the same institutions as those of metropolitan France, and that it was in this need that the policy of assimilation originated.

A major source of ambiguity lies in the nature of the settlement as a *colonie de peuplement*, a colony with a substantial permanent settler population. The French could not follow the United States precedent of exterminating or pushing back the indigenous peoples. French society did not experience a population expansion in the nineteenth century which might have created a great pool of potential settlers; and France was confronted in Algeria with the powerful resistance of large scale organised societies. The result was a political entity, in part colony, in part settler society.

The Europeans were too numerous and long settled to see themselves as only an alien minority, as in Tunisia or Morocco, but they were not sufficiently numerous to put an end to the resistance of the Arab-Berber populations by their own power. Hence the capitalist bourgeoisie of European origin in Algeria did not have the same interests as their American sister in separating from the metropole. Geographic proximity, the complementary character of the Algerian and French economies were also relevant. Moreover, only the metropole could guarantee to them the exploitation of the indigenous masses, source of their great profits. Manifestations of separatism, latent among the European bourgeoisie of Algeria, but appearing periodically (whenever there was a question of according rights to the Arab-Berber population) were always tempered by their fear of finding themselves *tête à tête* with the populations they exploit. In the last analysis, the preferences they enjoy on the French market, and the French army, are *the only bonds* which ultimately hold the European bourgeoisie of Algeria to what they nevertheless call their 'mother country' (Arnault, 1958: 272).

The commitment to Algérie française was an expression of this dependence of the settlers on France: they were too vulnerable to seek independent status for Algeria. But they could still muster sufficient power, by virtue of numbers and economic influence, to exert pressure on the French government, and they intervened effectively in the politics of metropolitan France to advance their interests and to enhance their power. Their success, however, was not simply the result of their own unaided efforts. There was appreciable support for their policies within France itself in the concept, strangely enough, of the universal rights of man and the civilising mission of French society and culture,[5] in the deeply

5. Dunn (1972: 159) writes that 'French policy was assimilationist in its teleological self-justification because universalist natural rights were central to the constitution tradition and the language of political aspiration of French politicians from the time of the revolution and of Napoleon onwards. All men in the state of culture in which they were actually to be found were not, regrettably, equal; but by being judiciously civilized, gallicized, they could be generously enabled to become so.'

ingrained view that Algeria was an integral part of France, and in some convergence of economic interests and conservative policies. Colonialism was not simply a phenomenon of European settlement in Algeria.

Thus the belief that 'if only the King knew', the abuses would be remedied, or the belief that it was only necessary to appeal to liberal France, was quite naive. It was one of the motivations of the demand for representation in the French parliament. The experience of parliamentary participation however proved disillusioning and no doubt served to convince Muslim liberals that the 'colonialist enemy', as Ouzegane phrases it (1962: 109), was in Paris at the same time as in Algiers: and, of course, the 'colonialist enemy' was also in the Algerian administration, in the French recruited, as well as the locally recruited, administrators. Julien (1952: 397 and 1961: 27-28) writes that only rare governors are able to resist the bureaucratic conspiracy and the temptation of popularity. Democrat, or even revolutionary at home, the Frenchman becomes conservative and traditionalist in the presence of the indigenous peoples. Most governors turn themselves into the devoted servants of settler interests, acting as proconsul with little concern for the directions of the metropolitan government. As for those who take up the cause of the Algerians, they are ridiculed with derisory indigenous nicknames, and if they persist in their policies, they are destroyed with support from Paris. Nora (1961: 45) describes a procession of governors, one who falsifies elections, another transformed by Algeria from a socialist minister into a McCarthyist proconsul. Ouzegane (1962: 240) refers to the strange dizzy derangement which destroys the psychic equilibrium of some of the French governors, unable to resist the colonialist *baqla*, and the neronian radiance of the summer palace. It must indeed have been difficult to stand up against the passionate ideological convictions, the aggressive commitment to French preponderance, and the blandishments of pomp and glory and adulation.

Yet France did intervene decisively to extend citizenship rights in 1919, and again under the Statute of Algeria in 1947; and the final settlement with the National Liberation Front was imposed by France against the will of the settlers and in the teeth of OAS terrorism and of mutiny within the army. But the reform of 1919 was a compromise, under which citizenship necessitated renunciation of Muslim status. Ageron (1970: 365) argues that for the first time a majority of the Algerian elite was open to a policy of assimilation, and that the failure of that policy goes back to 1919 and the years immediately after the First World War. The Statute of Algeria introduced important reforms, though again greatly compromised as a Statute, and rendered derisory by the failure of France to ensure that the reforms were implemented, even if this meant a thorough cleansing of the Augean stables of Algerian administration. And the final settlement was only imposed after years of a bitterly destructive and brutally atrocious war, and under mounting international pressure.

Brief mention should be made of the view that internal divisions among the Muslims themselves contributed to the failure of parliamentary action. Certainly the fratricidal conflict between factions of the nationalist movement, the MTLD, was a major precipitant of the revolutionary violence in November 1954. In July 1955, the Algerian delegation of the National Liberation Front in Cairo, in an analysis of this internal crisis within the MTLD, explained the decision of the revolutionary movement to launch direct action as based on the consideration that it was the best means for restoring the unity of the party while advancing the national struggle (Abbas, 1962: 213-215. See also Lacouture, 1961: 311, who points out that the revolutionary organisation was called the *'comité révolutionnaire d'unité et d'action,'* and Le Tourneau, 1962: 376-377). The proclamation launched by the revolutionaries on 1 November 1954 discusses in its preamble the crisis within the national movement, and the need to rescue it by revolutionary action from the impasse into which it had fallen through factionalism and personal conflicts. Their movement was named the National Liberation Front, for the reason that it disengaged itself from all partisans and offered all social strata, political parties and movements the possibility of integrating themselves into the struggle for liberation (Courrière, 1968: Text of FLN proclamation, 443-446). But the failure of French liberalising initiatives, and the chicanery and corruption and harassment and persecution, would have rendered virtually impossible creative involvement in party politics, and would have been cause enough for internal division.

Some hypothetical general laws

As the situation unfolded, it is difficult to see how Algerian Muslims could have achieved equality without the resort to revolutionary violence. The actual course of events seems to have led quite inexorably to revolutionary conflict. From a comparative point of view however the important question is whether there are general laws which govern social situations of this type, channelling actions along the course they took. Was it inevitable that the parties should have acted as they did, or could they have acted differently? Were there in fact missed opportunities, or was it inherent in the system that the settlers should have opposed basic reforms consistently, save as a last resort, or that the colonial government should have compromised in its legislation and then condoned the sabotage of its compromised measures?

There is an appreciable literature on the Algerian revolution, which argues the existence of general laws governing social situations of this type, and necessitating the choices made by the antagonists. Some of this literature is directed specifically to missed opportunities for successfully pursuing a policy of assimilation. However, my own interest is in the relevance of these 'general laws' for the question whether independence, or equality between settlers and natives, could have been achieved without highly destructive violence. I am assuming that assimilation was not a feasible policy, and that the events of the Second World War and the ensuing world movements of decolonisation would have led Algeria inexorably to independence.

The type of society under discussion is a *colonie de peuplement*, which combines substantial settler population with metropolitan government. Ouzegane (1962: 212) comments that the Algerian revolution would represent the first occasion on which a colony '*de peuplement européen*', in liberating itself from foreign domination, would give political hegemony to the indigenous majority.

The first hypothetical general law concerning these societies relates to the inevitability of violence as the instrument of radical change. Nora (1961: 37) quotes a prophetic statement by de Tocqueville in *Notes sur l' Algérie*, 1841. 'As I listened sadly to all these things, I asked myself what could be the future of a country given over to men of this type, and where would this torrent of violence and injustice ultimately end, if not in the revolt of the indigenous people and the ruin of the Europeans.' This prophecy seems based on a common sense assumption that violence and injustice breed violence. The more generally formulated proposition is that regimes established and maintained by violence can only be radically changed by violence. Fanon's thesis of the necessity for violence in decolonisation has become a political cliché in many circles advocating violent change. In my own view, this argument has no more logical cogency than the practices of sympathetic magic.

The second law follows from the first: it postulates the impossibility of radical change by reformism. Ouzegane (1962: 107) describes national reformists as enemies ·of cataclysmic violence, who reduce decolonisation to a purely juridico-political problem: he adds that they conserve the illusion that it is possible to reconcile the right of the strongest with natural justice. The reliance on such procedures as the progressive extension of the vote, and increase in representation, is certainly very characteristic of reformism, as is also the concern with the amelioration of social and economic conditions. The essential mark of reformism, as an evolutionary strategy of change, is that it proceeds in a constitutional way within the established framework of authority. It is precisely the possibility of significant change by this means which is rejected. The general proposition is that the colonial laws, and the procedures for making the laws, were designed to establish and maintain an exploitative domination, and that there is no possibility of reforming the system by its very own laws and lawmaking procedures. From this perspective, one may argue with reference to Algeria, that there were no errors in the past, no opportunities missed, since a colonial history cannot convert itself peacefully into a national history (see Nora, 1961: 117).

Related to the rejection of the possibility of reforming an oppressive system through the use of its own 'instruments of oppression', is the third general law that where reforms are introduced, they are invariably too little and too late to be significant. This seems plausible enough. It derives from the more general proposition that a privileged group will not voluntarily renounce its privileges. Hence reforms in the system will only be introduced under pressure, and the response of the ruling group is to resist this pressure for as long as possible, and to concede the very minimum. This is all the more likely where the colonialism of the metropolitan power is incarnated in a substantial settler population, directly experiencing the benefits and gratification of racial domination.

At a different level of analysis, the inherent contradictions of the system of colonial-settler rule are viewed as rendering reformism totally ineffective. There is said to be a dialectical relationship between settler and native. The original flagrant disparity serves as the foundation on which colonialism inevitably builds and consolidates the structure of inequality, so that there is within colonialism an internal contradiction which can only result in its explosive end. The demise of *Algérie française* is not due essentially either to the Europeans or the Muslims of Algeria: it is the necessary final term of a historic process (Aron, 1962: 7-8).

In what is above all a conflict of collectivities, individual character and effort become insignificant. Thus Nora writes (1961: 75) that not all Algeria is fascist, not all the French are ultras, not all the soldiers torture: but fascism, ultras, torture are France in Algeria. Abbas writes to somewhat similar effect that it is pointless to place responsibility on the 'bad French' and to exclude the 'good'; responsibility is collective, the product of a regime, the fruit of an erroneous concept. Man makes institutions, but institutions also make man: not all the French of Algeria were bad buggers to being with: it is the colonial regime, applied by the French bourgeoisie, which has made them what they are today (Abbas, 1962: 109-110).

The fourth general law then is that inherent in colonialism are the antithetical processes which must inevitably destroy it.[6] Since misery and despair are the direct and necessary consequence of the economic exploitation of colonialism, there can be no economic transformation while the system endures (Sartre, 1956: 1381). Economic exploitation makes necessary the overthrowing of colonialism. Social exclusion and inferior status, humiliation and servitude, create bonds of solidarity among the colonised, encouraging sentiments of a shared identity and a common destiny. Cultural repression and denigration foster a cultural renaissance and stimulate cultural pride. Political domination and foreign rule engender the antithetical reaction of nationalism.

If these propositions are accepted, then there was no basis in Algeria for policies of significant reform, and there were no missed opportunities for evolutionary change. This is not a view which I accept, and I return to the problem in my final chapter.

6. See Sartre (1956: 1371-1386) for a discussion of colonialism as a system.

4

Point of No Return

The analysis of the point of no return, like the problem of missed opportunities, has a retrospective reference. It is an attempt to rewrite history, altering its course by wishing away an event. What might have been the relations between the races if the Blum-Viollette project had become law, or if there had not been an episode constituting a point of no return? The posing of the problem of a point of no return also implies that there were other possibilities of action and development, that consequences were not totally determined by the structure of the situation: and it suggests a theory of polarisation, certainly if one accepts Fanon's view (1963: 89-90) that in all armed struggles there exists the point of no return, almost always marked by 'a huge and all-inclusive repression which engulfs all sectors of the colonised people'.

The phrase is usually applied in situations of extreme mutual violence, some highly repressive and violent action being taken as the point of no return for violent counteraction. Presumably there is only one point of no return, but there may be many missed opportunities. However, no logical necessity links the conception of lost opportunities to non-violent change, or the conception of a point of no return to the involvement in deadly violence. It makes perfectly good sense to describe the failure of Camus' courageous attempt to bring about a truce on the killing of civilians,[1] as a lost opportunity for initiating discourse between

---

1. See Mohamed Lebjaoui (1970: 38-55) for an account of Camus' appeal in Algiers in January 1956 for a truce on the killing of civilians.

the combatants; and conversely, the point of no return seems an appropriate enough term for the situation described by many revolutionary leaders in which the failure of petitions and of submissions and of constitutional approaches finally leads to the decision to engage in violence, as offering the only possibility left open for radical change. But in general, the association of these two conceptions with non-violent evolutionary change and with violent cataclysmic change respectively seems valid.

I select for discussion three 'points of no return' in the Algerian conflict. The events at Sétif, in May 1945, are often described as such. If Sétif was indeed a point of no return, then the description of later events in the same terms seems gratuitous, and the Statute of Algeria could hardly have represented a missed opportunity. Fanon (1963: 90) describes the '12,000 victims of Philippeville' in August 1955 and the institution of urban and rural militias in the following year,[2] as constituting points of no return. The third 'point of no return' was reached on 11 December 1960. Henissart (1970: 46) writes of the Muslim demonstration on that day, that French historians are nearly unanimous in pinpointing it as the turning point of the entire Algerian war.

1. Sétif

There is appreciable evidence for the significance of Sétif. Favrod (1959: 76) describes all the nationalist chiefs as unanimously of the view that the revolution of 1954 was decided during the events of 1945. The leaders he met in Cairo, Tunis, Bonn, Rome and Geneva, gave him the nightmarish account of the days and nights in May, when the destiny of Algeria was sealed in blood and tears. This would seem to be somewhat exaggerated, but there can be little doubt that the extreme repression of those days was one of the catalysts of revolution for some of the leaders and their followers (see Chevallier, 1958: 67 and Quandt, 1969: 79).

2. Fanon seems to be referring to the 'Dispositif de Protection Urbaine' established in March 1957. (See Courrière, 1969: 511-512.)

Abbas (1962: 208) writes that for a section of the nationalists a trial by force had become inevitable; the violence that liberates must oppose the violence that oppresses.

For Algerian soldiers, who had served with great valour and distinction in the French forces during the Second World War, it must have been deeply traumatic to return to the inequalities of Algerian life and to the harrowing accounts and evidence of French atrocity during a period of most ruthless repression and most brutal reprisal. Courrière (1968: 46) writes that:

(May 16)

At this time the heroic 7th regiment of Algerian sharpshooters is disembarking at Algiers. It has lost in Alsace more than a third of its effective fighting force. The men, almost all from the Constantine area, are returning home, covered in glory. They are about to see their families, their wives, their children, the peaceful villages of which they had dreamed in the mud of Alsace, under fire from German canon. They discover the pits in which are buried those shot down at Guelma, and the lime-kilns of Heliopolis and Villars. Still holding in their hands flowers from France, they find the most atrocious hatred in their own country. Throughout Algeria, while Adjutant Ben Bella of Marnia, Sergeant Ouamrame of Dra-el-Mizan, and Adjutant Boudiaf de Msila[3] still wear their war medals, the soldiers learn about Sétif, 8 May 1945. Everywhere else it was the day of victory.

The initial race riot arose out of the public celebration of victory. In almost all the important centres, compact groups of Muslims participated in the celebrations, brandishing the green-and-white flag of Algerian nationalism, and calling for the liberation of the nationalist leader, Messali Hadj. In Sétif, it was market day, and many peasants poured in from the surrounding areas. An authorised Muslim procession moved towards the centre, accompanied by the ululations (*you-yous stridents*) of the women. The marchers carried forbidden banners. An inspector of police seized one of the banners, precipitating a fracas, during which shots were fired. (According to some accounts, he lost his head, and shot the bearer of the banner.) A strong contingent of

---

3. These became leaders of the revolution.

Muslims spread through the city, savagely attacking and murdering the Europeans they encountered. Troops intervened and restored order by midday, but not before 21 Europeans had been killed, some fearfully mutilated.

During the night, at Sétif and in the neighbouring areas, there began what Courrière (1968: 41) describes as the abominable process of serial assassination. Armed bands of Muslims roamed the countryside, killing, raping, mutilating, pillaging, burning. French reprisals were even more savage, more vast and massive. At Sétif, the authorities proclaimed martial law: any Arab not carrying the regulation armband was killed: in the countryside, Senegalese troops and legionnaires pillaged, burnt, raped and slaughtered in full freedom: a cruiser bombarded coastal areas: planes destroyed forty-four villages (Julien, 1952: 302ff).

Military units carried out summary executions. Civilian commandos also engaged in summary executions, and organised reprisal massacres. Lacouture writes (1961: 292) that the settlers established themselves as judges with a speed and efficiency, which spoke eloquently of their organisation and preparation: for several days in the region of Sétif, they set in motion a veritable Ku-Klux-Klan, liquidating the natives with a great celerity born from deep knowledge of the milieu. Military tribunals, in a campaign of massive judicial repression, arrested more than 4,500, mostly in the department of Constantine: they sentenced almost 2,000, passed death sentences on 151, of whom 28 were executed (Le Tourneau, 1962: 350-351. Ageron, 1969: 94, gives the number of sentences as 1,476. Nouschi, 1962: 143, provides a different set of figures). In the final account, the French dead numbered 103: and there were some hundred wounded and mutilated. The French authorities estimated the Muslim dead as 1,500: the FLN placed their death toll at 50,000.

Accounts vary appreciably on points of detail and diametrically on interpretation, as is to be expected in plural societies of this type.[4] At one extreme is the view, represented by

4. Compare for example the reports of Le Tourneau (1962: 348-354) and of Nouschi (1962: 140-143). Aron examines some of the conflict of evidence on Sétif in an extended and balanced account.

Abbas for example, that the riot was engineered by settlers and administrators as part of a conspiracy to annul the liberalising measures of the French government and to suppress the new political movement, *Les Amis du Manifeste et de la Liberté*, with a membership of more than 500,000. Abbas offers much circumstantial evidence in support of this view. At the other extreme is the theory that the manifestations at Sétif were part of a planned general insurrection, as shown by the outbreak of violence not only in the immediate vicinity, but also at relatively distant points, and by the discovery of several depots of arms.

The intermediate position is that there was no planned insurrection, but that the riots at Sétif sparked off a spontaneous uprising. The argument in support of this theory is that the time was, as it were, ripe for insurrection. There was the general structural context, in which it was almost inevitable that the more numerous but least favoured community should seek greater equality through the power of its numbers and of its violence (Le Tourneau, 1962: 353). There was the stimulus of the Second World War; the diminished prestige of France following its defeat in 1940 and its accommodation with fascism; the proclaimed war goals of national liberation, and the beginnings of a world movement for self-determination and independence; nationalist agitation within Algeria; the greater militancy among Arabs, and the founding of the Arab League in March 1945. Some commentators attach significance to a grave crisis in the Algerian economy at this time (e.g., Nouschi, 1962: 141), a view Le Tourneau challenges. In any event, many factors according to this theory contributed to create a revolutionary situation. Insurrection was in the air, it was being planned, but it exploded prematurely and abortively following the riots at Sétif.

It is rather doubtful that Sétif represented a point of no return. At any rate, all the political parties seemed willing, in 1948, to participate in the elections under the Statute of Algeria. They may have felt that '*le pire n'est pas toujours sur*' (the worst is not always certain) and that the Statute of Algeria offered some scope for significant change. Or it may have been a matter of expediency for the more radical nationalists, overwhelmed by the severity of the repression and hesitant to engage in violence. For some of those who later became leaders of the revolutionary war, Sétif seems to have been a motivating factor; and it must have predisposed many in the Muslim population to throw in their support for the revolution in the final struggle. The French would have experienced the realisation of their most terrifying nightmares in the frenzied hatred with which they were pursued in the early riots, and in the atrocities to which they were subjected. Sétif would have seemed argument for resistance to reform and to the sharing of power; it would have provided justification for the belief that only force was effective in the governing of native peoples; and it would have offered a model for future repression.

II. *Constantine*

The massacres in the North Constantine area were a reenactment of Sétif, save that the initial atrocities were quite clearly and deliberately planned. In this account of the events, I follow the version given by Courrière in *Le Temps des léopards*.

The North Constantine division of the revolutionary organisation had been relatively quiescent, though the Constantine region itself was highly politicised. On 8 May 1955, the tenth anniversary of Sétif, a commando exploded a bomb at a casino, adjoining a cinema in Constantine, causing many casualties. There was an attack on army headquarters at El Arrouch, and on 10 May, revolutionary forces succeeded in isolating for some hours the urban centre of El Milia. Official policy was to put down brutally all new manifestations of rebellion, not only by attack on the rebel forces, but also by collective sanctions against those assisting them. The guerilla forces suffered heavy losses in men and morale as a result of military action. In the urban centres, repression had the initial effect of winning over to the FLN Algerians, until then, indifferent to nationalism. But civilian repression rapidly changed its character from arrests here and there to the pogrom, the *ratissage*, 'the killing on sight of suspected civilians, the burning of homes, and above all, the attack on the dignity of the men through their wives' (Courrière, 1969: 179). Some of the settlers played an active role in the repression, preparing lists, designating villages. To be pointed out by an informer was certain death. Villages, where it was thought that the FLN had taken refuge, were set on fire. The terrorised population began to withdraw from the FLN.

Under these circumstances of being driven to earth, with revolutionary action throughout Algeria at a low ebb, the leaders of the North Constantine zone resolved on the desperate remedy of blind massacre. This they scheduled for 20 August, anniversary of the deposition of the Sultan of Morocco.

On the appointed day, many thousands of Algerians gathered in the suburbs and outskirts of Philippeville, under the control of armed uniformed revolutionary (ALN) soldiers. In the centre, there was all the colourful *brouhaha* of a small Mediterranean town, gaily anticipating the pleasures of the weekend. Then suddenly panic. Men and women, beside themselves, seeking shelter, bursting into cafés, derisory protection. About them, a devastating flood of Arabs armed with hunting guns, scythes, bill-hooks, sharpened shovels, knives, advancing inexorably, crying oùt their long-suppressed hatred. The mob on the march, the enraged mob smashing everything in its path, the unjust, brutal, odious maddened mob, pushed and guided by the ALN, the mob let loose in a bestial urge to kill.[5]

At Constantine, the bloody events start with the assassination of Ferhat Abbas' nephew, an opponent of the FLN and of violence. Bombs explode throughout the city, at the restaurant Gambrinus, in the business area, and at the ABC cinema. At Aïn Abid, the mob breaks into the home of M. Mello, cutting the throats of a four-day-old baby, a ten-year-old child, Mello, his wife, and seventy-three-year-old mother-in-law.

At El Halia, a mining centre in which fifty European families lived among two thousand Arabs, under conditions of complete equality in employment, and seemingly in perfect harmony, massacre was at its most atrocious (Courrière, 1969: 186). Armed

5. This is a somewhat free rendering of the gist of Courrière's account (1969: 183ff).

with sticks of dynamite, gasoline, guns and hatchets, peaceful fathers of families become quite demented and slaughter European workers, foremen, engineers. Miners and people from neighbouring villages attack the women and children with relentless fury. When the military finally arrives, wading through pools of blood, they find women and children with their throats cut and disembowelled by billhook, men and women sexually mutilated. The twenty-five men of the ALN who directed the operation took no part in the action, but kept aside in neighbouring ravines. All told, 36 centres of colonisation were attacked, and 123 persons assassinated, 71 being European (Ageron, 1969: 101).

Savage repression and atrocity follow upon the atrocities of aggression. In Philippeville, the police and paratroops immediately counterattack. In Constantine there is savage slaughter of Arabs. At the end of the attacks controlled by the FLN, 1,273 Muslims have been killed and over 1,000 taken prisoner. And the reprisals continue. Europeans arm themselves, firing on anyone of bronze complexion, wearing a *cheich* or a veil. There is interrogation, torture. At the stadium in Philippeville, responsible civilians lead out all the young Muslims they can find to be shot down. Most of the prisoners are executed. Villages from which some of the assailants originate are destroyed by mortar. According to the count of the revolutionary forces, based on an extensive census, with names and addresses of the victims, 12,000 Muslims were dead or missing (Courrière, 1969: 187): an application of the *lex talionis* – but 100 Muslims for each European.

This was not a conflict between the forces of law and order, on the one side, and rebels or maquisards or bandits or revolutionaries on the other. It was a holocaust of deadly destructive fury between racial groups. This was shown on the Muslim side, by the many indiscriminate attacks on Europeans, indiscriminate not for the purpose of striking terror, but in the indifference to the position or personal attributes of the victims. The enemy was the European: and the attackers were not only the ALN; the Muslim population participated on a large scale.

'In all Algeria,' Courrière writes (1969: 189), 'there is no longer a European who, in the days following the massacre, does not think, on seeing an Algerian, even one he knows, even one he loves well: "After all, he too may be about to do the same. He too may slit my throat." '

On the European side, it was a population that was engaged, as objects of the terror, and as vigilante terrorising avenging groups. And the target was also a population group, as shown in the indiscriminate arrests, the summary, arbitrary, executions, the *ratonnades*, the collective reprisals, the imposition of collective responsibility. For the first time, the country began to live in a state of war, with interminable controls, and patrols and military barrages.

The Constantine massacres sharply polarised Arabs and Europeans. Mutual atrocity was part of the immediate experience of the groups. The FLN had demonstrated its power. Moderate representatives of the Muslim population moved toward the nationalist position, as a result either of intimidation or of reaction to the collective repressions. As to the Europeans, whereas in the past it was mainly politicians who had demanded repression without mercy, now almost all Europeans regarded Muslims as suspects and demanded radical measures against them.[6]

But perhaps there might still have been the possibility of reconciliation. The Governor-General Jacques Soustelle had followed a policy of order before justice in repressing the Muslims, ignoring the disorder from injustice. He was, however, committed to a policy of integration, and sought to introduce reforms with this end in view. He was not, however, able to gain support for his proposed reforms. Were there perhaps other possibilities of reconciliation? Or was the polarisation irreversible, a point of no return?

6. See the discussion by Le Tourneau (1962: 400-401) of the resolution of the 61 representatives, and of the general reactions of Europeans in Algeria.

III. *11 December 1960*

The third point of no return I have selected is the Muslim demonstration on 11 December 1960. This was in fact a counter-demonstration to the campaign organised by the *Front de l'Algérie français* during President de Gaulle's visit to Algeria on the 9-13 December.

For some time, de Gaulle had been moving toward a policy of Algerian self-determination and independence. On 14 June, 1960, in a radio and televised talk, he had renewed offers of peace, invited the leaders of the 'insurrection' to join with him in arriving at an honourable truce, and spoken of self-determination for the Algerian people, the transformation of *Algérie algérienne* into a modern country in fraternal relations with France. On 4 November, he had issued a statement declaring that the objectives of his government were no longer an Algeria governed by metropolitan France, but an *Algérie algérienne*, an emancipated Algeria, an Algeria where responsibility would vest in the Algerians themselves, an Algeria with its own government, institutions and laws, if this were the wish of the Algerian people, as he deemed it to be (Le Tourneau, 1962: 442). On 7 December, the French Prime Minister had announced that the questions of Algerian self-determination and of constitutional changes in Algeria would be submitted to a referendum on 8 January 1961.

Courrière (1971: 101) writes that the appeal of 14 June caused consternation in military circles in Algeria, and was a point of departure for the Generals' revolt in April 1961. It was the stimulus to the formation of the *Front de l'Algérie française* on 15 June, for which plans had been germinating for some months. The FAF was committed to the goal of Algerian integration into France. To promote this objective, it sought to bring together European settlers and non-FLN Muslims in a powerful organisation. De Gaulle's visit to Algeria provided an unexpected opportunity for the settlers to intervene decisively in the politics of metropolitan France, by mass demonstrations with army support and by the assassination of de Gaulle himself. The

FAF called for a general strike. On 9 December, its commandoes attacked the police and security forces. On 10 December, the strike and demonstrations continued, but without the hoped-for intervention by army units on behalf of the demonstrators.

It was on 11 December, in the course of this FAF campaign, that great masses of Muslims poured into the streets of Algiers, shouting for de Gaulle, but also proclaiming, with a great unfurling of thousands of nationalist flags, their allegiance to the FLN and their goal of an independent Algeria. The Muslim manifestations, it seems, had been organised by the French administration as a counter-demonstration in support of de Gaulle, but they had then taken on a militant nationalist character (Courrière, 1971: 188-190). Muslim counter-demonstrators broke through roadblocks, invaded European areas and pillaged European villas. They sustained heavy casualties as civilians and troops fired on them, but they had demonstrated their own independent power.

Henissart (1970: 46) writes that the disillusionment with the army, the psychological jolt of the counter-demonstration and the ensuing despair of some soldiers and civilians led, stage by stage, to the formation of the European terrorist organisation, the OAS. He quotes Paul-Marie de la Gorce to the effect that 'all the basic characteristics of the OAS are compressed in the history of those twenty-four hours ... 11 December 1960, explains the existence of the OAS, its psychology, its methods and even its mythology.' The effective point of no return, then, from this perspective, is the founding of the OAS in February 1961, as a terrorist organisation, consolidating a variety of activist organisations.

The desperate Armageddon mood which increasingly characterised the OAS is already conveyed in its first tract:

The sacred union is now made.
The resistance front is united.
Frenchmen of all origins,
The last hour of France in Algeria is the last hour of France in the world, the last hour of the West.

Today is the moment when everything may be lost or saved. Everything depends on our determination. Everything depends on the National Army.

We know that the last combat approaches. We know that for the combat to be victorious, there must be the most total unity, the most absolute discipline. Therefore all the clandestine National Movements and their resistance organisations have decided unanimously to join their forces and their efforts in a single combat movement.

L'*Organisation Armée Secrète* (Secret Armed Organisation), OAS.

Algerians of all origins,

In fighting for Algérie française, you fight for your life and your honour, for the future of your children. In this way, you will participate in the grand movement of national renewal.

In this fight, you will follow the orders of the OAS exclusively, from now on. Be assured, that if we all rise up together in arms, against the abandonment of Algeria, and if we know how to merit it, victory is certain.

In calm and confidence,

All to stand firm, ready and united.

Long live France.

L'*Organisation Armée Secrète* (Courrière, 1971: 234-235).

The objective was not simply to establish a common front of terrorist and activist organisations, but to unite Europeans under the banner of the OAS. To this end, the OAS used some of the same techniques as the FLN to discipline their potential following. They imposed taxes, they issued orders and levied fines for disobedience, they exploded plastic in reprisal against recalcitrants. Later they moved to systematic murder, assassinating liberals and other deviants. The commitment of the great majority of the settlers to the same policy of Algérie française as the OAS and the ruthless efficiency of its techniques, gained for the organisation effective control over the European population.

The disaffection in the professional army, which culminated in the Generals' revolt in April 1961, also contributed to participation in the terrorist movement. Virtually victorious in the field over the FLN, the army reacted against the French Government's decision to hold cease-fire negotiations with the revolutionary provisional government on 7 April 1961. Any satisfaction over the postponement of the cease-fire talks was quite destroyed when de Gaulle, in a press conference, declared that an Algerian state would be created, and that French interest and policy lay in decolonisation. To many professional soldiers, serving in an army which had been shamefully defeated in the Second World War, and recently in Indochina, this seemed the final humiliation, the final abandonment. It also seemed a great betrayal of solemn undertakings to the settlers in favour of Algerian integration with France and the continued presence of France in Algeria, to which must be added the betrayal of the great numbers of Muslim supporting troops (*harkis*) in the French army, and of Muslims in self-defense units.[7] Discontent in the army was such that the OAS might reasonably hope for army support as the crucial factor which would make possible the overthrow of the French government and the reversal of de Gaulle's policies.

Strategy was directed to intervention in the flow of events by local terrorism, and by terrorism in metropolitan France. On 19 May, on the eve of the peace negotiations at Evian, the OAS exploded 19 charges of plastic in actions against Muslims and liberal Europeans in Algiers. On 13 June, the OAS expressed its joy in the setback to the Evian negotiations, by a plastic bomb in the very heart of the city, this being immediately followed by the most extraordinary concert of motor-car horns and casseroles the city had ever experienced (Courrière, 1971: 388). On 31 October, in contemptuous and provocative anticipation of FLN demonstrations on 1 November, anniversary of the launching of the revolutionary struggle, and as an expression of OAS power, there were more than 70 explosions in Algiers.

As events drew toward independence and Muslim rule, there

---

7. Courrière (1971: 256) gives a figure of 200,000 Muslims in the army, and 50,000 in self-defence units. The disarming of the harkis at the end of the war meant virtually delivering them over to vengeance. It was only after the first throat-slittings, and the first sadistic tortures, by the last-minute recruits to the maquis (*maquisards de la dernière heure*), that the harkis were regrouped in a large camp. Some 14,000 were repatriated in France (Courrière, 1971: 623-624).

was progressive escalation of increasingly desperate violence. At first the OAS had used plastic bombs to intimidate, to destroy shops and apartments, but not to kill. Then, during the cease-fire negotiations in Evian on 1 June 1961, came news of the assassination of the central commissar charged with the investigation of OAS activities (Courrière, 1971: 388-389). The OAS had now turned to murder. In August, the OAS killed 6, in September 9, in October 13, in November 28 and in December 98 (Courrière, 1971: 473).

The understanding at Les Rousses, in February 1962, between representatives of the French and Algerian governments, concerning the procedures for a cease-fire, and the reservation of rights for Europeans, was the signal for a virtual declaration of war by the OAS. The directive of General Salan, leader of the OAS, opened with the words that the irreparable was about to be committed, and it called for insurrectional zones in the country, the heightening of revolutionary tension, systematic attacks on police and security forces, the use of explosives, and the launching of street mobs when expedient. This was the green light for atrocity. Algiers now averaged between thirty and forty violent deaths a day. 'Moslem pedestrians became the chief targets, in general because they symbolised the FLN, the enemy; and in particular because they happened to fall athwart a gunman in the streets ... Murder in the streets no longer shocked, it was an hourly occurrence; the manner of dying sometimes differentiated victims, but the grisly process itself was mechanical. From balconies, Europeans watched the gunning-down of Arabs and commented on it as on a sporting match. When an Arab fell, young *pieds noirs* did not break off conversation with acquaintances' (Henissart, 1970: 319-320).

With the signing of the cease-fire at Evian on 18 March 1962, the OAS affirmed its determination to pursue the combat; it ordered a general strike; it commanded its followers to harrass all enemy positions in the main cities of Algeria, and it called on comrades in the armed forces to join its ranks. There was further escalation of violence. Terrorist groups moved to even greater atrocity, to the indiscriminate slaughter of Arabs, of workers, domestic servants, peddlers. On 20 March, they fired mortars into groups of Muslims enjoying the sun in the Place du Gouvernement, in Algiers. Delta commandoes totally prohibited any movement of Muslims into the European sections of the city. At Oran, there were lynchings, *ratonnades*, and mortar attacks; it was certain death to penetrate the European areas.

The OAS now came into direct military confrontation with the army and police. One of its leaders had issued an ultimatum to French army and security forces, warning that French troops intercepted in an area corresponding to the Algiers working-class suburb of Bab El-Oued would be considered a foreign and hostile occupation force (Henissart, 1970: 336). In the course of this attempt to establish Bab El-Oued as an insurrectional zone, a military bastion, an OAS commando shot down seven soldiers and wounded eleven, precipitating fierce reprisals against the people of Bab El-Oued. This was followed by a massacre of demonstrators seeking to raise the state of siege imposed on Bab El-Oued and to challenge the military barriers in a trial of strength. Bab El-Oued was reduced to a devastated suburb in which despairing men and women mourned their dead and their lost hopes (Courrière, 1971: 562-581). As to the army, the OAS had on this occasion committed the irreparable. It had shattered all hope that the army might remain passive or intervene on behalf of a settler Algérie française.

The OAS, now reduced to an amalgam of desperadoes, deaf to reason (Courrière, 1971: 594), plunged into a final desperate phase, the period of Operation Apocalypse. In Algiers, in the last week of April 1962, the OAS murdered 73, in the following week 203 (Henissart, 1970: 393). On 2 May, as more than a thousand Muslim longshoremen waited at the docks in Algiers, a truck loaded with scrap iron exploded and killed 62: on the same day mortar shells rained down on two Muslim quarters, killing 30 more. That day, the OAS killed 110 and wounded 147. Some days later, only the heroism of the fire brigade averted a major catastrophe when OAS commandos precipitated a petrol carrier loaded with 16,000 litres of fuel against the Casbah.

Milkmen, fruit vendors, fishmongers, day labourers, gas-station attendants fell where they worked or on their way to work ... Street directions were bizarre. Newcomers to Algiers were told: 'Turn to the right, where they killed the baker'; or 'The house you're looking for is on Rue Charras – you'll see a body outside the door.' ... The streets of Algiers ... became a theatre of operations for roving gangs of young, pitiless thugs who scoured one neighbourhood after another for Moslem victims among a population frozen with fear. These gangs were modern counterparts of the mobs of ruffians who emerged from the Paris slums under the Terror. This was, in fact, a new Terror, and it lasted approximately a month. The atmosphere was steeped in racial malevolence, decay and nihilism, and its slogan could well have been the Spanish Civil War cry 'Viva la muerte!' ... Murder was, so to speak, taken over by the young. (Henissart, 1970: 393-395)

At the trial of Salan in May 1962, witnesses charged that the OAS had carried out more than 2,000 attacks, killed 1400, of whom 85% were Muslim, and wounded more than 4,000 (Henissart, 1970: 411-412).

Insofar as the OAS had a policy, it was to destroy all attempts at rapprochement between the two populations and to create a veritable apartheid. In Algiers, the OAS issued instructions to evacuate Muslim domestic servants and other Muslim workers from European areas. On 10 May, the OAS slaughtered seven Muslim women servants on their way to work in European homes. Apartheid was becoming reality as Muslims fled in haste from homes in the environs of European quarters, and Europeans abandoned homes in the Muslim quarter of Belcourt and in the mixed peripheral suburbs. The area between the European heart of the city and the now totally Muslim surrounding areas had become a veritable no-man's land (Courrière, 1971: 622).

With the beginnings of the great exodus, the arrest of many OAS leaders and the further disintegration of the movement into anomie and chaos, there remained only a sort of *götterdämmerung* of ultimate atrocity. On 7 June, in the apocalypse of a scorched-earth policy, the university library in Algiers was blown up and 600,000 books burnt, to the accompaniment of paeans of joy; plastic bombs exploded in the faculty laboratories, and in two amphitheatres, followed by explosions in the post office and town hall of El Biar, in two colleges in the centre of Algiers and one wing of the prefecture. As a crowning exploit, the OAS bombed the Summer Palace. On 15 June, the new city-hall in the centre of Algiers was destroyed by an enormous charge of explosives. At the same time, the operating blocks and the radiology laboratories of the Mustapha Hospital exploded (Courrière, 1971: 637, 641). In Oran, on 25 June, OAS terrorists set ablaze the immense oil storage tanks of British Petroleum. *Pieds noirs*, shouting with joy, crowded the waterfront to watch the gigantic blaze. The flames cauterised their wounds (Henissart, 1970: 454).

The FLN was by no means quiescent during this period. The terrorism and counter-terrorism of each of the groups were incitement to this extreme escalation of violence. Funeral obsequies for victims of FLN terrorism provided occasion for *ratonnades*, while OAS terrorism set off a renewed wave of FLN terrorism. On 20 October 1961, the FLN threw grenades into three cafés and attacked other targets; in the days which followed, they carried out 24 attacks, killing 19 persons: and in November they began to direct terrorism against the OAS (Courrière, 1971: 461-466). Yet the FLN was sufficiently in control of the Muslim population to defeat attempts by the OAS to provoke a blind massacre of Europeans, which would have forced army intervention. But the FLN could not indefinitely hold back its followers, and the terrorist attacks continued to multiply, though not to the level of OAS terrorism. In March, 1962, there were 866 attacks in Algiers, of which 611 were imputable to the OAS; in April there were 647 OAS attacks as compared to 32 for the FLN, and in May, 864 to 80, a ratio of 10 to 1 (Courrière, 1971: 595). Finally, on 14 May, the FLN itself organised reprisal raids, following, in 17 areas of the city, the same scenario of tossing a grenade into a bar and firing on the survivors (Courrière, 1971: 631; see also Henissart, 1970: 406-407). In the OAS riposte on 15 May, there was 1 death every 10 minutes in the streets of Algiers.

The terrorism of the OAS proved in fact to be a point of no return, though even during the period of its terrorism there seemed to be other possibilities. Most of the old historic leaders of the revolution in the provisional government favoured the continued presence of European settlers after independence (Courrière, 1971: 377). At the Evian meetings in May 1961, Krim Belkacem, leader of the Algerian delegation, declared that the cohabitation of Algerians and Europeans was an essential condition for the stability of an independent Algeria (Courrière, 1971: 384). On 1 November 1961, on the seventh anniversary of the launching of the revolution, the FLN called for a great demonstration in the course of which the Muslim population should show its desire to live peacefully with Europeans.[8] Following the mortar attack by OAS terrorists on an unsuspecting crowd of Muslims, on 20 March 1962, the FLN cooperated with the French army in preventing a racial confrontation (Courrière, 1971: 563). This was to become an established pattern of cooperation, as the French Government created interim institutions for a transfer of power, and sought to involve Europeans in policies which would make it possible for them to stay on in Algiers (Courrière, 1971: 595). There was even a last-minute truce offered by a section of the OAS, and accepted for the FLN by Krim Belkacem in an attempt to prevent further chaos and to preserve the last chance for the two communities to live together (Courrière, 1971: 641). On 29 June, in Oran, European town leaders met FLN delegates at a meeting which ended on a note of reconciliation (Henissart, 1970: 459). But it was now too late.

The majority of Europeans no longer had faith in anyone or anything. They had seen too many assassinations, too many settlements of account. They had too much for which to reproach others and too much with which to reproach themselves, to attempt the great adventure. These words of hope, of fraternity, of peace, one had rejected them too often on all sides, to adopt them today with any chance of success. At Algiers there was calm, but perhaps only a temporary calm. At Oran, everything was aflame ... Already there were kidnappings, the slitting of throats, in reprisal against the terror imposed

8. In the smaller cities, there were some hundred Muslim deaths as demonstrators clashed with the forces of order (Courrière, 1971: 469).

there by the OAS. Yes, all was finished, truly finished. ... By May, 100,000 Europeans had already left Algeria. This was the advance guard. In these months, more than 800,000 followed. (Courrière, 1971: 644)

IV. *General Laws*

In the same way that 'general laws' are invoked to support the argument that the missed opportunities were an inevitable consequence of the structure of the colonial situation, so, too, they are advanced as argument for the inevitability of massive retaliatory violence, constituting a point of no return. The core assumption is that violence is embedded in the structure of domination, and that violence is the immediate response of the rulers to militant challenge. Both Mahatma Gandhi and Frantz Fanon make this assumption, but with diametrically opposed prescriptions for action. For Gandhi it was necessary to steel the non-violent resisters to the sacrifices they might be called upon to make, so that they would be ready to resist to the death. For Fanon, the violence of the rulers served as argument for the historical necessity of revolutionary violence, 'the searing bullets and bloodstained knives'. And Fanon as we have seen, wrote of the 12,000 victims of Philippeville in 1955, and the instituting of urban and rural militias in 1956, as the huge and all-inclusive repression which almost always characterises the point of no return.

In point of fact, decolonisation is not necessarily a violent process. In many countries, decolonisation was not particularly violent, nor was it marked by the massive retaliatory violence of the rulers.[9] But under certain conditions, such as prevailed in Algeria, it seems plausible enough to argue that it was inevitable that the Europeans would respond with extreme violence to any challenge to their domination, and that these acts of repressive violence would set in motion an irreversible process of polarisation.

Some of these conditions are rather specific to the situation of

9. See my discussion of Fanon's ideology of violence (1969: Ch. 5A).

Metropolitan France at the end of the Second World War. I still find it totally incomprehensible that a France recently liberated from a repressive Nazi occupation should have engaged in most savage reprisals, after the riots at Sétif on the day celebrating the end of the war in Europe, against a movement, if it was such, for liberation from foreign occupation. Of course, the events would not have presented themselves in this light to the French. The right of colonial peoples to self-determination, in terms of the Atlantic Charter, was not yet taken too seriously, or as a high priority, by the colonial powers. In any event, there was the deeply rooted conception of Algeria as an integral part of France. The French could hardly gauge the extent, or the attendant threat to life, of an insurrection which had started so fiercely at Sétif. Moreover, the German occupation may have been brutalising, not humanising, and the suffering under it may perhaps have been an added stimulus to the violence of French retaliatory action against the Muslims. So, too, the defeat by the Germans may have provoked the army to assuage its own humiliation by a devastatingly powerful violence; and in any event, collaboration with Nazi Germany had demonstrated the strength of Fascism within France.

The repressive violence of the settlers, however, was certainly to be expected, and here general propositions might readily be formulated as to the conditions under which settlers are likely to engage in the huge and all-inclusive repression, representing a point of no return. These conditions would include the following: a *colonie de peuplement*, in which there is a large and deeply-rooted settler population, but still constituting a small minority; great discontinuities in culture, social situation and life chances between settlers and indigenous peoples; a system of privilege rooted in inequality under the constitution, in the differential political incorporation of the two sections, so that even minor reforms may have implications for the entire political structure of domination; a history of repression, establishing violence in the idiom of group relations; and a challenge to the traditional privileges of domination.

The conception of 'a point of no return' implies reciprocal

violence, in a continuing process of polarisation; but the settler hope would be that the massive violence it uses, the collective punishments it imposes, the admonitory massacres it perpetrates, would eliminate revolutionary challenge and impose a stable accommodation.

5

No Exit?
Polarisation in Extremis

An even more extreme polarisation is presented by Burundi. Here
there appears to be no escape from the deadly embrace of ethnic
groups, no possibility of release from the inferno of mutual hatred.
Massacre is established as a routine of political competition and
conflict escalates to the search for an ultimate solution in genocide.
If at a visceral level, the Tutsi minority feels that the loss of political
power would spell inevitable extermination, and if the Hutu
majority seeks to reverse this power and avenge its dead,[1] how are
Hutu and Tutsi to come together in somewhat peaceful
coexistence? How are they to participate in common political
institutions? Can Tutsi really find security in the suggestion offered
in Dossier Pax Christi that the Hutu have no need for genocide to
assure them proportional representation, and that those who have
suffered over long periods, hesitate to inflict suffering?[2] Are there
no powerful voices within the country raised in denunciation of

1. '*A l'heure actuelle, ce sont encore les passions qui parlent, et qui parlent à peu près seules:
les masques une fois jetés, ce que disent d'euxmêmes les protagonistes de l'affrontement en cours se
résume clairement dans les positions viscérales suivantes. Pour le pouvoir tutsi, garder le pouvoir
pour ne pas être livré à la mort. Pour l'opposition hutu, prendre le pouvoir et venger les morts*'
(Centre d'information sur le Tiers-Monde, *Dossier Burundi*, March 1973, p. I-1).
2. '*Mais les Hutus n'ont pas besoin d'un génocide pour s'assurer une représentation
proportionelle. Leur nombre suffit. L'horreur de l'exemple donné au monde par la folie meurtrière
de l'orgueil tutsi suffira, on peut l'espérer, à les maintenir sur une voie sage et à eviter la
réprobation du monde. Il n'y a pas que la vengeance qui puisse habiter le coeur de l'homme. Celui
qui a longuement souffert hésite à faire souffrir*' (Lucie Bragard, *Génocide au Burundi*, Dossier
Pax Christi, December 1972, p. 9).

massacre as a political principle, no social forces strong enough to impose ·a cooperative solution? Can only external intervention offer the possibility of a solution? And is there any basis for the hope that outside powers will change their policies of promoting deadly confrontation, as they pursue their own world interests through strategies of internal polarisation?

I

The reprisals by Tutsi against Hutu in 1972 were widely described as genocide. Some analysts deny the validity of this charge. In a report sponsored by the Carnegie Endowment for Peace, an authoritative United States source is quoted as expressing the view that 'it is not and never has been the policy of the United States Government that Burundi could be fairly accused of genocide. Genocide is a specific, legal term with a precise meaning. It boils down to trying to kill a whole people. The Burundi Government didn't try to do that: they couldn't. You can't kill off 80 percent of your population. Perhaps they engaged in mass murder; they weren't guilty of genocide.'[3] Other analysts used the phrase 'selective genocide' to stress one aspect of the massacres, the systematic destruction of Hutu above the level of the ordinary peasant, whether by virtue of education, however modest, or occupation, or possessions. The genocide was thus seen as selectively directed toward the liquidation of those Hutu strata from which leaders and political activists might be recruited.

The sequence of events, following the account given by Lemarchand,[4] is as follows. The immediately precipitating event was a revolt by some groups of Hutu against Tutsi domination,

3. See Bowen, Freeman and Miller, 'No Samaritan: The U.S. and Burundi', *Africa Report*, July-August 1973, 36.

4. Lemarchand, *Selective Genocide in Burundi* (1974a). Many accounts have appeared in the world press, including the *New York Times, Le Monde, Le Soir, Remarques Africaines, Africa Report*, and in scholarly journals. See *inter alia*, Weinstein, 'Conflict and confrontation in Central Africa: The revolt in Burundi, 1972' (1972); Weinstein and Schrire, *Political Conflict and Ethnic Strategies: A Case Study of Burundi* (1976); and Jeremy Greenland, 'Black racism in Burundi' (1973).

with participation of 'Mulelists' (rebels from Zaire). This revolt appears to have been interwoven with conflicts among the Tutsi elite, between monarchists and republicans, between rival royal clans and regional competitors for power, but the exact nature of this involvement is somewhat obscure. In the unfolding of events, it became of marginal relevance, as the conflict took the form of direct confrontation between Hutu and Tutsi, and as the Tutsi consolidated their ranks.

In the capital, the revolt was initiated by attacks on such strategic targets as military camps, police and the radio station. In the southern provinces, it took the form of the slaughter of Tutsi families, and of Hutu who refused to assist in the massacres. There were the inevitable atrocities – the killing of babies, disembowelling of pregnant women, mutilation, hacking and burning to death. Estimates of the dead ranged from 2,000 to 50,000, with 2,000 seemingly the more accurate estimate.

The reprisals were vastly more massive. They were carried out by the army, the police, and bands of so-called revolutionary youth or of self-constituted execution squads. Again, there were the unspeakable atrocities. The use of unsophisticated weapons, garden hoes and scythes, inevitably means atrocity, but sophisticated weapons may be the instrument for the satisfaction of the most brutal cruelty and for the expression of bestial strength in the intimate physical demolition of helpless victims, as in the clubbing to death with rifle butts. There were reports of disembowelling, mutilation, the hacking off of hands,[5] burial

5. There were reports of Hutu atrocities in the cutting short of the legs of the Tutsi victims and of Tutsi reprisals in the cutting off of hands. The French revolutionary song quoted by René Lemarchand (1970: 91), as a frontispiece to his account of the revolution in Rwanda, has a grotesque significance.

Il faut raccourcir les géants
Et rendre les petits plus grands;
Tout à la vraie hauteur
Voilà le vrai bonheur!

(We must shorten the giants
And make the small folk taller;
Everything at its true height –
That is real happiness!)   French Revolutionary song, 1793

alive, execution with hammer and nails. Greenland (1975 b: 4) asserts that most Hutu died from having their skulls crushed by wooden truncheons. The difficult logistic problem of disposing of vast numbers of bodies was eased in some areas by the use of bulldozers, or the enforced participation of Hutu in their own mass burial. Tutsi teachers and students furnished lists of Hutu students to be carted away for massacre. The *New York Times* of 11 June, 1972 reported that students were seen assaulting Hutu on the university grounds, beating them to death with rocks and clubs. A mild relaxing recreation, relief from the tedium of academic study! *Africa Diary* (July 1-7, 1972, p. 6025) reported that 'in Bujumbura Tutsi students had joined forces with the troops to massacre the Hutu. At the university students had lynched 20 of their comrades. Two Hutu had been strangled to death by fellow-students. At the Ecole Normale Supérieure, half the students, male and female alike, had been murdered. In five other boys' schools more than 200 had been killed.'

In his report on *Selective Genocide in Burundi*, René Lemarchand (1974a: 18) writes that '... the most astonishing feature of the repression is the rapidity with which it transformed itself into a genocidal-type operation aiming at the physical liquidation of nearly every educated or semi-educated Hutu', and he quotes Jeremy Greenland on the logistics of the operation:

Local Tutsi, sometimes soldiers, sometimes civil servants, arrived and motioned Hutu teachers, church-leaders, nurses, traders, civil servants into Landrovers with their guns. Bands of Tutsi combed the suburbs of Bujumbura and carted away Hutu by the lorryload. Throughout May and half June 1972, the excavators were busy every night in Gitega and Bujumbura burying the dead in mass graves. In secondary schools teachers stood helpless as many of their Hutu pupils were removed ... Those arrested were usually dead the same night, stripped and practically clubbed to death in covered lorries on the way to prison, then finished off there with clubs at nightfall. Using bullets would have been wasteful.

Wingert (1974: 69-70) cites Dr W. Stanley Mooneyham, president of World Vision International, on the operations in the schools:

A truck roars up to a school building and skids to a halt in a cloud of dust. Soldiers, armed with rifles and bayonets, stand before the gentle teacher and the defenseless children. The corporal demands that all students between 13 and 19 years line up against the wall. From this group they pick 122 boys, tie their hands behind their backs and throw them like logs onto the truck. Heads crack against the truck floor. One child is piled on another. The truck prepares to leave and the children weep. As the truck drives away, the missionary teacher hears the children singing 'Nearer My God to Thee' in their own language. The soldiers in the back of the truck crush all the children's skulls with their riflebutts. About a mile from the school, the truck stops on a bridge and tips the entire human cargo into the river.

The American Universities Field Staff summarised the extermination of the Hutu elite with the following list of victims:

The four Hutu members of the cabinet, all the Hutu officers and virtually all the Hutu soldiers in the armed forces; half of Burundi's primary school teachers; and thousands of civil servants, bank clerks, small businessmen, and domestic servants; at present (August) there is only one Hutu nurse left in the entire country, and only a thousand secondary school students survive.[6]

Estimates of the Hutu massacred in the reprisals range from 100,000 to 200,000.

II

The varied perspectives of the parties themselves are given in a number of dossiers. The Government of Burundi published its own version in a white paper in which the president acknowledged that there had been excesses. But they were very few. In troubled times, there were always bandits to settle personal scores. The Bishop of Burundi was quoted to similar effect. There was much exaggeration, he said: it was necessary to understand the reaction of Tutsi who found themselves plunged into a psychosis of self-defence, seeing themselves threatened with extermination. And if there were excesses in the repression,

6. Quoted in Bowen, Freeman and Miller, *Passing By: The United States and Genocide in Burundi, 1972*, p. 6.

this was easy to understand, but it should be remembered that the authorities and the army censured these excesses.

The root cause, according to the white paper, was to be found in the deliberate policies of the colonial power. Before colonisation, Burundi had attained a profound national unity, being at the point of becoming a model of ethnic integration. Burundi was so highly integrated that one could no longer determine which ethnic group was the source of particular elements of the national culture, whether language, music, oratory, decorations, chants or symbols of power. The very terms Hutu and Tutsi had lost their ethnic connotation, mixed marriages having become so common. It was to be expected that in the presence of a people so conscious of its unity, and governed by a traditional authority so well organised and accepted, the colonial power would prefer to maintain the traditional political and administrative structure. But this alliance was acceptable only so long as the traditional authorities served as the docile instrument for the realisation of colonial objectives. Whenever they refused to submit to the dictates of colonisation and sought to achieve national objectives, the colonial power resorted to two devices, sowing division between ruling families, and, particularly on the threshold of independence, sowing ethnic division among the people.

Of these, according to the white paper, incitement to tribalism was the most murderously deadly. Until 1947, reports of the colonial power had praised the profound ethnic unity of Burundi, and the moral and political qualities of its ruling class. But all this changed after the Second World War, under the obsessive fear of African liberation. Colonial scientists now went out of their way to present the colonial past in a sombre light, emphasising those aspects most calculated to arouse ethnic hostility, and indoctrinating ethnic stereotypes through the deforming prism of colonial literature. Colonial administrators pursued the same objective, the sowing of ethnic division. Identity cards had to give the ethnic and even clan affiliation. Students were obliged to mark their ethnic group on examination papers, many of them answering at random, since they were so completely oblivious of ethnic origins. Colonial and neocolonial propaganda sought to absolve Belgium from any responsibility for the errors of the past. If democratic processes had advanced little during the fifty years of colonisation, if on independence there was not one doctor, not one engineer, not one professor, not one lawyer, if almost the entire population was illiterate, blame must attach to one ethnic group (the Tutsi).

Dangerously inflammatory too was the colonialist political conception equating democracy with ethnic majority rule, and basing national and political solidarity on the ethnic majority. In opposition to the multi-ethnic conception held by African states, this colonialist theory emphasised the homogeneity of the most numerous ethnic group. The fate reserved for other groups was not only political death: it was, quite simply, total death. But in fact, the colonialists and their agents did not care about democracy: it was merely a screen for their antinationalist and anti-African strategies.

The Government white paper then reviews the history of ethnic conflict from the time of the movement toward independence. Belgian colonialists, and more particularly the Belgian *Confédération des Syndicats Chrétiens*, emerge as the diabolical manipulators of ethnic conflict. The Machiavellian strategems included the training of cadres opposed to independence and dedicated to betrayal of the national cause; the creation of syndicates, cooperatives and political parties adopting, as their programme of action, collaboration with colonialism and the politics of total struggle; the distribution of funds for the corruption of weak patriots; the adoption of repressive measures against UPRONA, the party of independence and national unity, running in desperation, when these measures failed to prevent the victory of UPRONA, to encouragement of the assassination of its leader, the Prime Minister Prince Rwagasore.

On the independence of Burundi in July 1962, the colonialists faced the problem of creating tribalism where none existed, as the electoral triumph of UPRONA demonstrated. Their new strategy was to create tribalism, or to create the appearance of tribalism, by reliance on a dialectic between provocation and order. Thus, the chiefs of the tribalist movement resorted to a series of provocative acts in the form of brawls, assassinations and attempted *coups d'état*, which forced the authorities to intervene and restore order, the intervention being greatly exaggerated in propaganda reports and misrepresented as tribalism. This was the pattern of events in the Kamenge episode (in January 1962, preceding independence), when members of the *Jeunesses Nationalistes Rwagasore* reacted to the provocation of the Christian Syndicates of Burundi. It was repeated in the assassination in 1965 of Ngendandumwe, the Hutu Prime Minister, and in the attempted coup later in the same year, when terrorist bands massacred thousands of women and children, of the old and the innocent, perpetrating atrocity. This was the first time in the history of Burundi, according to the white paper, that Hutu had attacked their brother Tutsi and Twa, not because they were more rich, more politically powerful, of different religion or language, but simply because they were of different ethnic group and because this was the wish of the Belgian syndicalists. In the view of the government, similar processes were to be observed in the planned genocide of 1969, and in the attempted genocide by Hutu of Tutsi in 1972.

The white paper recounts the events of 1972 under the heading, *la 3ème tentative ou le déchainement des Syndicalochrétiens belges*, seemingly ascribing the major responsibility to this intervention from abroad. According to the scenario (*'le film des événements'*) presented in the report, bands of some twenty-five thousand rebels, both nationals and strangers, armed with poisoned machetes, clubs, automatic weapons and Molotov cocktails, descended on different areas of Burundi, mutilating the young, subjecting women to unspeakable atrocity, savagely murdering the men and the aged, pillaging and burning their homes. It was selective massacre, directed, that is to say, against the Tutsi. The Government found comfort, however, in the fact that some who were not members of the ethnic group designated for extermination preferred to die rather than assassinate their brother countrymen, while others fled. The large number of victims (almost 50,000 corpses were counted), the extensive preparations, the plans and documents seized, amply establish that the aggressors did not wish simply to overthrow the republican government, but that they had planned the systematic extermination of an entire ethnic group, the Tutsi. Yet despite this atrocious slaughter of thousands of innocent people, the authorities had not applied the *lex talionis*. Only the guilty were punished. Far from there being any question of genocide against the Hutu, the defence of the country against the aggressors had been largely assured by civilian defense groups comprising a majority of Hutu. There was no genocide against the Hutu: and only those guilty of the genocide against the Tutsi were punished.

III

A totally different perspective, diametrically opposed to the version presented by the government, emerges from the two statements issued by the *Mouvement des Etudiants Progressistes Barundi* (MEPROBA) in Belgium in May 1972 and February 1973. The first statement, *Génocide au Burundi*, presents as the basis of the problem, the propositions that the differences which appear as ethnic derive more fundamentally from the exploitation and oppression of the Hutu by the Tutsi, who had colonised the country long before the Belgians; that the Belgians are implicated in the conflict to the extent that they contributed to the sharpening of the contradictions between Hutu and Tutsi, by the use of the latter as the instruments of colonial domination; and that even at the present time, Tutsi domination serves the interests of Belgian and other neocolonialists. Elaborating on the role of ethnic differences, the paper comments that, to be sure, two ethnic groups oppose each other, and it would be easy to talk of ethnic conflict. But in fact, one group, the Tutsi, forms a dominant minority in the service of foreign interests and its own class privileges, and seeks by all means to push the majority class of Hutu away from any share in the direction of national affairs.

This is a difficult conception, that the reality is a class struggle, its manifestation in ethnic conflict a mere appearance, an illusion. When Hutu massacre Tutsi, is it only the appearance of Tutsi they massacre, but is the reality the destruction of the upper class? And when Tutsi massacre Hutu peasants, Hutu workers, Hutu traders, Hutu officers, Hutu civil servants, Hutu cabinet ministers, are they engaged in a class struggle, eliminating the lower classes? Or are they eliminating the 'nation-class' of Hutu, to borrow the term by which Cabral reconciles the class struggle with national liberation? And is the uninformed observer misled into perceiving the victims as Hutu? And perhaps when the Hutu slaughter Tutsi of all stations in life, they too are engaged in eliminating a nation-class. And if it is a class struggle which is being waged, why does MEPROBA title its dossier 'Genocide in Burundi' and not 'Class Warfare in Burundi', and why does it use such terms as 'Tutsisation' to describe the process of replacing Hutu officials by Tutsi, and why indeed is the entire discussion phrased in terms of the relations between Tutsi and Hutu, and not of ruling class and proletariat or subordinate class? The Government, in its repudiation of the fundamental distinction between ethnic groups was more consistent, since it avoided appreciably the use of ethnic labels, though there are many references to tribalists, and a sharp attack on the tribalism of an association of Hutu students, described as financed and indoctrinated by Belgian Christian-Syndicalists, and as constituting the nursery of leaders in the attempted coup of 1969 and the invasion of 1972 (pp. 30-31). However, it seems that MEPROBA had second thoughts on the basic character of the conflict, since its later memorandum reports as one of the conclusions of a conference on Burundi, the denial of an identification of ethnic cleavage with class cleavage (*Génocide séculaire*, p. 15).

The papers give a brief description of the economy of Burundi as one of the poorest countries in the world, densely overpopulated, surviving on the basis of archaic agriculture, with some export crops (coffee and tea), but little development of industry, a small working class of barely 10,000 workers, and an inflated administrative sector relative to public resources. There follows a review of the early history, which is in fact an account of the relations between the ethnic groups: the Twa, the original inhabitants, hunters and potters (now constituting 1% of the population); the Hutu, later arrivals, establishing themselves in small kingdoms and engaged in agriculture (some 85% of the population before the massacres); and finally the Tutsi, infiltrating or invading warriors, nomads and pastoralists. The account stresses two aspects; first, the extreme inequality under Tutsi domination in the traditional system, with the Twa in the role of pariahs, and the Hutu in servitude under relations of clientage revolving round the ownership and care of cattle; and secondly, the maintenance of this traditional structure under both German colonisation and Belgian tutelage.

In their analysis of the contemporary conflict from the first legislative elections in September 1961 to the massacres of 1972, the authors attribute great significance to the revolution of 1959 in neighbouring Rwanda for an understanding of the recent political evolution of Burundi. They assert that this bloody revolution, in which the Hutu overthrew the monarchy, and which resulted in the exile of a good part of the dominant Tutsi stratum, continuously preyed on the minds of the Burundi rulers, fed their fears, and stimulated the search to prevent, at any cost, a similar fate in their own country. Denying that responsibility attached only to the imperialists and the Belgian Christian syndicalists, they charge that it was above all the Tutsi rulers who over the last ten years had raised ethnic solidarity to the level of political doctrine.

The process of basing political strategy on ethnic conflict is traced through a series of traumatic events. According to the version given in *Génocide au Burundi*, these start with the assassination on 13 October 1961 of the progressive leader, Prince Rwagasore, by members of a rival royal Tutsi lineage. Savage reprisals followed against Hutu leaders, five of whom were murdered, the mayor of Muramba being buried alive, while five trade union organisers were arrested and executed. *Génocide séculaire* gives a slightly different account, reporting that three months after the assassination the *Jeunesse Nationaliste Rwagasore* conducted a punitive expedition against trade union members of the opposition party, killing four and severely wounding others, the Hutu mayor Miburo being buried alive on the order of the then prime minister, a Tutsi.

On independence, in July 1962, signs of tension appeared: in the vacuum resulting from the lack of a leader and of a programme with sufficient appeal to transcend the deeply embedded cleavages, it was only to be expected that politicians would regroup on the basis of ethnic membership. The ruling party UPRONA split into two wings: the Monrovian, largely Hutu, seeking to affirm the majority position of the Hutu, and the Casablancan, bringing together traditional and modernist Tutsi as well as Hutu, under the leadership of Tutsi extremists, traumatised by the example set in Rwanda, and disturbed by the rise, and militancy, of Hutu.

A number of minor crises then intervened. The Tutsi prime minister arrested and imprisoned some of the Tutsi supporters of the Monrovian group. On his replacement in June 1963 by a Hutu prime minster, Ngendandumwe, there was a demonstration by Tutsi against the criminal prosecution of the Tutsi murderers of the Hutu trade unionists. The King responded by dismissing three Hutu ministers from Ngendandumwe's balanced inter-ethnic cabinet. Ngendandumwe resigned and was succeeded by an extremist Tutsi prime minister. The new government immediately released the recently convicted murderers, an action which gave rise to dissatisfaction among the parliamentary supporters of Ngendandumwe, leading to the arrest of a number of Hutu leaders.

The next major event was the attempted coup in 1965. Ngendandumwe was recalled to power at the beginning of 1965, only to be assassinated shortly after he had presented his newly constituted government. In the ensuing general elections, a large majority of Hutu was returned, but the King nominated his cousin prime minister, and severely curtailed the powers of parliament, provoking an abortive coup by some army and police officers. Michel Micombero, on whom the King conferred all necessary powers, visited severe reprisals upon the Hutu.

Almost all the Hutu army and police officers were executed, Hutu leaders were murdered, Hutu propagandists in the recent elections imprisoned or murdered, and whole communes razed to the ground. After the declaration of a Republic, and under a political formula of reconstruction and national reconciliation, Micombero continued to pursue the policy of 'Tutsisation' in the army, the administration and the schools, and of the liquidation of the Hutu population. Extreme atrocity attended the summary judgments of the judicial process – the gouging out of eyes, the amputation of limbs, the skinning alive, electrodes applied to genitals, tortures recalling the Nazi concentration camps. In 1969, the new regime used the pretext of a plot to eliminate many Hutu elite; in 1970 it arrested Hutu students accused of plotting against established institutions. In 1971 the regime announced that it had foiled a plot by the Banyaruguru (Tutsi mainly of the North): and in May 1972 it launched a campaign of genocide against the Hutu.

The papers charge that the genocide, in which 300,000 Hutu were slaughtered, was planned as far back as 1963, and that the whole course of events seemed to indicate that the peasant jacquerie which served as the pretext for genocide was the result of deliberate provocation. Two days before the uprising, the Minister of Interior and Justice had informed a meeting of officials at Lake Nyanza that, on analysing the passage of events in Burundi, and the menace represented by the large population of Hutu in the Nyanza area, the authorities had decided to reduce their numbers, leaving as only survivors, the uneducated peasants. In the reprisals, almost all the Hutu ministers and civil servants were executed, as well as soldiers, workers and merchants. At Rumonge, the military razed everything to the ground, killing men, women, children and the aged. Aeroplanes from Zaire launched their rockets against everything that moved. French helicopters machine-gunned all concentrations. Fanatical hordes from the Rwagasore youth movement ran through the territory, killing, pillaging, burning. Tutsi students denounced their fellow Hutu students, provoking riots so as to provide the occasion for military intervention. Not a single Hutu student was left in the official superior and secondary schools of Bujumbura, the capital.

Meanwhile the great powers remained silent. Indeed they helped the Government – soldiers and aeroplanes from Zaire, French helicopters, the army equipped with Belgian munitions. How then could the Government lay the blame on imperialism, when the diplomatic representatives in Burundi from both the East and the West had contributed to the reinforcement of the army! The responsibility lay with the rulers, who had elevated ethnic solidarity into political doctrine. Even the African states had given the Burundi government their political support.[7]

IV

The opposition between these two perspectives extends to the historical roots of the problem in the contrast between the idyllic picture of traditional ethnic integration presented in the Government white paper, and the centuries of serfdom and oppression perceived as the fate of the Hutu under Tutsi domination. There can be no questioning the fact of ethnic massacres and countermassacres, but designation of their ultimate source is controversial. Are they the creation of such Machiavellian conspirators as colonialists, neocolonialists and tribalists, or are they rooted in the very structure of traditional Burundi society?

7. On 8 September 1972, MEPROBA wrote to the heads of African states meeting in Tanzania as follows: 'Tutsi apartheid is established more ferociously than the apartheid of Vorster, more inhumanly than Portuguese colonialism. Outside of Hitler's Nazi movement, there is nothing to compete with it in world history. And the peoples of Africa say nothing. African heads of state receive the executioner Micombero and clasp his hand in fraternal greeting. Sirs, heads of state, if you wish to help the African peoples of Namibia, Azania, Zimbabwe, Angola, Mozambique and Guinea-Bissau to liberate themselves from their white oppressors, you have no right to let Africans murder other Africans ... Are you waiting until the entire Hutu ethnic group of Burundi is exterminated before raising your voices?' To this MEPROBA adds the despairing comment: 'We ask ourselves in what measure African heads of state have harkened to our appeal, since Micombero's hordes continue tranquilly to execute their ignoble plan! History will not fail to judge the silence of African peoples when thousands of their brothers fell under the blows of an anti-African caste.'

Analysis of a wide range of dossiers and commentaries offers support for both points of view. The *Dossier Burundi* of the Permanent Secretariat of the Clergy projects an image of integration well advanced in traditional society and indeed progressing to new levels under colonial rule. Hutu and Tutsi are described as having lived together harmoniously, and having become so intermingled physically and culturally that in the recent '*événements*', many of the victims of the attacks by machete were Hutu mistaken for Tutsi. Conscious of sharing the same fate, in adversity as in prosperity, Hutu and Tutsi had developed in their settlements the fraternal solidarity of good neighbours. They held equal political status under the rule of the Mwami and the princes of royal blood, and they participated without discrimination in the service of the court. It was thus sheer distortion to suggest that the Hutu had at any time been the slaves of the Tutsi. As for colonisation, the policies pursued by the colonisers did tend to consolidate the power of the ruling princes and to rigidify political administration. But ethnic interpenetration nevertheless continued to progress under the stimulus of Christianity and of education. Inter-ethnic marriages multiplied and a new class arose, defining itself no longer by ethnic group and clan, but by reference to values derived from intellectual interests and economic progress. The phenomenon of ethnic conflict belongs to a later period, that of decolonisation.

Le Centre d'Information sur le Tiers-Monde released its own *Dossier Burundi* in March 1973. This consists of a '*prise de position*' by CITM and a history of Burundi and its ethnic conflicts by a group of Hutu.[8] The former, in essence a radical Third World perspective, attributes much of the responsibility to the external forms of Christian-Social ideology and of neo-colonialist strategic interests in the rule of the moderates. The history traces the origins of the conflict to its roots in traditional society, which is described as having established Tutsi superiority over Hutu, comparable to that of the lords over their serfs in the Middle Ages. There was certainly nothing harmonious in this master-

8. With Nicodème Sinzobahamvya.

slave relationship. The Tutsi provided chiefs, sub-chiefs and notables. The Hutu constituted in general the mass of subjects in the service of the notables and sub-chiefs, while the Twa were the veritable pariahs of the society. This social structure was reflected in the very language of Kirundi. The word 'hutu' signifies servant, the verb 'kwihutura' means release from the condition of 'hutu' by becoming enfranchised in taking a Tutsi wife, and 'kutwakara', literally to become a Twa, is a synonym for 'to degenerate'. As for the most recent conflict, responsibility is to be attributed to the rulers of the country, men whose cruelty and machiavellianism are well known, extremists committed to a sinister plan for the extermination of the Hutu. What followed was not a civil war, but a massacre by the regular army of a part of the population in the name of racism.

These different political perspectives are refracted through the prism of ethnic identification. They offer insight into the conflict partly as analytical perspectives on the conflicts, but more significantly as aspects of the conflict itself, expressing the profoundly antagonistic attitudes of the combatants.

In contrast to these polarised perceptions of the massacres, there is the balanced perspective presented by René Lemarchand, a scholar of great ability and integrity who has worked for many years in Rwanda, Burundi and Zaire. He opens his account of *Selective Genocide in Burundi* with the statement that at the present time, the pattern of Tutsi dominance extends to virtually all sectors of life, restricting access to material wealth, education, status and power, and he adds the comment that 'for anyone even remotely familiar with the relatively open and flexible system of stratification that once characterised Burundi society, the transformation is little short of astonishing'.

Professor Lemarchand's perspective emphasises the diversity and complexity of structures which provided a basis for linkage between different sections across ethnic boundaries. The ruling families, the princes of royal blood, became identified as a separate ethnic group, characterised by internal rivalries and bitter feuds in precolonial times. The Tutsi themselves fell into two major sections, a 'higher-caste' of Tutsi-Banyaruguru, and a 'lower-caste' of Tutsi-Hima, largely corresponding to regional differences between the North and South. Cutting across the various divisions in Burundi society were the social rankings attached to different patrilineages within each ethnic group, and a system of clientage drawing Hutu and Tutsi into 'a web of interlocking relationships extending from the very top of the social pyramid to its lowest echelons, with the Mwami acting as the supreme Patron'. Ethnic divisions were not significant for social prestige, and only marginally significant for wealth. The many cleavages provided the basis for a great diversity of shifting alliances and conflicts, no single line of cleavage was dominant, and ethnic conflict was in fact seldom if ever activated. Thus Professor Lemarchand concludes that if the term 'tribalism' has any meaning in the context of Burundi society, 'it is a very recent phenomenon, traceable to the social transformations introduced under the aegis of the colonial state and the consequent disintegration of those very structures and mechanisms that once gave cohesiveness to society as a whole'.

In assessing these views, there is the initial problem of determining what criteria are to be applied in arriving at a judgment as to the potential significance of ethnic differentiation for conflict. Is the crucial test to be the eruption of violence, the outbreak of massacres, the attempts at genocide? One recalls the research of a sensitive observer, Jacques Maquet, whose central thesis was the acceptance of the premise of inequality in traditional Rwanda society, and the difficulty in reconciling this thesis with the later history of ethnic massacre and counter-massacre in the period of decolonisation. It would seem reasonable to assume that the Rwanda conflict was deeply rooted in the traditional structure of the society, even though it did not manifest itself in overt violence. Perhaps the same assumption must be made that the potentiality for the holocausts of ethnic violence was also deeply embedded in the traditional structure of Burundi society, notwithstanding the greater mobility, fluidity and diversity of inter-ethnic relations in Burundi.

For purposes of this discussion, it is not necessary to attempt the almost impossible task of assessing the precise significance to be attached to ethnic differentiation in traditional Burundi society. I will assume that the roots of the conflict reach back to the traditional structure, and that the potentiality for inter-ethnic violence was increased by the policies of the mandatory power: and I will ask what factors over the first decade of decolonisation transformed a situation of the containment of conflict into 'selective genocide'.

V

In a strange way, representative government, which would seem to offer procedures for the just reconciliation of ethnic and other interests, was one of the catalysts of 'selective genocide'. The competition between political parties gave a new dimension of political significance to ethnic identity. Democratic representative government rewards the majority, and if the electoral process is ethnically defined, then representative government becomes the rule of the ethnic majority. This was the charge the Burundi government directed against the colonialist and tribalist conception of democracy, which it equated, in exaggerated terms, with the conception that only the ethnic majority had the right to control public affairs, and indeed to survive. So too, the bishops in their pastoral letter complained that ethnic division was supported by the democratic conception that it is the law of numbers that prevails, that the majority must govern as if the majority of votes was in itself the very foundation of right and justice.

I take it to be highly probable that with representative government in ethnically or racially plural societies, there will be politicians ready to exploit to the maximum the politics of ethnicity for personal power, whatever the political formula under which they act. But I take it to be equally axiomatic, that the ethnic appeal will have little resonance, unless there is a significant structural basis of division and discrimination. Ethnic politics cannot be fabricated out of a harmonious integration by pure ideology; nor is the mere presence of members of different ethnic groups within a society a sufficient basis for ethnic appeals.

The ethnic political parties emerged with the inception of electoral politics immediately preceding independence, but initially they proved quite insignificant, the major conflict being between parties led by members of competing princely families in a continuation of precolonial rivalries. Yet in the space of some four years, the politics of ethnicity was firmly entrenched. Whether this was inevitable, or whether the tensions might have been resolved harmoniously, if the leaders had renounced the resort to violence, it is impossible to say. Violence was embedded in the conflict from the very outset.

The initial violence, strangely enough, was in the neighbouring state of Rwanda, where a peasant Hutu jacquerie against the ruling Tutsi erupted in 1959, and where reprisal massacres followed Tutsi attempts to regain their power in 1963. It dramatised with all the spectacular and gruesome brutality of a Last Judgment, the glittering rewards, and the horrendous torments, of massacre, and it intensified ethnic consciousness in Burundi. The *Dossier Burundi* issued by the clergy, comments that the shedding of blood in Rwanda served to recall people to reason, thereby contributing to the initial rejection of tribal electoral appeals in Burundi in 1961. But the clergy go on to explain that the resulting cohesion was fragile: Hutu extremists, lacking the ideological appeal which might win them electoral popularity, fell under the fascination of the Rwanda precedent, while Tutsi in Burundi began to fear that they might suffer the fate which had overtaken the Tutsi of Rwanda. The *Dossier Burundi* of CITM makes the same point, but from a perspective sympathetic to the Hutu, that the events in Rwanda had aroused their hopes of shaking off the feudal yoke and of achieving equality of opportunity, while they had awakened among the aristocratic Tutsi the fear that the Hutu in Burundi would now raise their heads.

It is exaggerated, however, to suggest that in 1972, the Hutu of Burundi paid for the blood of the Tutsi in Rwanda. Internal violence, starting with the trauma of Prince Rwagasore's assassination, and the terrorism by 'Nationalist Youth' against Hutu political and trade-union leaders, released a cycle of assassinations, executions, attempted coups, reprisals, massacres and counter-massacres, escalating ultimately to 'selective genocide'. But the brutalities of political change in Rwanda (from a radical point of view, the 'good massacres'), did contribute to the ethnic fears and hatreds and to the ultimate holocaust (the 'bad massacres') in Burundi. René Lemarchand comments that 'by giving the Burundi situation a false definition to begin with, a definition patterned on the Rwanda situation, Hutu politicians evoked a new behaviour among themselves and the Tutsi, which made their originally false imputations true. Ethnic conflict thus took on the quality of a "self-fulfilling prophecy".'[9]

Some sources stress the role of Hutu and Tutsi elites. Thus the bishops, in their pastoral letter of January 1973, deplore the changing values of Burundi society, and the use of nepotism, racism or tribalism, and regionalism for personal gain. They comment that though the main problem appears to lie in these divisive processes and policies, they themselves are persuaded that the root cause is the egoism of Hutu and Tutsi elites. I have no difficulty in accepting an emphasis on the significant role of the elites in inflaming and manipulating ethnic hatreds, as Tutsi political leaders sought to maintain their dominant position and as Hutu politicians challenged that domination and the increasing 'Tutsisation' of high office. But I would add that they were harnessing real social forces, embedded in the structure of the society, and in the perceptions of many of its members.

There were many sources of conflict within the society, other than the division between Tutsi and Hutu. Weinstein and Schrire (1976: 55) refer to the urban/rural cleavage, to the opposition between tradition and modernity, and between monarchists and republicans, to competition for control over the political system and for economic resources, to class stratification, as evidenced in the divergent interests of higher and lower Tutsi status groups, and to the increasing regional antagonism among Tutsi. In an extended analysis, they argue that the Hutu revolt in April 1972 was

---

9. *Selective Genocide in Burundi*, p. 8. For a detailed analysis of the politicisation of ethnicity in Burundi see Lemarchand, *Rwanda and Burundi*, particularly ch. 13.

essentially or most significantly a peasant revolt in southern Burundi against the encroachment of alien life patterns and under the spur of economic grievances. But these other conflicts were either less salient than, or they fed into, the conflict between Hutu and Tutsi. Whatever the position in traditional Burundi or in colonial Burundi, the ethnic division had become the dominant cleavage in the society, the encompassing principle of political organisation and action.

Inevitably in so divided a house, outside powers found opportunity for intervention, thereby adding fuel to the internal fires.

VI

The term 'selective genocide' is a euphemism. There was much indiscriminate slaughtering of Hutu. But to the extent that it was selective, it eliminated not only the elite, but also the potential elite among the Hutu. Is this then the solution, the intellectual sterilisation of a whole population? And will this arrest the cycle of reciprocal violence? Will it lay the foundation for acquiescence in domination, or for evolutionary movement to equality of participation? And if not, are doses of 'prophylactic violence' to be administered again and again? Is another cycle of terrorism and counter-terrorism, of massacre and countermassacre inevitable? Is there no other way? Is there no escape from the deadly embrace of ethnic hatreds?

Part Two

POLARISATION

6

Polarising Ideologies

Ideology and action are like partners in a modern dance, gyrating in harmony or in disharmony, or wrapt in their separate, exclusive closed worlds. Ideologies may guide future action or merely rationalise past events. They may be marginal to action which is planned under the spur of other stimuli; pure rhetoric,[1] with little resonance among the general populace. Or they may mould the consciousness of the masses and their predispositions to act. Where ideologies influence events, reactions and ideology may be quite consonant, or the course of events may be quite the reverse of expectations dervied from the content of the ideologies. It is thus hazardous to argue from ideology to action: and in this chapter, I am presenting abstract systems of ideas, which portray the society as polarised between two major sections, or which seem to be directed to that end. I am assuming, however, that, in extreme racial or ethnic conflicts, ideologies are a significant element where they are widely disseminated, and where there is a convergence between ideology and action.

I

An uncompromising dualism constitutes the core of ideologies of polarisation. This dualism may rest on some simple factual definition of the situation, as in Courrière's description of the

---

1. See Jacques Ellul (1969: 208-236) for an interesting discussion of words masquerading as revolution, and rendering the very concept banal. In this chapter, I am developing ideas I originally presented in 'Ideologies of violence among surbordinate groups' (1969: 153-167).

attitudes of supporters of the French terrorist organisation, the OAS, in the last phases of the Algerian war. For them, he writes, everything had to be all white or all black: not to be committed to the goal of a French Algeria was to be all black. And it was entirely in the general interest that the OAS should assassinate the liberals and those other evil men who wished to deliver their lovely country into the hands of the bandit National Liberation Front (Courrière, 1971: 451).

Often, however, or at any rate in elaborated ideologies, the dualism is linked with some conception of a general process which ranges the parties in implacable opposition, denies the possibility of mediation, and provides unambiguous identification and hostile characterisation of the enemy.

Among subordinate groups, theories of the class struggle and of colonialism are major sources for conceptions of a general process of polarisation. The Communist Manifesto provides an archetypal model. There is the dialectical opposition between the interests of owners and workers, an historical process which heightens this contradiction, drawing the members of the society inexorably into two hostile camps, until the dominant group is overthrown by revolution. Any conception in other terms represents false consciousness. In Fanon's theory of decolonisation, the colonial world is already by its very nature polarised between colonisers and colonised. It is a Manichean world, a world cut into two reciprocally exclusive, racially defined sections, between which there is no possibility of conciliation, decolonisation being quite simply the replacing of one 'species' of men by another 'species', to be accomplished through murderous struggle.

Ideologies of dominant groups seem to be less theoretical. They may take the form of stark alternatives, as in the conception that group relations are governed by the choice between domination and subordination; or there may be a conception of an impassable chasm in evolutionary levels, or of an eternal dichotomy in terms of this-worldly or other-worldly salvation between the saved and the damned. Ideologies of polarisation among dominant groups are perhaps more pragmatic, and yield more directly the monstrous characterisations which serve to encourage or justify holocausts of violence. It seems too that as the conflict becomes more deadly, the hate-laden stereotypes are likely to prevail over the theoretical underpinnings in the ideologies of both dominant and subordinate groups. And indeed, in some situations, theories of a general process of polarisation, or of dialectical opposition, may be a specious superstructure on an historical enmity.

Given the factual complexity and variety of social relationships and of interests cutting across the racial or ethnic divisions, the conception of an uncompromising dualism calls for an ideological simplification of structures and issues. The mediating structures, the bridges, the intermediaries come under attack from both sides. There is no middle ground, no possibility of arriving at an understanding. The French Governor 'believed he could come to an understanding with Abbas (the Algerian Muslim leader). The man was moderate, sympathetic. The report proved the contrary. With 'them' there was only one method, to be the stronger. Their proverb was quite unequivocal: "Kiss the hand you cannot cut off"' (Courrière, 1969: 159). As to the bridges, 'a traitor and a bridge are very much alike, for they both go over to the other side' (Rev. Dr. Ian K. Paisley, one of the leaders of the Protestant ultras in Northern Ireland – Rose, 1971: 101).

There is a corresponding simplification of issues. The diversity of interests which provide an actual or potential link between the racial or ethnic groups is transformed ideologically into a conception of totally opposed life situations. This transformation is facilitated in plural societies by the pervasive domination of one racial group over another in a great variety of structures. Since members of the subordinate race experience political inequality, economic exploitation and social exclusion, issues of conflict in these varied contexts tend to be superimposed, providing a realistic basis for conceptions of a total conflict of interests. So too, for members of the dominant race, the extensive exercise of privilege is strong argument for a dichotomous conception of race relations.

Reformism must be exorcised, since it might strengthen

common interests, or create new interests across the racial
barriers, thus fragmenting the polar opposition of racial groups,
and inviting more flexible and evolutionary perspectives.
Members of a minority dominant group may draw on the
distilled wisdom of the polarising cliché that reform spells
annihilation, or that it is the trigger for the discharge of insatiable
demands, while the subordinates may view reformism as a
machiavellian device, a counterrevolutionary strategy for
perpetuating domination.

Whatever the structure of the ideology, the nature of the
theory, the quality of the characterisation, and the mechanisms of
simplification, the end result is to present the alignments and the
issues in the form of stark alternatives, readily crystallised into
polarising slogans. The alternative, *Algérie algérienne* or *Algérie
française*, hardly leaves room for conciliation when Muslim
Algerians equate *Algérie française* with colonial Algeria (Fanon,
1968: 89), and when French Algerians express the ancestral fear
of minorities in the belief that equality between one million and
nine million spells massacre, and that Algerian independence
means '*the suitcase or the coffin*' (Courrière, 1971: 191, 122).

II

The advocacy of violence seems to be an invariable component
of ideologies of polarisation. Presumably this is what they are
about. The violence envisaged may not be that of the bearers of
the ideology. It may be delegated to the invading force of an
outside power, or to a deity as in millenarian movements. But the
necessity and desirability of violence, and its justification are
nevertheless present.

The necessity for violence has been debated so often that it is
now crystallised into a set of axioms. For subordinate groups, the
essential elements are first the alleged failure of non-violence.
This rests on the assertion that the subordinates have explored all
possible forms of non-violent action without success, and that
there are no constitutional channels for change. Ruling groups, so
the argument continues, simply laugh at non-violence, which

merely enhances their power, and they are impervious to moral and reasoned appeals. Their domination rests on violence, they respond by violence to non-violence, and years of non-violent struggle end in the futility of violent suppression. Thus, in 'Requiem for non-violence', Eldridge Cleaver (1969: 74, 138) claims that the fact that white America could produce the assassin of Dr Martin Luther King, was viewed by black people as a final repudiation of any hope of change by peaceful and non-violent means; the bullet that killed Martin Luther King murdered non-violence. Given the violent nature of domination, and the refusal of ruling groups to relinquish power, it is argued that domination can only be overthrown by violence. This conclusion by no means follows from the premises, but it is bolstered by the appeal to historical necessity, no people ever having won its freedom without bloodshed.

These arguments for the necessity of violence may be supplemented by a variety of tactical considerations. Violence is seen as the only effective technique for raising political consciousness in a populace under conditions of political repression which deny freedom of association and other basic political rights. Even where there are constitutional channels for political action, violence may seem more efficacious as a means for heightening revolutionary consciousness with greater speed and smaller sacrifice. In the absence of solidarity among the subordinates, violence may be deemed necessary for the forging of unity. This violence may be visited directly on members of the subordinate group by attacking the non-conformists who seek to maintain cooperative relations across the racial barriers or in other ways reject discipline. Or the violence may be invited by provoking indiscriminate reprisals from the ruling group. The less polarised the society, the greater may be the felt need for violence internal to a particular racial or ethnic group.

Necessity and justification are interwoven. If violence is necessary to freedom, then violence is morally justified, assuming, that is, the overriding value of a state of freedom. If there is an historical necessity for revolution, if revolution is the midwife of history, then violence is not only a necessary part of the historical process, but again morally justified. What unspeakable atrocities of tyranny and torture have been committed in the name of freedom or of historical necessity, how many millions slaughtered under their banner!

Ellul (1969: 103-108) includes justification among the basic laws of violence. He writes that 'the man who uses violence always tries to justify both it and himself. Violence is so unappealing that every user of it has produced lengthy apologies to demonstrate to the people that it is just and morally warranted. Hitler, Stalin, Mao, Castro, Nasser, the guerillas, the French "paras" of the Algerian war – all tried to vindicate themselves.' Ellul is not arguing that the practitioner of violence feels uneasy, and experiences pangs of conscience, but rather that in acting violently he is so unsure of himself that he must have an ideological construct that will put him at ease intellectually and morally.

I find it difficult to believe that violence is unappealing, when it has become the great spectacle in the mass entertainment of the Western world, as it was in Nero's time, and when its advocacy is well established in the featherbed seclusion of academic circles, engaged in autoerotic exhibitions of revolutionary heroism. It is surely common enough practice for ideologists of violence to surrender to frenzies of hatred. Indeed Ellul (1969: 104) argues that violence and hatred always go together, that violence is an expression of hatred, has its source in hatred and signifies hatred. Can one really accept that hate-ridden ideologists of violence feel insecure in their advocacy of violence and hence in need of ideological supports? To be sure, many advocates of violence do indeed have moral scruples, but the appeal to morality may also rest on political expediency. Given that the moral sense with which members of a society are imbued, restrains, in some measure, violence and the spilling of blood, the effective mobilisation of support in a dangerous enterprise would call for moral appeals to release the inhibitions against violence and to motivate personal sacrifice.

Whether or not moral justifications of violence universally attend its use, they certainly seem to be a very general feature of ideologies of violence. One cannot readily conceive of a serious social movement mobilising under the slogan 'Violence is Fun'. Sorel's *Reflections on Violence*, which later served as one of the inspirations or rationalisations of the Fascist idealisation of violence, seems now to have a somewhat genteel intellectual flavour, quite remote from contemporary calls to violence. The apocalyptic violence he sought was nothing more terrifying than that of the proletarian general strike: and he did not believe that it would result in any development of brutality, since the idea of the general strike might foster the notion of the class war by means of incidents which would appear as of small importance to middle-class historians (1967: 186). Moreover, his goal in the use of violence was the moral regeneration of society.

Fanon is infinitely more bloody-minded. His concern with racial or national liberation has much greater relevance for current social movements than Sorel's advocacy of proletarian revolutionary violence, and his call to violence has proved highly congenial to many revolutionary circles. In his essay 'Concerning violence', there is a lyrical exultation in violence. But Fanon does not exult in violence for its own sake. On the contrary, he offers us case studies in the psychopathology of violence, and he denounces the violence of the colonisers. It is the violence of domination which, in his view, necessitates and justifies the violence of liberation, and it is the dehumanising oppression of the colonisers which gives to the violence of the colonised its regenerative quality. For both these ideologists, Fanon and Sorel, the moral issues are quite central.

The justifications then of violence are the higher ethical imperatives of justice, liberty, and historical necessity. Domination is violent, unjust: the violence of domination is the cause of my violence, its justification; and ultimately, violence is less costly in terms of human suffering. Violence is liberating, purificatory, therapeutic — for the aggressors presumably rather than their tortured or annihilated victims. It is God's will, if we are to believe the revelations of some of the men of God. 'God is not the dominator, but the awakener of guerillas among oppressed peoples. Unless we participate in the struggle of the poor for their liberation, we can understand nothing about Jesus Christ ... How shall we observe Lent nowadays? By making each of us a revolutionary rupture with a society based on injustice, and by paralysing the death mechanisms of the money system – if necessary, by a well-planned general strike. Such is the Lent that pleases God, the Easter liturgy of today.'[2]

Implicit or explicit in these justifications is the distinction between just violence and unjust violence. As the village politician, Mr Nark, explains in *Death at the Bar* by Ngaio Marsh – 'You can slaughter in a righteous manner, and you can slaughter in an unrighteous manner.' And he adds, that 'it's all a matter of evolution. Survival of the fittest.' This addition seems inconsequential, but is his Darwinian justification so very different from the historical justifications by which communist violence must be condoned, because it accords with the trend of history, in contrast to fascist, capitalist or colonialist violence? (See Ellul, 1970: 108-109). Thus, Dos Santos, vice-president of the Mozambique liberation movement FRELIMO explained in an interview (reported in Southern Africa, May 1974, 16) that:

Fire burns, whether it purifies is another question! Whether it purifies or not depends on the type of violence. For example, the fire from the Portuguese burns and destroys. The fire coming from FRELIMO purifies and builds. Why does the fire coming from FRELIMO build? Because it is a revolutionary fire. A reactionary fire just destroys. It is not really the weapon that you have in your hand that counts but the men who carry it. So, if you are a revolutionary your fire purifies, and if you are a reactionary it destroys. If we speak just of violence there is no guarantee that it will purify anything unless it is directed for the good of the people.

The President of FRELIMO, Samora Machel, at the beginning of the production cycle for 1971-2, made a similar distinction between oppressive and liberating violence:

2. Quoted in Jacques Ellul's study of Violence (1970: 49-50) from his discussion of the theologians of revolution. In my comments on ideologies of polarisation, I am greatly indebted to him.

In the enemy zone, under capitalism, under colonialism, there is also production. There, too, man wields the hoe to break the soil. There, too, on the factory machine – which we do not as yet have in our zone – man makes things. Yet we say that production in the enemy zone is exploitation, whereas in our zone production liberates man. But it is the same hoe, the same man, the same act of breaking the soil. Why then is there this dividing line? Almost everyone knows the G3 gun. In the hands of the enemy the G3 is used to oppress and slaughter the people, but when we capture a G3, it becomes an instrument for liberating the people, for punishing those who slaughter the people. It is the same gun, but its content has changed because those who use it have different aims, different interests. (*Mozambique Revolution*, No. 49, October-December 1971, p. 20)

There is the good Darwinian violence and the good Communist violence. There is the good violence, engaged in as a last resort. There is the bad violence that enslaves, and the good violence that liberates. There is the unjust violence of the oppressors and the just violence of the oppressed who body forth the future.

But is it less agonising to be destroyed by a purifying fire or a liberating gun? And what of the inevitable atrocities, the massacres, the slaughter of innocents. Are they simply regrettable miscarriages of justice? Or is there an inexorable law by which many are destined for the rubbish bins of history? Or are they all guilty, the infants, the aged, the weak, the infirm, the poor, the downtrodden, the powerless, simply because they belong to the offending group? And suppose the liberating violence enslaves, or that it is one of the laws of violence that violence breeds more violence. The violence of Hutu against Tutsi in Rwanda, their massacre of whole communities, must be 'just violence', since it was the violence of an oppressed majority. Conversely, the slaughter of at least 100,000 Hutu by Tutsi in neighbouring Burundi, must be 'unjust violence', since it is violence perpetrated by a dominant minority. Yet the 'just' slaughter of Tutsi in Rwanda is in some measure a cause of the 'unjust' slaughter of Hutu, in Burundi.

Paradoxically, the overwhelming violence is the violence perpetrated by dominant groups, yet they take it largely for granted as being hardly in need of justification. Much of the violence is routine, embedded in the institutions of the society, its procedures and daily life. Legitimised as force necessary for the maintenance of law and order, it is distinguished, even when the violence is extreme, from the violence of the subordinates, in terms of the underlying morality that: 'Those who wish to defend the Constitution cannot be castigated in the same terms as those who wish to oppose it' (statement by Belfast Grand Orange Master, as quoted in '"Red hand" blamed in tit-for-tat killings', London *Observer*, 4 Feb. 1973).

Grandiose conceptions of the role of the dominant group justify violence (force) in its defence. Darwinism and other evolutionary theories have been at hand for some generations, serving much the same function as Marxism and myths of historical necessity in the ideologies of subordinate groups. These theories of domination often offer the 'moral conception' of the 'civilising benefits' brought by higher-order civilisations to inferior peoples groping in the darkness of barbarism. Myths of origin and divine mission transform atrocity into piety, into painful duty reverentially performed. If the subject peoples are not mindful of the beneficence of the master, it is because of the brutishness of their dispositions, the barbarousness of their cultures, or the incitement of outside agitators. The interests of the subject peoples themselves demand that they should be forcefully protected against their own inclinations and against corrupting influences from the outside world.

At a less grandiose level, argument for the necessity of violence emerges from the situation of minority domination. Whether dominant minorities project their own violence as characteristic of the subordinates, or whether they believe intuitively that violence must inevitably breed violence, or whether they are moved by quite realistic fears of the resentment of their subject peoples, expectation of barbarous violence from fanatical hordes becomes justification for the necessity of repressive violence. If this nightmare of fear erupts into reality, as it did in the Hutu revolt in Burundi in April 1972, or as happened also in Philippeville in Algeria, in August 1955, when the revolutionary leader of the Constantine region unleashed indiscriminate slaughter in a desperate attempt to revive the revolutionary struggle, then there is even more powerful argument for savage repression, for admonitory massacre, for cataclysmic vengeance.

III

Often these polarising ideologies of dominant and subordinate sections so intermesh as to move the ideological conflict into high gear. Like the curious affinity which exists between communism and capitalism as expressions of modern industrial and technocratic values, and which underlies their radical opposition, so, too, the polarising ideologies of revolutionary movements and of counter-revolutionary repression seem to draw on a common pool of conceptions. Themes are often interchangeable, and sustain the argument of the enemy.

Uncompromising dualism, with its attendant simplification of structures and issues, is common ground in the polarising ideologies of dominant and subordinate groups. The corollary to this radical dualism is the impossibility of reconciling the objectives of the contending parties.

There is a basic assumption that power cannot be shared. The charters of dominant groups establish their divine right to rule, or their Darwinian right, or some sort of Parsonian right, or a right in natural law, or historical right by reason of conquest. Thus, in the early stages of the Rwanda revolution, twelve leading Tutsi at the Mwami's court expressed their astonishment that the Hutu should claim division of a common patrimony. Since Tutsi kings had conquered Hutu country, and killed their petty chieftains, subjecting the Hutu to servitude, how could they now claim fraternity (Nkundabagenzi, 1961: 35-36)? The impossibility of sharing power flows from the right to rule, as in the above example, or from the unworthy nature of the subordinates, or from such beliefs as that the relationship between the races is governed by the stark alternative of domination or subjection.

In the polarising ideologies of subordinate racial groups, the impossibility of sharing power arises initially from the resistance of dominant groups. Often, there has been an earlier period of supplication or agitation for the right to effective political participation. Failure of this movement lends conviction to the belief that the dominant race will not share power, as in South Africa where the trend was toward increasing concentration of exclusive white power, or as in Algeria, where the settlers effectively resisted or sabotaged reforms. Hence the rulers must be compelled by violence to share their power or they must be violently replaced by the subordinates. The choice between these alternatives will depend in part on strategic appraisal of the distribution of resources, and the feasibility of a struggle for mastery. There may also be some general conception, along the lines of the Marxist dictatorship of the proletariat, that the domination is of such a nature that it offers only the choice between continued subjection or replacement of the rulers by their subjects, as in Fanon's ideology of decolonisation. Where the commitment is to the replacement of the rulers by their subjects, as in the Pan-Africanist goal in South Africa of African majority rule, the charter which confers the right to rule rests on prior occupation, on the right to self-determination and to liberation from the tyranny of foreign domination and exploitation.

The impossibility of sharing power excludes reform. While dominant polarising groups see reform as a stepping stone in the reversal of power, not as a process in the sharing of power, subordinate groups consider it a delusion to hope that the State, which is the instrument of their oppression, will bring about effective change, and they see reformism as a device in the maintenance of power. Yet however antithetical the ideological perspectives, they converge in an attack on reform; and the rejection or sabotage of reform by one section becomes argument by the other for the impossibility of reform.

Discussion, which might offer some hope of conciliation, is also excluded. It was this expression of extreme polarisation which Camus (1958: 176-177) sought to counter when he pleaded in Algeria for a truce on the killing of civilians.

'There is no longer the possibility of discussion.' This is the cry that destroys all hope for the future ... Imprisoned in their separate rancour and hatred, they can no longer hear each other. Whatever the proposition, it is received with distrust, immediately distorted and rendered futile. Step by step we move into an inextricable snarl of old and new accusations, of implacable vengeance, of unwearying resentments, replacing each other, as in the old family feuds where grievances and arguments so pile up over the generations that the most honest and human of judges can no longer sort out the issues.[3]

These ideological themes are sustained by characterisations of the antagonist, and strangely enough the characterisations also share many elements in common. Domination is usually justified in plural societies by ideologies of cultural difference, denigrating the culture of the subordinates and dehumanising them in a more or less radical fashion. These ideologies include not only the benefits to be derived by the subordinates from their contact with representatives of a superior culture and of a higher moral order, but rationalisations for the arbitrary determination of their fate, and for the use of the only language to which they are fully responsive, that of violence. The response to these ideologies by the subordinates is the glorification of their traditional values in a cultural renaissance, and the framing of counter-ideologies, attacking the qualities and culture of the dominant group, their impermeability to the appeals of reason and morality and their commitment to violence: these themes are linked to an assertion of the necessity for counter-violence. Thus each has an image of

3. This is a rather free translation of part of the following very moving passage in Camus' plea. ' "*Il n'y a plus de discussion possible*": *voilà le cri qui stérilise tout avenir et toute chance de vie. Dès lors, c'est le combat aveugle où le Français décide d'ignorer l'Arabe, même s'il sait, quelque part en luimême, que sa revendication de dignité est justifiée, et l'Arabe décide d'ignorer le Français, même s'il sait, quelque part en luimême, que les Français d'Algérie ont droit aussi à la sécurité et à la dignité sur notre terre commune. Enferme dans sa rancune et sa haine, personne alors ne peut écouter l'autre. Toute proposition, dans quelque sens qu'elle soit faite, est accueillie avec méfiance, aussitôt déformée et rendue inutilisable. Nous entrons peu à peu dans an noeud inextricable d'accusations anciennes et nouvelles, de vengeances durcies, de rancunes inlassables se relayant l'une l'autre, comme dans ces vieux procès de famille où les griefs et les arguments s'accumulent pendant des générations, et à ce point que les juges les plus intègres et les plus humains ne peuvent plus s'y retrouver. La fin d'une pareille situation peut alors difficilement s'imaginer et l'espoir d'une association française et arabe, d'une Algérie pacifique et créatrice, s'estompe un peu plus chaque jour.*'

the other as deaf to reason and moral appeal, given over to violence, and responsive only to greater violence.

Where there has been protracted conflict, the history of the relations between the enemies is certain to offer ample evidence of the unspeakable cruelty of the rulers. In Algeria, the French conquest took the form of total war, with the burning of crops, the destruction of thriving villages, the taking of women and children as hostages, pillage, rapine, slaughter, and episodes of the greatest barbarity, even by the standards of twentieth-century western civilisation. In living memory, at the time of the revolution, there were the massive and ruthless reprisals following the Muslim rising in Sétif in May 1945, suggesting continuity in the most brutal forms of repression.[4] But conversely there were the atrocities committed by Muslims, as in the Constantine region, to lend substance to a settler image of the savage cruelty of the adversary, calling for extreme repression by vastly more massive counter-atrocities. Here then, as Camus declared, were two populations 'bound together in an inevitable solidarity, in death as in life, in destruction as in hope, a solidarity governed by a terrible infernal dialectic which requires that those who kill members of the enemy group also kill members of their own group. Meanwhile each casts blame upon the other, justifying his acts of violence by the violence of the adversary. Thus two populations, both similar and different, but equally honourable, condemn each other to die together, with rage in their hearts, because they had not learnt to live together' (1958: 175). Thus the reciprocity of violence finds expression in the interlocking of ideologies, justifying the inevitability and the necessity of the resort to violence.

Specific historical relationships between the groups feed into their ideologies, and historical episodes and personalities acquire a symbolic significance. Here, too, the parties make use of, or confront, common elements in their historical experience, but

4. For a general discussion of the psychology of conquest, and of political and military continuities in the colonial wars in Algeria from 1830 to 1960, see Lacheraf, 1965, Chapters 3 and 7.

with diametrically opposed ideological connotations. In Northern Ireland, Catholics and Protestants reenact their history as part of the contemporary conflagration. O'Brien (1972: 176, 177, 270) writes of the summer season of traditional Protestant triumphal rites, of which the principal ceremonies, among a great number of lesser ones, are the 12 July Orange Parade in Belfast, and the parade of the Apprentice Boys in Derry on 12 August. 'The long siege of Derry by King James's Catholic Army, and its relief by King William's Protestant Fleet in 1689, belong with the Battle of the Boyne at the centre of Ulster Protestant iconography, religion and patriotism ... And every year on 12 August, the Protestants triumph on top of the walls, looking down on the descendants of the unsuccessful besiegers, inheritors of a siege that has never been altogether abandoned.' And of a cycle of commemorations, he writes further that 'we all seemed to be like sleepwalkers, locked in some eternal ritual reenactment, muttering senselessly as we collided with one another, wrestling in the dark'.

In Algeria, in 1961, the National Liberation Front chose 5 July, anniversary of the French invasion of Algeria, as the day for demonstrations against partition (Courrière, 1971: 403). Six months earlier, young demonstrators in the Casbah of Algiers had flourished banners with the two words, *Sétif – 1945* (Aron, 1962: 142). To Muslims, *Sétif* had become a horrifying synonym for savage French repression, while for many French settlers, it symbolised the deep fears of a dominant minority, and the only effective strategy for survival.

In South Africa, the great triumphal day for the Afrikaners is 16 December, on which they commemorate the defeat of a Zulu army in 1836 by their voortrekker forefathers. In recent years the day has been renamed the Day of the Covenant, in recognition of God's complicity in the affair, and a great ceremonial is staged at the Voortrekker monument. For the African resistance movement, it served as a day of protest against apartheid. In Rwanda the Tutsi commemoration of their conquest was symbolised in the adornment of the ceremonial drum, the Kalinga, with the genitals of defeated Hutu chiefs. In the period of revolutionary struggle, the Kalinga became one of the focal points in the Hutu attack on Tutsi domination.

Marches, anthems, ceremonials, add the fuel of past conflicts to contemporary conflagration.

7

Cycles of Polarisation

Polarisation may be a deliberate policy, or an unpremeditated consequence of strategies pursued. There are certain clichés of action, almost involuntary idiomatic actions, which feed into the process of polarisation. Action and reaction, premeditated and involuntary, may so intermesh as to move violence to higher levels of destruction through escalating cycles of polarisation in a process Courrière describes as *'l'engrenage de la violence'*. These cycles of polarisation are the subject of this chapter.

The case studies selected here are of extreme and massive polarisation. To be sure, total polarisation is almost inconceivable in societies where the plural sections have lived together for generations. Even in Algeria, after five years of civil war, and the involvement of half a million French troops, there were 171,000 Muslim Algerian soldiers in various French auxiliary units (Heggoy, 1972: 260-261); and further evidence of the forces making for coexistence are to be found in the strange 'fraternisation' of 13 May 1958, and in the desire of a section of the revolutionary leaders to integrate the European settlers into an independent Algeria. But the struggle was waged over many years, during the course of which it became increasingly defined in racial or ethnic terms, and polarised large masses on either side. Burundi appears to be one of the contemporary societies in which there is almost total polarisation, but there is little precise knowledge of what is taking place in the country, in contrast to the Algerian revolution where voluminous documentation and commentary offer extensive materials and insights for the analysis of the processes of polarisation.

Polarisation is conceived here as involving mutually hostile action. Thus I exclude situations of such disproportionate power between groups that the weaker is simply the victim of genocidal hatred, as in the case of the Nazi genocide against Jews, and the Turkish massacres of Armenians; and I reserve the term for an intensification of conflict by aggressive action and reaction. Polarisation then is a process of increasing aggregation of the members of the society into exclusive and mutually hostile groups, entailing the elimination of the middle ground and of mediating relationships. Episodes and issues of conflict accumulate. There are corresponding ideologies, as we have seen, presenting simplified conceptions of the society as already polarised into two antagonistic groups with incompatible and irreconcilable interests, rendering inevitable the resort to violence. In its extreme form, polarisation is marked by mounting violence and atrocious holocaust.

ALGERIA

I.

While the full working out of processes of polarisation does seem inevitably to result in extreme violence, polarised relations may develop appreciably by non-violent means, and without deliberate intention to polarise the society. Quite straightforward techniques of normal political action may contribute to this end. For the subordinates, as they seek to aggregate the members of their group for political action, these techniques would include the founding of exclusive organisations, the attempt to gain support through demonstrations and ideological appeals, and the antagonistic labelling of those who seek to mediate and to maintain cooperative relations. Often the political organisations take two forms, one based on reformist willingness to accommodate and work within the political system, and the other characterised by a revolutionary ideology. The failure of reformist strategies becomes then a significant factor in the increasing solidarity behind revolutionary action, and in the more extensive polarisation of the society.

The dominant section does not have the same need to aggregate its members in the early stages of polarisation. Its members are already appreciably aggregated, acting through, or represented by, effectively organised political structures. But the growing aggregation of the subordinates, and the challenge of their demands, are likely to heighten solidarity in the dominant section. The rulers could respond by a measure of cooperation, and negotiate with the 'extremists' in an attempt to win them over. But the tendency in plural societies is to suppress militant organisations and to liquidate the leaders. This was the history of the Algerian struggle with continuous but ineffective outlawing of the militant nationalist organisations. It was the history too of the South African revolutionary movement in the 1950s and early 1960s. The effect is to drive the movement underground, thus contributing to the search for an ultimate solution in violence. In Rwanda, the attempt by Tutsi elite to terrorise the militant Hutu leaders acted as catalyst for the Hutu peasant jacquerie against the Tutsi, which heralded the demise of their regime.

Where the struggle moves into a violent phase, consolidation becomes a more acute problem for the subordinates. Even in this phase, consolidation may be pursued by non-violent means. Thus during the Algerian revolution, the National Liberation Front (FLN) imposed on Muslims prohibitions against smoking and against drinking liquor. This was a discipline for affirmation of solidarity in the dedication to Islam: but it also had the effect of polarising, since it set an exclusive religious and cultural identity over and against the Christianity of the European settlers. Other disciplines included the imposition of a levy to provide funds for the revolutionary forces. Inevitably there would arise the need for sanctions to ensure compliance with these disciplines, such sanctions as cutting off the lips or noses of offenders. The revolutionary forces would also experience the need to silence informers and political opponents and rivals for power within their own group. Thus, as the revolution proceeded in Algeria, the sanctions grew increasingly violent and terrorising. At first attacks against Muslims were rare, but they became more and more frequent and atrocious, staged in the most macabre way to strike terror by horrible and repugnant mutilations, and by menacing messages pinned to the clothes of victims (see Soustelle, 1956: 23). The exemplary reprisals included the slitting of throats, disembowelment and sexual mutilation. Not all submitted to these fearful sanctions. Some defended themselves, or responded with counterattack, or ultimately formed auxiliary units in association with the French forces.

One of the most horrifying episodes of internal Muslim conflict was that centering round the settlement of Melouza in May 1956. The events illustrate some of the complexities in the processes of polarisation. They start with French reprisals for the killing of a captain during an ambush by an FLN group. French forces arrested and shot some suspects. They then displayed their bodies on the roof of a car which toured the region of Melouza, as a demonstration of the fate awaiting those giving aid to the FLN. The demonstration proved counter-productive. When the French forces left the area, the population passed over *en bloc* to the FLN, who then used Melouza as a base for extending their influence over the important settlement of Béni-Illemance.

This settlement was under the control of the rival nationalist organisation, the *Mouvement National Algérien* (MNA). Its Arab population resented demands by the Kabyle guerilla forces of the FLN for the payment of levies, and the rendering of aid which would inevitably expose them to French army reprisals. They resisted violently, killing an FLN officer and three liaison agents. They surrendered several noncommissioned officers to the security forces, and they hacked to death a sergeant and his secretary, seeking asylum in the village. In retaliation, the forces of the FLN enacted a fearful vengeance. They attacked the village of Béni-Illemane. They removed the men, 304 in all. They forced them along to a small neighbouring hamlet. There they drove their prisoners into the low stone shelters, some 30 to each dwelling. Then they massacred them with rifle, knife and pick, leaving the widows to search out the horribly mutilated bodies of

their husbands in the midst of this most unspeakable carnage (see
Courrière, 1970: 57ff).

II

The movement of violence by the subordinates against the
dominant group may be planned with the deliberate intention of
avoiding polarisation. Thus when a section of the African
National Congress in South Africa formed the organisation
Umkhonto we Sizwe (Spear of the Nation) for violent action,
there was the selection of sabotage as the initial means of violence
in preference to terrorism or guerilla warfare, which the leaders
felt would more fiercely inflame racial hatred. Clearly, the attack
on the property of members of the dominant group, or on the
institutional structures of administration and rule, incites to racial
hatred, particularly when it is part of a coordinated campaign for
the assault on privilege. But I think we can readily agree that the
threat to life is likely to inflame a more passionate and vengeful
hatred. As the Permanent Secretariat of the Clergy, Bujumbura,
Burundi comments in a dossier on the massacre in Burundi:

When a collectivity experiences the leverage of the instinct of preservation,
one may anticipate the worst excesses. One can truly say that this war has
shaken each Murundi to the very core of his being, either because of fear for
his own life, or because of the loss of relatives and friends, given the deep ties
which exist between Hutu and Tutsi (*Dossier Burundi*, December 1972, p. 9).

The attack on life seems to be the most powerful means for
polarisation. But even in the use of murder, there may be the
attempt to avoid unnecessary polarisation. In a book on his
experiences as a Lieutenant in the French army in Algeria,
Servan-Schreiber (1958: 94-96) refers to a distinction between the
'Stalinist' terrorists and the 'Bourguibists'. The former seek to
create the maximum damage, to destroy all attempt at
compromise or reconciliation, to root out the slightest sentiment
which might foster the desire for an *entente*. Hence if the choice is
between liquidating a notoriously brutal police officer, or a

Frenchman seeking to establish contact, the selected target is the conciliator. The 'Bourguibists' by contrast seek to arrive at an understanding with the French, to control hatred, to activate a moral conscience in their enemies, conducive to a short war. Hence their target would be the brutal police officer. Where the French respond to these provocations with a blind collective repression, they strengthen the hands of the 'Stalinists'. Where, however, a responsible French official restrains blind anger, and avoids retaliation against the innocent, he encourages the 'Bourguibist' tendency. At the same time, he becomes a target for the 'Stalinists'.

The choice of a sharply defined specific target such as the police monster or the good administrator implies some restraint on the stimulus to polarisation. The maximum impulse to polarisation is likely to flow from the massive killing of innocent people, slaughtered with total indifference to their personal involvement in the struggle, and selected quite haphazardly and indiscriminately. Here the targets are identified solely by their membership of the hated racial or ethnic group, as in the exploding of a bomb in the densely inhabited Muslim Casbah or the retaliatory tossing of a grenade into a milk-bar frequented by Europeans in Algiers. Whereas the murder of a police officer or an administrator can be received with a proper sense of outrage but with some equanimity, by those whose occupation does not inevitably expose them to danger, the mass indiscriminate slaughter now carries the threat of annihilation into their own lives. A haphazard, monstrous, unpredictable doom shadows their most harmless daily activities. In many societies the sense of outrage is heightened if the victims include women and children, the very aged and the very young.

Where there are such additional refinements of atrocity as cutting of throats and disembowelment and sexual mutilation, the effect is specially inflammatory. In these reactions, cultural differences in definition of atrocity and forms of atrocity become highly significant. Thus the French in Algeria, many of whom seem to have found their own atrocities of the gaping bullet wound, or the bomb shattered body or the contorted mutilation of torture quite acceptable, were nevertheless outraged by what they perceived to be the unspeakable barbarity of Muslim atrocity. Their accounts are full of the horror of the Muslim practice of slitting human throats in the manner of the ritual slaughter of animals. It may seem somewhat ludicrous that the sense of propriety of a torturer should be deeply offended by alien cultural idioms for inflicting all the torments of an agonising death under conditions of the most appalling humiliation and degradation. Nevertheless, these nice distinctions in barbarity deeply inflame hatreds and accelerate the process of polarisation.

The dominant group has a specially decisive role in the escalation of violence. If it is a general law that there is reciprocity in violence, that violence provokes violence, begets and creates violence, it can hardly be said that there is a general law of reciprocity in non-violence. Mahatma Gandhi assumed that the rulers would respond to the non-violent campaigns of their subjects by violence. The violence of domination is embedded in the laws which impart their sanctity to the domination. Violence is a quite natural response to any challenge to this sanctity of legitimated rule. The rulers may seek to provide further legitimation for their own violence by the use of provocateurs to incite the subordinate group to a violence, which then evokes, and is presented as justifying, the most savage and brutal repression. As we have seen, Ferhat Abbas (1962: 153-159) explains the riots in Sétif, in May 1945, in these terms, as a Muslim response to a deliberate provocation designed to provide justification for the suppression of his political movement, and the abandonment of proposed reforms. The intentions of the rulers in the use of repressive violence are to eradicate challenge to their domination and not to polarise, but regardless of their intentions, the consequence is likely to be further polarisation of relations, unless the repression is so massively effective in inspiring terror and in liquidating leadership as to dispose of resistance for all time or until a new generation renews the challenge.

Many of the reactions of the rulers have an idiomatic quality.

They often seem quite involuntary. They are embedded in conceptions of legitimate authority, of constitutional channels for initiating change, and of appropriate political action to maintain law and order. They may also be embedded in the very structure of situations which offer limited alternatives for action. Whether involuntary, or carefully deliberated, these idiomatic reactions frequently have the unintended consequence of polarising relations.

The imposition of collective responsibility is one of the almost automatic reactions to attacks on life and property in situations in which a minority rules over a large majority, not integrated into the life of the country or effectively administered, but remaining an anonymous mass. Courrière, in his account of the Algerian revolution (1969: 108-109), quotes the instructions issued in May 1955 by the Commander-in-Chief of the French forces to the commanding general in the Constantine area.

Every new extension of the rebellion should call immediately for brutal action, on the one hand against the rebel bands, and for sanctions, on the other, against accomplices, by virtue of collective responsibilities.

Example of collective responsibility: destruction of 99 telegraph poles near Oued Zenati. One knows that all the men in the douar carried it out. The douar should pay for the replacing of the poles destroyed. Then all the men are to be moved away (*éloignés*, that is to say, interned in the newly-created camps).

Second example: bridges destroyed by picks. Those who carried it out, if known, and the inhabitants of nearby *mechtas*, who cannot but be in the know, to furnish free the necessary labour, then eventually they are to be sent away. Requisition herds without prejudice (*sans préjudice*), pay as slowly as possible.

In the view of Courrière, it was this notion of collective responsibility which became after several weeks of application, one of the principal psychological trump cards, enabling the FLN to take in hand a population initially indifferent for the most part to the revolution. He adds the comment that it was the populations against whom these measures were applied in the

Constantine area that participated three months later in the terrible massacres of 20 August.

The frustration and anger of the regular army forces, as they seek to engage an intangible, invisible guerilla enemy, suddenly materialising in an ambush, then disappearing into the mountains or into peasant anonymity, may be directed against hamlets in the area, again on the principle of collective responsibility. Courrière (1969: 173) likens the regular abusive searches of hamlets to the rage of a buffalo, stung on the nostrils by a mosquito, crushing everything in its path. What an aid for recruitment to the FLN!

Little by little, the population feels itself, by the very force of events, regarded as an enemy, even if it is not an enemy. Imperceptibly, from week to week, sympathy grows for the maquis. The people see the French army, representative of the occupying power, pursuing men belonging to their own race, and quite naturally they lend their support to the maquis. Moreover the fate reserved for the indomitably pro-French among them gives cause for reflection. They can no longer remain isolated. Either they move over to the FLN or they join the ranks of the mobile rural protection groups which soon become transformed into harkas [French auxiliary units]. (Courrière, *ibid.*)

The ordinary soldier may face a problem similar to that which impels the government to impose collective responsibility. The peasant he encounters in the field, the workman he meets in the street, may in fact be a rebel soldier or a rebel terrorist. To take the Algerian example, if he treats all Arabs as innocent until proved guilty, he may be gambling with his very life. Concern for security drives him then to see all Arabs as suspect, and to take anticipatory and often violent action against the innocent. The consequences can only be a more massive and deadly polarisation. (See Servan-Schreiber, 1958: 47-48, 63-64, for a discussion of these issues.)

The same principle of collective responsibility or collective guilt is applied, though not deliberately as such, in indiscriminate arrests. It is an extremely difficult problem for the rulers to suppress urban terrorists who disappear into the anonymity of a protecting population. They may seek a solution through indiscriminate arrests in a terrorising enforcement of authority, and in a desperate attempt to extort information. In a sense this reaction is not too different from the taking of hostages. Courrière (1969: 448-476) describes the process during the Battle of Algiers. The FLN had decided to call a general strike on 28 January 1957. This was preceded by a number of terrorist outrages in the form of bombs exploded in cafes frequented by Europeans. The strategy of the strike was to demonstrate, preparatory to the meeting of the United Nations Organisation, that the FLN were in fact the representatives of the Algerian people.

The French administration had resolved to break the power of the FLN and to abort the general strike. The resident minister ordered the transfer of police powers to the military. Paratroopers invested the Casbah and during the night of the 14/15 January, they arrested residents named in a police list of suspects. Something of the indiscriminate nature of the arrests appears from the disproportion between the 1500 arrested and the 250 listed as suspects. Nevertheless, despite the oppressive presence and actions of the paratroops, the Muslim population of Algiers followed the orders of the FLN and launched the general strike on 28 January. The paratroopers then ruthlessly drove Algerians to work. In the Casbah, they forced open stores. They rounded up the inhabitants. They assigned the most menial tasks to those of a slightly higher social level. Teachers, directors of schools, intellectuals were compelled to collect the garbage with their bare hands. Again, the paratroopers arrested indiscriminately. An impatient movement, a proud gait, a glance of revolt, were grounds enough for arrest and interrogation. Systematic and most barbarous torture yielded information.

The strike was defeated. But the Muslim population was irrevocably welded together. Bourgeois, workmen, dockers had been arrested and tortured indiscriminately. There are no longer distinctions of class. There can no longer be any possibility of a third force with which to negotiate. (*ibid.*, p. 476)

The fullest working out of the principle of collective

responsibility is in the vast resettlement schemes so often imposed on subject peoples, as in Malaysia, Soviet Russia, Algeria, Angola and Mozambique, and as an anticipatory counter-revolutionary measure in South Africa. Resettlement schemes may have the effect of utterly eradicating the possibility of resistance, but the uprooting of populations and their transplanting to areas, usually inadequately prepared, and with rudimentary facilities, cannot fail to be highly traumatic and polarising. Bourdieu (1964: 13) describes the displacement of over two million Algerians, and the exodus to the towns, as among the most brutal known to history.

Ordinary members of the dominant group, not charged with military, or police, or judicial functions, may arrogate these functions to themselves in indiscriminate attacks on the subordinates. The attacks are hardly guided by a considered principle of collective responsibility, but they take much the same form. They are directed against any member of the hated group, regardless of his guilt or innocence. Where there is some pretense of trial, it is likely to be so perfunctory and prejudged, as hardly to depart from action based on the attribution of collective guilt. Vigilante groups form and slaughter freely. Idioms of action become established. Thus in Algeria, the huge European processions forming part of the funeral cortege of the victims of Muslim terrorism, would suddenly go on the rampage, in *ratonnades* against Arabs. Or a Muslim terrorist atrocity against innocent Europeans in a public place would be visited by a similar retribution. Or collective retribution might be triggered off by some political development, such as peace negotiations.

While these summary slaughters on the basis of collective guilt usually have a passionate wild spontaneous quality, they may also be influenced by elements of directed purpose. Thus the authorities may themselves encourage mob action, as in the Turkish massacres of the Armenians, or the Russian pogroms, or the Tutsi slaughter of Hutu in Burundi or the Hutu slaughter of Tutsi in Rwanda. Or the mob may itself attack politically significant targets, as in 1961, in Luanda, Angola, when Portuguese settler militia, with army and police support, gathered into their bloody harvest many educated Africans, as a reprisal against an African massacre in the north (see Davidson, 1973: 189-195). This policy of the attribution of guilt to the educated as a category, had been initiated earlier by the Portuguese authorities in trials held in 1959, later described as 'the beginning of a systematic and exhaustive aggression, reaching a paroxysm in 1961, against every man of colour who had distinguished himself *in whatever way* ... It was the onset of a persecution, as stupid or impious, of all those who could read, had books, possessed a radio, wore spectacles. ...' (*ibid.*, p. 167). The convergence of mob and official atrocity against a selected target in a context of indiscriminate slaughter was carried to its extreme in Burundi in the virtual elimination of a whole stratum of the educated, however modest the level of education.

In the imposition of collective responsibility, the authorities may be driven by a conception of the necessity to re-establish law and order, as an imperative overriding the concern for justice, particularly in a situation where the rebels are anonymously sheltered in a strange and hostile population. But they confront the dilemma that the policy, if it fails, will become an effective recruiting agent for the rebel cause. An analogous dilemma arises, where the authorities maintain, parallel to their practices of collective responsibility, institutions for the administration of criminal justice, guided by traditional concern for the clear proof of individual responsibility and guilt. Suppose now that the guilt of a terrorist for some deadly atrocity has been judicially established, and sentence of death passed. Conceptions of criminal justice would call for execution of the sentence, and there would be great pressure for vengeance by an outraged public belonging to the dominant group. The rebel forces might retaliate by carrying out their judicial execution of a captured soldier, a highly polarising act, rebel justice being perceived as particularly flagrant atrocity in contrast to the merciful and principled justice of the authorities. But whether or not there is retaliatory action, the execution of a revolutionary can be a highly traumatic ritual and profoundly polarising.

Courrière (1969: 539) describes the reaction to an execution during the Battle of Algiers, quoting Germaine Tillion:

The entire prison … hears the preparations. One knows what is about to happen. One calls out to the dead. And in the neighbouring Casbah people take up the chant of the dead, crying out, weeping, praying. It is an intense communion in deepest suffering.

And these deeply polarising executions provoke retaliatory atrocity.

III

I have been describing elements in the process of polarisation, which are embedded in the structure of the society, in the nature of the situation, in the concepts of authority, and in the exigencies of the struggle. Particularly conducive to violent and extreme polarisation are systems of domination, in which a relatively small minority rules over large numbers of subordinates of different culture, who are not integrated into the dominant society, but remain, from the perspective of the rulers, a largely anonymous mass. These are societies which are often already appreciably polarised, with pervasive cleavages. The dominant group suppresses militant organisation among the subordinates, so that it becomes hazardous to mount a challenge to domination. The revolutionaries are thus likely to be driven to somewhat desperate measures in order to command a following among their own people, and their attempts to aggregate their fellow countrymen serve as a stimulus to greater solidarity in the ruling circles. Since the subordinates lack the resources for a military campaign, when they finally move to violent action, they may feel that they have no alternative but to rely on the sudden stealthy surprise attack, and on acts of terrorism.

This was appreciably the situation in Algeria at about the time of the revolution. The context was that of the first stages in a worldwide movement for decolonisation and national independence. Joseph Kessel, in his introduction to Courrière's *Les Fils de la Toussaint*, comments that the day when the Algerian revolt exploded was one of the most grave and decisive of the century for the destiny of France. Inscribed in it were the attacks without number, the combats without end, the tortures and the fearful destruction, the civil and military rebellions, the attempts at a *coup d'état*, the change of regime, the exodus of an entire population, and the secession of a vast territory, part of the soil of France according to century old teaching in the schools. Imagine then the astonishment in discovering that the movement which threw Algeria into a war lasting eight years and gave it independence was the work of six men, six in all, without troops, arms, money, external backing or even local popular support. 'When one discovers the penury, the misery of the means, and when one reflects on the immense goal of the enterprise, the disparity seems beyond all reason, indeed quite lunatic.'

Kessel's statement slightly exaggerates the paucity of manpower, resources and support, but they were certainly infinitesimal in relation to the objective of national independence. The success in mounting the national liberation movement must be attributed in part to the structure of the plural society with its pervasive cleavages, which offered, and finally yielded to the revolutionaries, a massive following. In part it was favoured by a global situation, encouraging movements for decolonisation, and by an increasingly effective international public opinion, which contributed to the defeat of France when she had virtually conquered in the field. In part, too, there was increasing aid for the military struggle from neighbouring territories. But above all, it was the struggle itself, and the processes of polarisation it set in motion, in the context of a divided society, and a changing world ethos, which enabled the revolutionary forces to win sufficient support to engage a powerful French army.

Some of the elements or units in the process of polarisation, as we have seen, have a quite idiomatic character. This is especially true of many of the responses by the rulers in the exercise of their authority for the maintenance of law and order. The Burundi government, in the white paper it issued on the 'events' of April and May 1972 refers to a dialectic between provocation and the reestablishment of order (pp. 22-23). It charges that this was the technique used to give a tribalist colouration to events in a society not characterised by tribalism. By attacks, assassinations, *coups d'état*, the leaders of the tribalist movement had compelled the intervention of the authorities to restore order, and this intervention was then falsely represented as motivated by tribalism. The strategy was to create tribalism by use of the dialectic between provocation and order.

This dialectic between provocation and order was a powerful instrument for polarisation in Algeria, as the French authorities responded to sabotage, guerilla ambushes and urban terrorism by such idiomatic sanctions as the imposition of collective responsibility, indiscriminate arrests and interrogation, and executions in due process of law and justice. Torture was perhaps not one of the idioms of French government. In any event, it became a routine during the Battle of Algiers, not simply in the form of a little gentle torture in search of information but carried to the deadly extremes of torment. It would seem that for many torturers, the joy of torturing soon breaks through all restraint against the ultimate ecstasy of the hapless body so brutally tortured that it can no longer be returned to human society.

During the course of the struggle, there is a routinisation of elements in the polarising process. Such routines would include, in the Algerian case, the Muslim terrorist attack followed by the settler *ratonnade*, or Muslim terrorism, funeral gathering and *ratonnade*, or Muslim massacre and massive French settler vigilante massacre, with large-scale army reprisals, or French terrorist attack on an innocent public and Muslim reprisals in the same form, or French terrorists picking off a selected Muslim target and Muslim counter-terrorism against a selected French target, or French judicial executions and Muslim extra-judicial executions. The extreme of routinisation was reached in the final stages of the Algerian revolution when self-appointed settler executioners slaughtered victims in the most casual way, before seemingly indifferent spectators of their own group, or when terrorists engaged in exterminatory excursions, firing from their cars on members of the opposite group, as if hunting down animals.

These routines quickly take on the character of customary patterns of conflict. They draw, of course, on elements of traditional culture – French legal culture, concepts of authority, modes of sanction, techniques of violence, military and police technology. In the Muslim case, too, these traditional elements of culture and technology influence the modes of violence. The slitting of throats is of course the ritual mode for slaughtering animals and it may have a special significance when used against enemies. Similarly the disembowelling and sexual mutilations, or the slicing away of organs and limbs as a sanction against breach of discipline, draw upon traditional patterns. Sometimes a particular mode of handling a conflict becomes powerfully established as a precedent. This seems to have been the case with the massive reprisals by the French at Sétif in 1945, which served, in the minds of many settlers, as the appropriate model for effective sanctions against a population, supposedly responsive only to extreme violence. For the Muslims too, Sétif represented a crucial experience, but one which typified French brutality and oppression. The massacres in the Constantine area in August 1955, were in some sense a replay of Sétif. French reprisals took the same form of slaughter by vigilante groups and massive reprisal by the military. There was, however, a difference in the role of Muslims, who provoked the retaliation by a planned recourse to massacre, rather than by the seemingly unpremeditated race riot at Sétif in the course of a demonstration and confrontation with French police.

These idioms and routines are a measure of polarisation between the sections. They are also part of the process of polarisation, and have a powerful cumulative effect. In addition, they interact, often intermeshing like gears, to generate greater power in escalating cycles of polarisation. The sequence in Constantine is an example of this intermeshing of elements in a deadly destructive atrocious cycle. It started with terrorist attacks and the imposition of collective responsibility, then moved to most atrocious massacre and even more atrocious and overwhelming reprisal, leaving a profound cleavage between the population groups, not only in the directly affected area, but throughout the country. Or to take a further example from the work of Courrière (1969: 114-115). At the funeral of a very fine administrator killed by terrorists in May 1955, the Governor-General vows vengeance and swears his determination to accomplish the mission of France. Courrière comments that it was putting into high gear the cycle of terrorism-repression. There were the exactions, the liquidations and the mutilations of pro-French Muslims by the FLN. Then there was the French response in the form of resettlement camps and torture. This evoked on the Muslim side, blind killing, and the striking down of Europeans for the first time. 'To this, the response is certain to be new repressions, and again the killing of innocent people. Innocent people on the other side ... Terrorism strikes blindly, so does repression. The cleavage so greatly feared becomes established. The gulf grows deeper and deeper.'

The most basic process underlying these elemental patterns is the reciprocity of violence, that violence begets violence. (See the discussion of the laws of violence by Jacques Ellul, 1970, 93-108.) This reciprocity of violence seems to be in the nature of an archetypal response. It is often quite involuntary, but it may be carefully deliberated, and indeed legally sanctioned, as under the *lex talionis*. Of course, there are qualifications to the generality of the law. The violence of the aggressor may be so overwhelming, that there cannot be an effective reprisal, or the counterviolence may be directed not against the aggressor, but against a substitute target, as in scapegoating. Or institutional mechanisms are called into play which deflect the reciprocal violence. Or a Gandhian type ethic restrains the violent response. But where there is a divided society, an appreciable breakdown in common understandings, a long history of violence, and some equivalence in the capacity for violence, then the reciprocity of violence would indeed seem to be a basic process readily set in motion by either of the parties. This was the process the OAS sought to launch when it embarked on a strategy of indiscriminate atrocity designed to provoke Muslim retaliation in the form of blind massacres, which would call for intervention by the French army, and so polarise relations as to defeat the impending referendum. The strategy failed because of the iron discipline imposed by the FLN against reprisals, though there was a series of hit-and-run raids on 14 May 1962, when 'cars with FLN commandos of three or four youths sped through the European quarters, machine-gunning bars, automobiles and passersby'. On 15 May, 'there was jubilation within the OAS. Terrorism and provocation were beginning to pay off. The next step was to kill a still greater number of Muslims. There was to be no end to the deadly cycle of retaliation and counter-retaliation until the reigning anarchy made a referendum altogether impossible' (Henissart, 1970: 406-407).

The reciprocity of violence tends to express itself also in an equivalence of means, moving from murder to the reciprocity of more extreme forms of violence. Of course, in Algeria, Muslim violence could not be compared to that of the French. The great destructive power of the French army was engaged in the conflict. Civilian reprisals, too, were on an infinitely more massive scale. At the level of terrorism, however, there was more equality in the capacity for atrocity, and it is particularly in terrorism that the reciprocity of violence and the equivalence of means received their clearest expression, with cultural differences, to be sure, in the proprieties and niceties of atrocity. The equivalence of means, in the case of the OAS, even extended to the reproduction of the organisation used by the FLN in the Battle of Algiers (Henissart, 1970: 146. See also pp. 273 and 305 for further examples of replication of techniques).

The effect of the reciprocal violence and of the intermeshing and escalating cycles of violence, is, increasingly, to aggregate the members of the society into exclusive groups, bound together by interdependence and deadly enmity. The extreme of aggregating and polarising violence is reached when violence blindly attacks men, women and children engaged in innocent pursuits; when it kills or mutilates in total disregard for position or direct involvement in the struggle, identifying its victims solely as members of the opposing group; when it strikes suddenly, unpredictably, terrifyingly, injecting the fear and horror of unspeakable anguish into the daily routine of living.

The ultimate point is the point at which the reciprocities of violence create an irreversible situation, a point of no return. But it would seem that in the Algerian revolution, this was not reached until the very last holocaust of OAS terrorism.[1]

ZANZIBAR

I

In Zanzibar, Rwanda and Burundi, as in Algeria, one must distinguish between two levels of domination, that of the colonial power and that of a dominant minority. However, contrary to the situation in Algeria, the dominant minorities in the Belgian mandated territories of Rwanda and Burundi and in the British Protectorate of Zanzibar were of different nationality from the colonial overlords, and the territories were never conceived as an integral part of the metropolis. In consequence, the minorities had little opportunity for the sort of involvement in metropolitan politics, which had been such a feature of French-Algerian relationships.

Both in Zanzibar and Rwanda, the struggle against internal colonialism (if that is the correct phrase to describe Arab domination in Zanzibar, and Tutsi domination in Rwanda), took precedence over the struggle for liberation from British and Belgian rule. Lemarchand (1968: 22) writes that 'because the need to assert these values (of progress, democracy and social justice) internally, or intrasystemically, assumed a higher priority than the need to assert them in opposition to European colonial rule, nationalism as a broadly unifying force remained for all intents and purposes an epiphenomenon'. Extreme polarisation developed in both these territories in the movement towards independence and in the attendant struggles for power, though the massacre of Arabs (or to use a more romantic and moral term, the revolution) only took place after independence. In Burundi,

1. Mostefa Lacheraf (1965: 279) writes on this point that 'l'histoire retiendra que c'est l'O.A.S. qui fut a l'origine d'une situation irréparable et de l'exode massif de ses compatriotes'.

the genocidal polarisation was the product of a protracted struggle *after* independence.

In Zanzibar, with its very complex racial and ethnic structure, polarisation was essentially between two sections, both minorities, namely Mainland Africans and Arabs, and then mainly on Zanzibar Island, not on Pemba Island. Before the massacre, expulsion and flight of its victims, Zanzibar (that is, the two islands of Zanzibar and Pemba) had a population of some 300,000 with roughly one-fifth Mainland African, about one-sixth Arab, over half Shirazi (or indigenous African claiming mixed African-Persian descent) and small numbers of Indians and other minorities. Its economy rested largely on the marketing of cloves, and on subsistence agriculture and farming. There was some employment by government and in commerce, but little in industry and that mainly in the processing of foods. (See Lofchie, 1965: ch. 3, Middleton and Campbell, 1965: ch. 3 and Kuper, 1974: ch. 7.) Zanzibar Town, the centre of government and of population, was of appreciable size, with 58,000 inhabitants in 1958.

Violence did not play a major role in the polarisation between Arabs and Mainland Africans in Zanzibar. There were no campaigns of terrorism and counter-terrorism, no development of assassination as a political weapon, no escalating cycles of indiscriminate murder and reprisal. Lofchie (1965: 205) writes that a tradition of political violence had long been established in Zanzibar, violence having become a recurrent method of resolving conflict before the era of nationalism. He refers to riots in 1928 between Omani and Manga Arabs, to an attack on administrative offices by Manga Arabs in 1936, and to a fierce combat with police by villagers attempting to free farmers convicted for refusal to cooperate in a cattle innoculation programme against anthrax. But these episodes of violence, between different sections of the Arab population, or in resistance to administrative measures, do not particularly relate to the polarisation between Arabs and Mainland Africans, save of course, to the extent that Arabs held administrative positions and were identified with administration, and to the extent that

Manga Arabs may have come to symbolise Arab violence.

The violence which arose out of the electoral contests was more directly significant for the polarisation between Arabs and Mainland Africans. Extremists in the youth groups of the major parties baited and assaulted members and leaders of the opposite party; there was frequent intimidation and coercion, with severe beating of several candidates in the two 1961 elections (see Lofchie, 1965: 205-206). Highly polarising were the riots in the elections of June 1961 between supporters of the two major parties in Zanzibar Town, and the extension of rioting to the rural areas, where numerous bands of Africans roamed the plantation area of Zanzibar Island, looting, pillaging, devastating clove plantations and murdering. The official death roll from 1 June to 8 June, was placed at 68, of whom 64 were Arabs, mainly Manga Arabs, petty traders and small shopkeepers who lived either on the plantations or in villages in the plantation area. In addition, about 400, almost equally African (presumably African and Shirazi) and Arab, were treated in hospital (Report of Commission of Inquiry into Disturbances in Zanzibar during June 1961). Several thousand Arabs from outlying districts took refuge in Zanzibar Town. The British acted firmly, declared a state of emergency, flew in troops from Kenya and the Middle East, and restored order. It is important to note that Pemba Island remained peaceful. The last elections before independence, held in July 1963, went off quietly, under close surveillance by the Government.

Violence certainly contributed to the polarisation, but in no way comparable to its role in Algeria, Rwanda or Burundi. The polarisation resulted essentially from normal political processes acting on a structure highly conducive to racial conflict between Mainland Africans and Arabs.

The main arena of the conflict was Zanzibar Island. Here in the first place, the racial composition favoured Mainland Africans. They constituted about one fourth of the population, being almost three times as numerous as Arabs. Some 25,000, according to the 1948 census, representing almost 60% of the Mainland African population of Zanzibar Island, were concentrated in the urban conurbation of Zanzibar Town (Middleton and Campbell, 1965: 21). The general layout of the urban area and the distribution of the different sections, rendered the Arab population, and the administrative centres, highly vulnerable to attack. Arabs had engaged heavily in the slave trade, with Zanzibar the main market for the transhipment of slaves. There thus lay between Arabs and many Mainland Africans the enmity of ancient wrong and this ancient wrong was compounded with present discrimination in Zanzibar, before the revolution.

If one views the different sections of the population as categories, that is to say, if the internal differentiation within each section is ignored, then the following preliminary account, given by Lofchie (1965: 14), may serve to locate the racial and ethnic groups, though quite crudely, in the structure of Zanzibar society.

Arabs constituted a privileged political and economic elite until the African revolution; they were the owners of the largest coconut and clove plantations and occupied many of the highest administrative positions in the Zanzibar civil service. Asians (persons of Indo-Pakistani descent) formed Zanzibar's commercial and middle class; they dominated wholesale and retail trade, import and export businesses and enjoyed nearly exclusive occupancy of the middle tiers of the civil service. Africans were historically the broad underprivileged mass of the Zanzibar population; they were the unskilled manual and agricultural labourers, tenant farmers and petty agriculturists.

Distinguishing within the African category, the Shirazi, corresponding to the indigenous population, and the relatively recent immigrants, the Mainland Africans, Lofchie writes that:

Social differentiation between Shirazis and Africans of mainland origin is generally clear and precise. Even in cases where an individual is of mixed mainland and Zanzibari background, his own self-description and common acceptance usually locate him in one group or the other ... (Mainlanders) tend predominantly to be employed in the towns, either in domestic service or in manual work as government labourers; those engaged in agriculture are usually squatters on land to which they have no permanent rights. Shirazis are a more rural community and tend predominantly to be fishermen and farmers on privately owned or community-held land (pp. 82-83).

To this we might add, that Mainland Africans, drawn from many different peoples on the continent of Africa (Nyamwezi, Zaramo, Makonde, Dengereko, Nyasa, Yao, Maniema and Zigua) were somewhat distinctive in culture. The Permanent Secretary to the Chief Minister, in his evidence before the Commission of Inquiry into the 1961 disturbances, emphasised cultural difference as the distinctive mark of the Mainland African.

If a person's way of life is still that of a mainland African then he would be accepted by most people and regarded as a mainland African. For example, if he is a troublemaker or the way he speaks Swahili, he does not speak the local idiom, he would then be regarded as a mainlander. His actual national status is not at issue. It is what he is in fact. Has he become assimilated ... He would be identified as a mainland African if he had not become assimilated. (Notes of Proceedings on the Eighth Day, 27-28)

The cultural differences included some difference in religious affiliation. Though only a small proportion was Christian (some 2,000 according to a survey made in 1948-1949), they could nevertheless be presented, in the crude categorisations of political conflict, as of alien religion in a Muslim country.

These broad differences between Arabs and Mainland Africans laid the basis for a heightened polarisation of race relations, under the stimulus of constitutional political processes in the movement to independence. The distinctive feature of these political processes was the extent to which the political divisions were expressed in racial and ethnic terms.

II

The early manifestations of the role of racial and ethnic origins in political conflict are to be found in the sectional associations. These exclusive associations started in the first decades of British rule. The Arab Association, formed to secure financial compensation for slave owners affected by the abolition of slavery, and later representing the general interests of the Arab landowning community, dates back to the beginning of the twentieth century. Indians founded the Indian National Association shortly before the First World War. Conflicts of interest between the landowning elite of the Arab Association and the financial and commercial elite of the Indian Association led, in the 1930s, to a very sharp struggle in which Indian leaders launched a boycott of the clove industry in protest against Government legislation and Arabs began to organise a succession of counter-boycotts, while armed bands of Arabs roamed the rural areas, intimidating Indian shopkeepers (Lofchie, 1965: 104-126). In the electoral contests from 1957 onwards, Indians being a small minority, could not play a significant role, as an ethnic unit. Though they were able to act successfully as a kind of interest group on rare occasions, their dominant style of behaviour was nonpolitical (Lofchie, 1965: 79).

The remaining ethnic associations were the African Association, composed of Mainland Africans and founded in 1934, and the Shirazi Association formed in 1939. In contrast to the Arab Association, neither Association actively intervened politically until after the Second World War.

British constitutional policies in the Zanzibar Protectorate contributed to the significant role of racial and ethnic identity in the political process. The Protectorate Council, established in 1914, included four representatives of the Arab and Asian communities. The Legislative Council, created in 1926 as an advisory body with some legislative functions, had eight unofficial members, nominated by the Sultan on the advice of the British Resident, and comprising three Arabs, two 'Africans' (Shirazi), two Indians and one European. It became customary for the Arab and Indian Associations to present panels of names for consideration in these appointments (Middleton and Campbell, 1965: 43). The African Association and the Shirazi Association 'contested bitterly over the allocation of the nominated seats in the Legislative Council reserved for representatives of the African community. The fact that until

1956 these places were in every case awarded to a leader of the Shirazi Association offended mainland African leadership and created a deep split between the two groups' (Lofchie, 1965: 168).

British constitutional reforms proceeded by careful progression toward independence. For the first time, elected members, six in number, were included among the unofficial representatives on the Legislative Council, the elections being held in July 1957. The next step began in 1961 with responsible government in the form of a legislative majority of locally elected representatives, and the assumption by local leaders of ministerial responsibility in the fields, *inter alia*, of agriculture, health and education. In the terminal phase of colonial status, internal self-government, introduced in 1963, provided for a National Assembly, consisting only of locally elected representatives, and for the exercise of sovereignty, limited by British control over defense, foreign affairs, and internal security until independence in December 1963. These were the constitutional reforms which heightened the polarisation between Mainland Africans and Arabs, and which *perhaps* acted finally as catalyst for massacre.

The long-standing practices of racial representation had encouraged communal separatism. It appears, however, to have been a standing feature of the society, also outside the political arena. Lofchie (1965: 179) refers to the innumerable racial and communal bodies, and the fact that even sports, social life and the local press were organised on communal lines. Inevitably, political parties exploited these communal loyalties in their struggle for power.

The main contestants were Mainland Africans and Arabs, the former relatively recent immigrants, the latter long established. It is not easy to understand why the Shirazi, the indigenous majority, did not play a more active role in a struggle for leadership on their own account. Perhaps, since so many of them were cultivators and fishermen, they were not easily mobilised into political strife. They represented a middle group in the structure of the society, responsive in some ways, and resistant in others, to the appeals of the main antagonists. On Zanzibar

Island, they were in competition with Mainland Africans as
squatters, and with Mainland Africans, Arabs and Indians as
producers of food for the markets. They were not driven by
racial hatred of the Arabs, though there were differences here
among the Shirazi, the Hadimu Shirazi on Zanzibar Island
having experienced the greatest deprivation and subordination
under Arab rule. Loyalty to the Sultan, however, was a unifying
bond. The Shirazi did not identify with Mainland Africans, and
indeed there were many tensions, economic, political and
ideological between the two groups. In general, the Shirazi
seemed less activated by ethnic sentiment, and though they did
form a Shirazi political party, it proved quite unstable.

Neither of the contestants for power could succeed under a
democratic system favouring the rule of numbers, without
Shirazi support, and a major feature of the struggle was the
attempt of the contestants to woo the Shirazi. Both came forward
as nationalist parties, but their nationalism fused with separatist
loyalties, in such manner as to exclude their main antagonist.

The Zanzibar Nationalist Party (ZNP) was the first in the
field. Arabs dominated the ZNP which represented their interests
or the interests of the Arab elite. The ideology of the party was
that of multiracial nationalism. This offered a basis for the
affiliation of other ethnic and racial groups. 'Any specification of
the differences between Zanzibar's ethnic communities was
considered unpatriotic and disloyal. Indeed, communal
differentiation was explicitly identified by official ZNP party
dogma as a colonial legacy' (Lofchie, 1965: 155). Lofchie adds
the comment that this mystique of imperialist responsibility for
segregation made any articulation of the glaring economic
differences between the various racial groups a basic violation of
nationalistic political norms. At the same time, this inclusive
ideology was so elaborated as to exclude Mainland Africans. It
emphasised the unity in Islam of Zanzibari, and represented
Mainland Africans as an alien threat to the goal of a culturally
autonomous Islamic state. The slogan of Zanzibar for the
Zanzibari provided a basis for the incorporation of nationals and
the exclusion of aliens.

The Mainland African leaders based their appeal on an equally exclusive ideology. Their constituency was explicitly African, that is both Mainland African and Shirazi. They emphasised the unity of Africans, confronting the threat of Arab domination. Their goal of an independent African state was diametrically opposed to the policy of the ZNP. Combining racial and class criteria, they represented themselves as the champions of the depressed African majority.

The main impetus for the founding of an African political party (the Afro-Shirazi Party) and for a political alliance with the Shirazi came from the Mainland African community (Lofchie, 1969: 312). The forging of this alliance was attended by numerous difficulties. Lofchie comments (1969: 285) that 'Zanzibar's indigenous inhabitants did not view themselves as Africans and sought to distinguish their identity, culturally and historically, from mainland Africa.' He writes further of an endemic power struggle between Mainland African and Shirazi leaders, superimposed over a complex pattern of regional jealousies. '... its fundamental component was a mutual distrust of the virtue and motivations of the two communities. The Shirazis believed that the ASP could never attract the vast majority of Shirazis as long as it was dominated by Mainlanders. At the same time, the Mainlanders were determined to prevent control over the party from falling into the hands of men whose loyalty to the cause of African nationalism they found suspect' (1965: 233).

For the 1957 elections, the African and Shirazi Associations formed a union, but without merger. Many Shirazi were reluctant to join a political party in which their identity would be subordinated, they held different views on the place of the Arab community in Zanzibar society, and they were repelled by the anti-Arab militancy of Mainland Africans. The Pemba Shirazi held that they represented the great majority of Africans on Pemba Island. They did not wish the name of the new party to make reference to the racial composition of its members, and they wanted a non-racial political organisation which would be nationalistic rather than anti-Arab in character (Lofchie, 1965:

171-172). The Pemba Shirazi therefore stayed outside the electoral union. After the elections, in which the Afro-Shirazi Union (on Zanzibar Island) and the Shirazi Association (in Pemba) gained five of the six seats, the Pemba Shirazi agreed to a limited form of cooperation. The two elected representatives from Pemba thereupon joined the Afro-Shirazi Union, then renamed the Afro-Shirazi Party (ASP).

The alliance between Mainland Africans and Shirazi proved unstable, and in 1959, some of the Shirazi leaders left the ASP to form the Zanzibar and Pemba People's Party (ZPPP). Middleton and Campbell write (1965: 55) that 'the former series of threats, intimidations and openly hostile acts which had long characterised the relations between the Shirazi and African elements of the old ASU continued, now more in the open than before'.

The ZPPP contested the elections in January 1961. It emphasised the special interests and needs of the Shirazi majority. Its objectives were constitutional monarchy, rapid evolution towards independence and non-racial government. This new formation also proved unstable. The number of seats in the January elections had been increased to twenty-two. The ZNP, which had made a remarkable recovery, gained nine of the seats, the ASP ten, and the ZPPP three. The Shirazi party thus held the balance of power. It thereupon split its support between the main rival parties, thereby creating a deadlock which necessitated new elections in June 1961. These were the elections that precipitated considerable violence. In both the June 1961 elections and the July 1963 elections, the last elections before independence (10 December 1963) and the revolution (12 January 1964), the ZPPP formed a successful electoral coalition with the ZNP. The effect of this coalition was to deny the Mainland African party an electoral victory. In the July 1963 elections, the ASP gained only two of the fourteen constituencies on Pemba Island. Nevertheless, it had increased its support on Pemba Island, by toning down its anti-Arab propaganda, and giving greater emphasis to religious and patriotic themes. As a result, it gained 54% of the votes, not sufficient immediately to inherit the

political kingdom, but sufficient for disillusionment with
constitutional processes and parliamentary institutions.

III

The riots and murders attendant on the general election in June
1961 were the subject of a Commission of Inquiry appointed by
the British Resident. The Commission heard evidence from thirty
witnesses at hearings extending over sixteen days in September
and October 1961. The Government of Zanzibar, the Zanzibar
Nationalist Party, the Zanzibar and Pemba People's Party and
the Afro-Shirazi Party were represented at the inquiry. They
called witnesses, including senior government officials and party
leaders, and they presented by way of argument their analyses of
the causes of the conflict. The Commission conducted the
proceedings with great care and integrity, and reported its own
findings.

The disturbances indicated a high degree of polarisation. The
Police Commissioner stated that he was quite sure that if the
ZNP had retaliated, there would have been racial war (Notes of
Proceedings on the 5th Day, p. 25). On reading the evidence, it
seems to me very likely that, but for the British presence, the
revolution might have taken place in June 1961. Given this view
of the significance of the events, and given the extensive
documentation available, the disturbances would seem to provide
a valuable point of entry into the analysis of the processes of
polarisation in Zanzibar.

The Commission found the immediate precipitating cause to
be the seizure, assault and removal from the voting queue of
individual members of the Zanzibar Nationalist Party by
supporters of the Afro-Shirazi Party. This was motivated by the
belief, quite mistaken, but honestly and firmly held, that the
ZNP had achieved its success in the January 1961 election as a
result of large scale 'cheating', double voting and 'personation',
and that it had prepared a campaign of 'vote stealing' for the June
elections. The ZNP withdrew from two constituencies on
grounds of intimidation and assembled its supporters, some

armed with sticks, knives or swords, at Party headquarters. Afro-Shirazi supporters immediately reacted by arming with sticks and stones. The resulting confrontation became so serious as to call for the reading of the Riot Act by the Superintendant of Police. Dispersing Afro-Shirazi were assaulted by Nationalist Party supporters. 'Africans being attacked in this manner were heard to be saying, "The Arabs are killing us", and it seems clear that this developed into a wide-spread rumour that Arabs were killing Africans, and was responsible for much of the subsequent violence' (Commission Report, Para. 61). There were further disorders in Zanzibar Town, and looting of Arab houses and shops. From the town, murder and pillage spread to the rural areas. By 6 June, the authorities had reestablished effective control, but in the few days of rioting, many Arabs had been killed, and many Africans and Arabs had been seriously injured.

The British showed quite remarkable foresight and skill in their handling of the disorders. Reading through the evidence, one recalls the British dedication to the maintenance of law and order, and their efficiency in its preservation. In May, the Government held meetings to discuss security arrangements for the elections, and agreed with the political parties on the points of procedure to be announced to the electorate. A maximum publicity effort was made to bring these procedures to the notice of the public. A Security Committee kept the political situation and the security arrangements for polling day under constant study. An Election Committee, attended by leaders of the political parties, also concerned itself with aspects of security. Neither the Security Committee nor the Election Committee found any indications that trouble need be expected on election day, though they thought there might be minor incidents, and perhaps serious trouble after the announcement of the results. The Commission was informed 'that whenever the likelihood of trouble occurring on election day, 1st June, was discussed at Election Committee meetings, the representatives of the political Parties present would invariably say, "We Zanzibaris are peaceful people. There won't be any trouble" ' (para. 116).

Notwithstanding these favourable indications, the

Government made careful arrangements for the disposition of its own police force on election day and for the immediate availability of forces from the mainland in case of need. A General Service Command of Police, on four hours stand by in Kenya, was summoned and arrived on the evening of election day, and a second General Company on the following morning. With the extension of the disorders to the rural areas, the British Resident arranged for the dispatch of troops. Two companies of the 5th King's African Rifles became available on 3 June, and three further companies of the 5th and 6th King's African Rifles on 4 and 5 June, one being sent for a few days to Pemba where some degree of tension was reported. That there were so many deaths and casualties, after all the preliminary precautions and with so much force at the disposal of the authorities relative to population, is strong argument for concluding that in June 1961, a race war or race massacre was narrowly averted by the resolute action of the British authorities.

Though the disturbances were so closely linked to the political struggle, they seem to have arisen outside of the political party structure. The Senior Superintendent in charge of the Criminal Investigation Department gave evidence that there was no reliable information that agitators were sent out from Party Headquarters to stir up trouble in the rural areas, though he did say that in one or two cases local political leaders were actively involved (Seventh Day, 23-24). The Permanent Secretary to the Chief Minister expressed the view that the leaders of the party had nothing to do with the organisation of the actual gangs, and also that they did not seem to have much control over the gangs he had observed (Eighth Day, 12). The commission concluded that there was no premeditated plot by any person, group of persons or political party, and it rejected the charges to this effect made by the Zanzibar Nationalist Party against the Afro-Shirazi Party. The leaders of both these parties, at the request of the authorities, had done their best to persuade their supporters to remain calm and to disperse. It seems clear, too, from the small number of African deaths, that Arabs had reacted with restraint. They had been involved in confrontations with Africans, they had assaulted Africans, but on the whole they had stopped short of murder.

As to the different groups of Africans involved, the evidence is not very clear. There are innumerable references to Africans, but without indication whether Mainland, Shirazi or both: there are references to Shirazi, to indigenous Africans (presumably Shirazi),[1] to tribal Africans (seemingly Mainland), to Mainland Africans, to Zanzibar Africans, and to specific mainland groups, such as the Makonde from Tanganyika and Mozambique, who shared with Manga Arabs a reputation for violence and were described by the Commission as 'a somewhat primitive tribe of mainland Africans'. The Commissioner of Police, in his evidence, makes precise distinctions between Africans and Shirazi, but refers also to Afro-Shirazi, apparently indicating supporters of the Afro-Shirazi Party. Where examining and cross-examining counsel do not share the same perceptions of the structure as the Commissioner of Police, the proceedings introduce ambiguity in his evidence.

The Commission, in its report, draws distinctions between indigenous and other Africans, but not consistently. Sometimes it uses the term African, presumably as an inclusive term. When discussing the confrontation in Zanzibar Town with Nationalist Party supporters, it refers to Afro-Shirazis, in-the sense it seems of party supporters. Since this was a confrontation between supporters of the main political parties, I think there can be no doubt that both Shirazi and Mainland Africans must have participated: some 10% of Hadimu Shirazi lived in Zanzibar Town (Lofchie, 1969: 315). The Commissioner of Police had testified that there were a large number of habitual criminals with many convictions, either born in the mainland or descended from persons of mainland origin, most of whom had been in Zanzibar for as long as 25 years. Under çross-examination, he also referred to the many hooligans in the Ngambo (African and

---

1. The Superintendent of the CID explained that he meant Shirazi by indigenous Africans (Proceedings, Seventh Day, 54).

Shirazi) section of Zanzibar Town, the majority of whom, he said, undoubtedly supported the Afro-Shirazi Party (Fifth Day, pp. 44 and 17).· The Commission linked these hooligan and criminal elements to the disturbances, arguing that it was 'reasonable to conclude that they were responsible for much of the looting, wounding and murder that took place. Some two to three hundred habitual criminals were housed in Ngambo' (para. 63).

In the rural areas, the Commission refers to gangs, composed of Africans of many tribes from the squatter labour on the surrounding farms, involved in incidents of violence on 2 June: it refers to looting Africans on 4 June, and to operations, on 5 June, by two bands of armed Makonde. One of these bands, of between 30 and 50 Africans, armed with spears, pangas, knobkerries and various other instruments, was dispersed by the Commissioner of Police, when breaking into a shop; the Commissioner reports that murders had been committed in this area. In evidence, the leader of the Zanzibar Nationalist Party expressed his belief that a considerable number, if not the majority, of those involved in the murders, were non-Zanzibaris (Tenth Day, 108). The Commission makes no pronouncement on this issue, but seems to be at pains to mention gangs consisting mainly of indigenous Africans, attacking and looting Arab shops and assaulting the occupants on 3 June. 'The temper of these gangs was described as being completely hysterical; one witness expressed the opinion that by then they had become "blood mad". Killings and lootings occurred at four different places' (para. 73).

Looking at the disturbances as a whole, there was clearly heavy Mainland African involvement, but with active participation by Shirazi. It is, however, quite impossible to give any precise picture of the extent of Shirazi participation.

In analysing the cause of the riots and murders, the Commission takes as its starting point the political background from the first common roll elections in 1957. It makes passing, idyllic reference to Zanzibar as a country in which different races lived together in peace and harmony before 1957 (apart from a few isolated incidents). In the evidence, this point of view seems to have been well accepted; even the leader of the Afro-Shirazi Party agreed that Zanzibar had the reputation of being a peaceful and quiet country, that people in Zanzibar prided themselves on that reputation, and that no one could have foreseen the tragic events that took place later (Fourteenth Day, 9). The Commission, in further comment, quotes from The Annual Report of the Provincial Administration for 1957 that the elections of that year were later described 'as having been probably the most peaceful in constitutional history' (para. 15).

Given the Commission's view of the harmonious nature of race relations up to the 1957 elections, one of the causes of the polarisation must certainly have been the political processes launched by constitutional change. The Commission comments, that whether or not by design, the two rival parties succeeded in working up the political temperature by August 1958 to such heights and bitterness that the Administration thought a mere spark would produce conflagration (para. 16). It refers to the report of the Provincial Administration that the year 1958 was remarkable for the extent to which politics infected almost every side of life in Zanzibar.

Traders, cultivators, labourers, fishermen, even housewives, were affected. Villagers in the rural areas argued among themselves. Funerals and religious ceremonies were boycotted by rival political parties! Women even pawned their clothing in order to raise the bus fare to political meetings. Such was the immediate result of the first common roll elections for these formerly peaceful islands. (Commission Report, para. 88)

The Commission describes the conflicts in this period between landlords and tenants, arising from some Arab landlord pressure on squatters to support the landlord's political party, with eviction as a sanction, and from tensions consequent upon a speech claiming that only the trees belonged to the landlords, not the land.[2] Its report draws attention to the attempt to replace

2. Middleton and Campbell (1965: 52) write that the squatters on Zanzibar Island proclaimed the ASU slogan 'The trees are yours, the soil is ours', this being in accordance with the norms of Shirazi traditional land tenure.

established Afro-Shirazi labour at the docks by labour favoured by the Zanzibar Nationalist Party (Lofchie, 1965; 187 states that most of the dock workers were Mainland African). There is comment on the closure of several hundred Arab owned shops, as a result of boycotts, and on the boycotting of buses owned by members of the opposite political party. The Commission makes special mention of the youth branches of the two main parties, the Youth Branch of the Zanzibar Nationalist Party training in a militant manner, wearing uniforms and on occasion usurping the functions of the police, while the Afro-Shirazi Youth League was described in evidence as 'completely undisciplined' and as having been a constant source of trouble to the police (para. 20).

Many of these issues were discussed in the Report of the Select Committee Appointed to Enquire into the Public Order Bill, Sessional Paper No. 7 of 1959. The report lists the major conflicts of 1958, showing that boycotting even included refusal by members of one political party to allow people of the opposing party to draw water at their wells, and that infiltration of politically controlled labour by the Nationalist Party extended to the meat and copra markets. An Appendix describes the activities of the youth groups but mainly those of the Youths' Own Union, affiliated to the Zanzibar Nationalist Party – marching, drilling, mounting of guards, interfering with traffic, insulting behaviour to grown-ups of the opposite political party. To this I would add the observation by Middleton and Campbell (1965: 52), relating to the same period, that the Youths' Own Union was rabidly anti-European and anti-African, and that vividly racist songs were a feature of its rallies.

The Commission sees the intervening period between 1958 and the riots of June 1961 as marked by fluctuations in tension, declining as a result of Round Table Conferences, of improvements in the relations between landlords and squatters, consumers and retail shopkeepers, and travelling public and bus owners, but mounting again toward the end of 1959 on the breakaway of three elected members from the Afro-Shirazi Party to form the Zanzibar and Pemba People's Party. There is further heightening of tension with political party conflict over the conditions for constitutional advance, and 'by July 1960, the tone of the Press, and political speeches, was so deplorable that the British Resident decided it was necessary to call together the political leaders to discuss the situation and, after prolonged discussion, they all agreed to sign a joint declaration, calling upon their supporters to mend their ways and to behave with traditional good humour and politeness' (Para. 31). Thereafter the situation improves but tensions mount again as a result of the stalemate in the January 1961 elections, the suspicions of the ASP that only electoral fraud could have accomplished the reversal of their earlier success, and their determination to make sure that no 'cheating' takes place in the June elections, a determination which sparked off the riots and the murders.

The fact that the murder victims were almost entirely Arab might suggest that the conflict was essentially racial. The Commission seeks to guard against this interpretation. It points out that most, if not all, of the murdered Arabs in the rural areas were Manga Arabs, a group with a reputation for violence ('the "bogymen" of Zanzibar'), living as small traders in fairly densely populated squatter areas. Moreover the disturbances provided an opportunity 'for paying off old scores'. Given this background, the Commission argues that the murders should not be interpreted as necessarily indicating the extent of racial antagonism between 'Africans' and 'Arabs'. The nature of the 'old scores' referred to by the Commission is suggested in the evidence of the leader of the Afro-Shirazi Party, who refers to earlier Manga Arab violence, and more recently to the eviction of squatters, the burning of their houses, and the throwing away of crops, Manga Arabs adding to their shopkeeping the leasing of crops, and, when well off, the ownership of farms (Fourteenth Day, 12). Lofchie (1965: 206) gives a somewhat different version. He writes that during the racial crisis of 1958, it appeared to Africans that Manga Arabs were to blame for the squatter evictions, for in numerous cases landowners justified the expulsions on the grounds that the squatters were boycotting Manga shops, and in a few instances, members of the Manga community fell heir to the land from which Africans had been removed. He adds also the comment that because of their violence Manga Arabs became widely and erroneously known as the secret military wing of the ZNP.

Consistent with its attitude to the interpretation of the murders of Manga Arabs, the Commission rejects the contention of Counsel for the ZNP and ZPPP, that the disturbances were 'overwhelmingly racial in character' since in its view, the evidence establishes that what has been described as the 'wind of change', and the impact of party politics, played a substantial part. It thus views racial conflict as one of the factors but not decisive. Earlier it had commented that the evidence showed conclusively that the Afro-Shirazi Party made its appeal to the electorate on a racial basis, and that the Zanzibar Nationalist Party introduced religion into the controversy. There is curious confirmation of its analysis of ASP ideology in the evidence given by the leaders of the political parties. The ZNP leader declared that he did not know his race, and he maintained his position under cross-examination, describing himself as a Zanzibari. By contrast, the leader of the Afro-Shirazi Party affected astonishment at the term Zanzibari ('The Zanzibari surprises me. What does Zanzibari mean?'), and he dealt quite bluntly with the two categories of Arab and African, much of his evidence, however, being in terms of political party conflict. Though in the Commission's view the racial conflict contributed to the disturbances, as did the 'wind of change', the major cause of the heightening of tension to explosion point was the 'bombardment of words', written and spoken, to which the people of Zanzibar were subjected, more or less continuously, after the first General Election in July 1957.

IV

In a strange way, the Commission foreshortens its analysis, taking as its starting point the common roll elections of 1957, and bringing into relief the electoral changes and the electoral conflict. It presents a picture of traditional harmonious race relations until 1957, but seems not to be astonished that group relations should have reached a point of near conflagration in one year, and of protracted riots and murderous violence some three years later. It emphasises the wind of change, but without discussing on whom it was blowing and in what direction. The impact of party politics is described as having played a substantial part in the disturbances. Racial conflict is seen as a factor, the Afro-Shirazi Party having made its appeal to the electorate on a racial basis. Yet the Commission does not analyse the racial basis of political alignments, nor the relationship between political party affiliation and racial identity, though there was much evidence in the proceedings on these issues. It would seem that the Afro-Shirazi Party could not have launched racial appeals, unless the membership was racially exclusive, and the evidence shows that the ASP, though non-racial in constitution, was overwhelmingly Mainland African and Shirazi. Lofchie (1965: 204) in discussing the 1961 disturbances, cites as specially relevant, that party and racial conflict had become practically synonymous, the fundamental division being between Arabs and Africans, to the extent that the Swahili terms for Arabs and Africans were used everywhere in the Protectorate to describe the ZNP and ASP respectively. We have no way of knowing, however, to what extent this represents the views of the Commission, though the Commission does quote a statement of the British Resident, that the Arab, Comorian, Shirazi and African Associations all looked to one of the existing political parties to protect their political interests. Most strangely of all, the Commission cites as a major cause the 'bombardment of words', as if this bombardment was unrelated to the racial conflict, the winds of change, and party politics, and as if it did not provide a vehicle for, and a stimulus to, political party and racial conflict.

These reservations notwithstanding, it seems to me that the basic approach of the Commission is sound, though requiring amplification. In seeking to explain the rapid polarisation before the disturbances of 1961, and its course during the succeeding years, I take as my starting point the social structure of Zanzibar with its marked discontinuities, associated with cultural differences, between a dominant Arab minority and a subordinate, but much more numerous Mainland African minority on Zanzibar Island, many being recent immigrants, not integrated, or only marginally integrated, into the society, and concentrated in the conurbation of Zanzibar Town. The winds of change, in the continental upheaval against alien racial rule, had acted with profoundly different impact on the antagonists. They moved Zanzibar Arabs to militant demands for national independence, but at the same time raised fears of African domination: in the political struggle there was continuous Arab concern over the threat represented by Mainland Africans. On the African side, the winds of change inspired a Pan-Africanist conception of Africa for the Africans, and a militant determination to shake off racial domination and to achieve African majority rule. There is some evidence of these perspectives in the proceedings of the 1961 Commission (Eighth Day, 17, 22, 57; Tenth Day, 104). As a result, a profound ideological polarisation set in opposition a small minority of different race, seeking to maintain a privileged position in a tiny island, narrowly separated from the mainland of Africa, and a Mainland African minority, many with ties to the mainland, viewing Zanzibar from the perspectives of militant liberation movements and of Pan Africanism, as an integral part of Africa under alien settler rule.

It was this background of structural, cultural and ideological discontinuity, that gave the electoral reforms introduced by the British their catastrophic impact. The whole process of electoral conflict set in motion an increasing polarisation between Arabs and Mainland Africans. Given the plural structure of the society, the pervasiveness of communal divisions, the effect of British policies of communal representation, the different cultural milieus, historical experience and racial background of the antagonists, and the ideological polarisation between different racial groups, it was inevitable that the campaigns should inflame racism. The ASP, the party of Mainland Africans, was in its composition a racial organisation, dedicated to exclusive racial goals, and identified with African nationalism and Pan-

Africanism on the mainland. It drew heavily on the historical
association of Arabs with slavery, and stories of Arab atrocity
pervaded the African villages and rural areas (Lofchie, 1965:
209). The ZNP sought to bring together in a Zanzibar national
movement Arabs, Shirazi, Indians and other small minorities. It
exploited images of a threat to Islam, and of domination by
foreigners, aligned to the mainland of Africa. Youth groups of
both parties, by their racist extremism, heightened the
antagonisms, already mounting under the tensions of racial fears
and the incompatibility in political goals.

The small scale of the society, with its many primary
groupings, with few structures cutting across communal lines,
with little industrial development, with the known identities of
its members, contributed to the polarisation, or in any event, laid
its stamp on the process. It seems to be this quality of Zanzibar
life which partly accounts for the penetration of almost every
aspect of life with partisan emotions.

Day-to-day activities became a battleground in which every individual act
was invested with highly symbolic significance as a demonstration of party
membership and solidarity. Performance of the most routine daily tasks –
marketing, working and commuting, for example – was viewed as an integral
facet of the national political struggle. Practically every individual construed
his personal behaviour as an opportunity for a direct contribution to the cause
of ultimate party victory. Supporters of opposed parties boycotted their rivals'
buses, refused to share their wells, and in numerous farming and fishing
villages ceased to work collectively. Sports and social activities were
organised and attended on strictly party lines. Even religious life was affected.
Funerals, weddings and worship itself were subjected to an almost
unanimously imposed segregation; each party's members refused to attend
ceremonies initiated by or identified with supporters of the opposite party. By
early 1958 no dimension of social behaviour remained politically neutral.
Even private quarrels and disputes which had long preceded the formation of
modern political parties were absorbed into the pattern of partisan conflict.
(Lofchie, 1965: 183-184)

The intense and somewhat total involvement in partisan
politics naturally led to undue pressures and episodes of violence.

The ZNP used its support by the wealthy and landowning classes to expand its membership through patronage, the promotion of trade unions, and the conferring or withholding of opportunities for employment. The ASP responded by economic warfare against ZNP supporters in the form of boycotts and party-managed consumer cooperatives. The trade union movement assumed an exclusive political form, with separate trade unions affiliated to the rival political parties, divided on the issue of Mainland African employment. Tensions reached such a point that 'towards the end of 1958 persistent outbreaks of disorder threatened to engulf the society in chronic racial warfare' (Lofchie, 1965: 188). After a brief intermission in racial conflict, largely as a result of the intervention of the Pan African Freedom Movement of East, Central and Southern Africa, sharp violence erupted in the elections of June 1961, leading to the riots and murders analysed above. Then followed the crucial elections of July 1963, which would set the pattern of political control in an independent Zanzibar. ASP members experienced the frustration of winning a majority of votes, but not a majority of seats. To this was added the further frustration of the repressive measures passed or initiated by the new government, measures which did not augur well for the possibility of democratic participation by the opposition.

This whole process would be sufficient to account for an extreme political polarisation, leading to revolutionary violence. However, the bizarre aspect of the matter, given the increasing polarisation between the political parties, is that the massacre (revolution) was carried out, not by or under the auspices of the ASP, but by a relatively recent Mainland African immigrant, acting on his own initiative, with support from the Afro-Shirazi Youth League, and launching a force he deliberately selected largely from Mainland Africans, with first generation Mainland Africans in most positions of authority. (See the account of the revolution by its leader, John Okello, 1967: ch. 6).

The violent assumption of power was a brief and rather simple affair, in which John Okello's small band captured the two police armouries, distributed weapons to supporters, occupied the radio station, and set about rounding up and slaughtering Arabs on Zanzibar Island. Violent mobs came out into the streets of Zanzibar Town. They must certainly have been appreciably Mainland African, but would also have included Hadimu Shirazi.[3] There was no revolutionary struggle on Pemba Island. One of the survivor's accounts mentions bands of Nyamwezi and Makonde roaming Zanzibar Town in search of victims, and describes the dominating role of Mainland Africans (Kharusi, 1967: Appendix II). In contrast to the speed with which power was seized, the brutalities, the interrogations, the tortures, the murders were a protracted affair. Lofchie gives an estimate of several thousand Arabs killed, and a total decrease in the Arab community by murder, repatriation and emigration of about 10,000 persons (Kuper, 1974: 127).

There is a theory that a second revolution was definitely being planned by the ASP, in collusion with high Tanzanian officials, and that possibly a third revolution by the Marxist Party UMMA was in preparation (Lofchie, 1967: 37). It is impossible, however, to know whether a revolutionary struggle would have been launched by one of these opposition parties, if it had not been for the bloody unanticipated intervention of a leader, quite marginal in the social and political structure of Zanzibar, though an ASP-led revolution seems not unlikely, given the state of polarisation between Mainland Africans and Arabs.

The processes of polarisation within Zanzibar society would certainly have made an impact on Okello and his followers. In his account of the revolution, Okello refers to the riots and deaths in the June 1961 elections, as an event which marked the beginning of bitterness between Arabs and Africans (1967: 82). This is, of course, a view quite contrary to the one I am advancing. At the end of 1962, after having given much thought to 'the political problems of the black Africans of Zanzibar', Okello decides that revolution is the only solution (85). In the

3. Lodhi (1973: 24) distinguishes between Hadimu meaning ex-slave or person of ex-slave origin, and Mhadimu, a Shirazi of Zanzibar Island, and suggests that because of the confusion in terms, many of the younger Zanzibar Shirazi mistook themselves to be of ex-slave descent and joined the ASP.

July 1963 elections, he campaigns for the ASP, observes the split between the leaders and the demoralisation of the party as a result of the electoral defeat, and decides that the time has come to arrange the revolution, and to free people of his blood from Arab slavery (92-94). In his overtures to the Youth League he declares that Africans, the majority, were 'grossly deceived, cheated and defeated by votes under the so-called British democratic system' (102). Later in his account, as he is recruiting followers, he claims to have uncovered Arab plans to expel all non-Zanzibari Africans, to confiscate their wealth, to rule the remaining Africans as slaves, to kill all male African babies, to sever Zanzibar from East Africa and Africa, proclaiming it as a land for Asians and Arabs, and to exact retribution from Africans in the ratio of 60 African deaths for each Arab killed in the 1961 disturbances (120). (Clearly Okello is expressing his own hatred of Arabs in a paranoic fantasy.)

These interpretations of the course of the political conflict on Zanzibar would have been sufficient to motivate a revolutionary struggle. But the seeds of Okello's revolutionary leadership were present long before his involvement in Zanzibar politics. Born in Uganda, he arrives in Nairobi in October 1954 at a time of massive repression against the Mau Mau revolt. He makes contact with some of the leaders of the Land Freedom Army, and joins the Nairobi African District Congress, learning African plans for the future of Kenya and techniques of political organisation (57-58). He moves to Mombasa and describes poignantly a visit to Fort Jesus, the former slave depot, monument of sacrifice for Africans and of shame for the descendants of the arab slave traders (64). He arrives in Pemba Island in June 1959, and shortly after has a Messianic dream that he is an annointed of God who will help redeem his black brothers from slavery (73). Continuously, the sentiments he expresses in his account are of militant African nationalism and Pan-Africanism, and of hatred for alien rulers and for Arabs, equating Arab domination with African enslavement.

I am suggesting then that Okello brought his revolutionary ideology with him from the mainland, that the perspectives of many of his followers were similarly moulded by identification with the political movements of the mainland, and that in a sense the societal context of the revolution was appreciably that of an East African social unit, including the small islands of Zanzibar and Pemba. Or to phrase the matter differently, the processes of polarisation in Zanzibar on the one hand, and the revolutionary conflict on the other, must be viewed to some extent in detachment from each other. Given the large number of Mainland Africans in Zanzibar, and the proximity to the mainland, it seems that there would have been an African revolution or coup even if the course of events in Zanzibar had not been so polarising.

RWANDA

Before the massacres in Rwanda and Burundi, both countries had the same ethnic or racial composition, a dominant minority of Tutsi (about 14%), a great majority of Hutu (85%) and small numbers of Twa. This basic structure was, however, rendered somewhat more complex by regional and other internal differentiations, which affected the actual process of polarisation between Tutsi and Hutu.

Both these territories are small in scale. The population of Rwanda was two and a half million, and of Burundi perhaps three and a half million. (Figures of population for Burundi fluctuate quite alarmingly from source to source.) The two societies were essentially agricultural. If a continuum is drawn of countries in Africa in terms of development and industrialisation, then Rwanda and Burundi would represent about the lowest point, South Africa the highest, and Algeria at the time of the revolution something in the way of a midpoint.

Rwanda and Burundi were, and continue to be, densely populated, and exceedingly poor, though Burundi has large deposits of nickel, which await exploitation. The economics of the two countries rested essentially on subsistence farming and herding. With a narrow margin over subsistence, famine constantly threatened. Coffee was the main cash crop and export.

There was some very modest exploitation of minerals, but industrialisation remained quite embryonic. Foreigners controlled commerce and industry, though in Burundi, after independence and before the massacres, a local petty bourgeoisie had emerged which engaged in the marketing of coffee and in wholesale trade (Mpozagora, 1971: 14). In general, the growth of a modern sector introduced new strata, comprising small numbers of professionals, of western educated intellectuals, of traders, and of 'proletarised' workers.

Bujumbura, the capital of Burundi, had been the centre of Belgian administration for the two territories. With trading and manufacturing activities, and a population of 55,000,[1] it was an appreciable centre and it played a significant role in the political struggles of Burundi. Of Kigali, the capital city of Rwanda, Lemarchand (1970: 16) writes that 'with a population of 4,000 and only one asphalt road, Kigali shares none of the characteristics of large, cosmopolitan towns. So minimal is the rate of urbanisation in and around Kigali, so limited is the incidence of commercial and industrial activities, that it is perhaps better described as an overgrown village.' In Rwanda, there were virtually no towns, but dispersed settlements with some large villages and hamlets. Unfortunately the small scale of a society is no barrier to massive massacre.

I

Many factors contributed to the polarisation between Tutsi and Hutu in Rwanda, but the catalyst was violence precipitated by the struggle for power in the movement to independence.

The social basis of the polarisation is to be found in the traditional structure of the society, often described as a caste society. Lemarchand (1970: 34-35) emphasises the significance of common values in maintaining this structure. He writes that 'the caste structure of Rwanda was based on a shared and "culturally

---

1. This is the figure given by Lemarchand (1970: 16). Melady (1974: 40) gives a figure of about 75,000.

elaborated" image of society, involving a combination of
exclusiveness and reciprocity, of inequality and solidarity' and he
refers to the concept of 'the premise of inequality' which Maquet
invoked to explain the integration of traditional society. Maquet
(1961: 165) defines this premise of inequality as based on the
conception that 'people born in different castes are unequal in
inborn endowment, physical as well as psychological and have
consequently fundamentally different rights'; and he argues that
the acceptance of inequality was a basic principle influencing the
whole structure of Rwanda life.

In the ordinary course of social life, it is difficult to estimate the
significance of different elements in the structure and culture of a
society. It is moments of crises, of disjunction, which illuminate
the normal, and make it more comprehensible.[2] The rapidity of
the polarisation in Rwanda society may suggest that acceptance
of the premise of inequality was not so deeply rooted, or that it
was coloured by much ambivalence. Alternatively, since the
picture Maquet presented was of traditional Rwanda society
before the full impact of European contacts, the suggestion that
the premise of inequality was undermined by these contacts seems
plausible enough.

The premise of inequality represents for Maquet an underlying
system of ideas which functioned as one of the elements
integrating Tutsi pastoralists and Hutu agriculturalists in the
traditional society. He mentions (1961: 148ff) a variety of
structures also serving integrative functions: the carrying of
similar clan names by Tutsi and Hutu, suggesting some minimal
solidarity; the participation of Hutu in the army; membership in
the same Ryangombe religious sect; a system of clientship linking
individuals in a unified economic system through which
agricultural and pastoral products were distributed throughout
the society; some slight social mobility for Hutu; a plurality of
structures in which individuals were affiliated; and the role of the
ruler, the Mwami, as representative of the deity, and as king,

---

2. See the discussion of this point by Jan Mejer in his dissertation, *The May Events:
A Theory of Disruptive Crisis*, University of California, Los Angeles, 1976: ch. 1.

father and protector of the country.

Many of the changes under the Belgian mandate were beginning to modify this system. (See the discussion by Lemarchand, 1970: ch. 4.) There was provision for sanctions against deprivation of goods in 1917, the abolition of domestic slavery in 1923, and amelioration in the conditions governing service by clients (d'Hertefelt, 1960: 460). Some opportunities for higher education, and some very modest development of industry, commerce and agriculture, had opened up new occupational categories among the Hutu – a small professional elite, a stratum of primary school-teachers, clerks, petty traders, innkeepers, truck drivers, bricklayers, etc., a rural proletariat and peasant labourers. The progressive abolition of *buhake*, under a decree of April 1954, was of even greater economic and political significance for many of the peasants. *Buhake* was a key institution of the traditional system, 'through which a client pledged his allegiance to a patron, who then acknowledged the homage of his future vassal by entrusting him with one or several cows' (Lemarchand, 1970: 127). Because of its intimate connection with political domination, change in this system of vassalage was bound to have radical implications for political change (Lemarchand, 1966: 592), more particularly since the use of delaying tactics by some patrons, and the failure to introduce the land reforms necessary to render effective the redistribution of cattle, must have been deeply frustrating to many Hutu, a frustration of rising expectations.

The introduction of elections by the Belgian government, under a decree of July 1952, represented a more direct attack on the traditional structure of power. The reforms were very cautious, presumably guided by recognition of the difficulties in promoting progressive democratic participation in a society characterised by the hereditary privileges of a dominant minority. They were also very complex, consisting of procedures for representation in consultative counsels at different levels of authority, the lowest being that of the Sub-Chief, and the highest that of the Superior Counsel. The first election in 1953 did not include a popular vote: this was, however, introduced in the 1956 elections in the form of adult male suffrage for the election of members of the electoral colleges in the sub-chiefdoms.[3] At this level, the Tutsi representation, as a result of the elections, was 33.08%, indicating, d'Hertefelt comments (1960a: 406), that a sufficiently large number of Hutu reinterpreted the western electoral system according to the norms of their traditional culture in such a way as to give the Tutsi a higher representation than might have been expected on the basis of their demographic significance. Still, the great majority of Hutu must have voted for the representatives of their choice, disregarding the vested rights of Tutsi to authority under the traditional system. This was made possible by the anonymity of mass elections (d'Hertefelt, 1960a: 407): confronted, however, by Tutsi notables in the electoral colleges, and perhaps under the influence of traditional considerations, Hutu members gave their support to Tutsi, with the result that there was an ascending representation at higher consultative levels, with a virtual monopoly by Tutsi of representation in the Superior Counsel (d'Hertefelt, 1960a: 407-408). This, too, must have been a situation of frustrated expectations for many Hutu, whose optimistic expectations for the future were denied by elections which merely confirmed Tutsi in their dominant position.

These electoral reforms were clearly significant for a restructuring of social consciousness. Munyangaju, one of the Hutu leaders, President in 1959 of the political party APROSOMA (Association pour la Promotion Sociale de la Masse), in a remarkably perceptive analysis of 'L'Actualité Politique au Ruanda' and its sharpening tensions, written before the peasant jacquerie of November 1959, sees in the elected counsels and their functioning, and in the suppression of pastoral serfdom under *buhake*, a major stimulus to a growing consciousness,· among the so-called inferior classes, of human dignity and of basic equality in the rights and duties of all citizens (1959: 13). The reforms, however inadequate in their implementation, the appearance of an educated Hutu elite,

---

3. See d'Hertefelt, 1960: 403-437, and Maquet, 1959: 57-67.

encouragement of, and support for their aspirations by European clergy, the increasing identification of the Belgian administration with Hutu interests, the visiting missions and interventions of the United Nations, the political movements in neighbouring territories, all helped to foster an egalitarian challenge to inequality.

These changes, however, only slightly modified the actual inequality between Tutsi and Hutu in the period immediately preceding the revolution. In analysing ethnic inequalities in plural societies, one may view the structure abstractly as consisting of a variety of positions, and then study the distribution of members of the different ethnic groups in these positions. Usually a selection is made of the more important positions in terms of power, wealth and prestige. The approach readily lends itself to stereotyping. Thus, if the incumbents of the major political positions are Tutsi, then this is generalised into a stereotype of Tutsi as monopolising political power, even if the great majority do not exercise political functions and have almost no prospect of access to political authority in any form. An alternative approach is to take as a starting point the actual ethnic groups, and to analyse their distribution in different structures. The first approach emphasises discontinuity, the second gives maximum weight to the continuities.

Taking the first approach, it is clear that Tutsi continued to monopolise the important positions in the society. It was from their ranks that chiefs, subchiefs and members of the highest councils were chosen. Hutu had only the most modest representation in these categories. Tutsi controlled the major resources of the country. They had privileged access to schooling.[4] They constituted a ruling stratum, an aristocracy of power and wealth.

II

The process of polarisation was marked by cycles of violence starting with the peasant jacquerie, which suddenly erupted in

4. See the figures presented by Lemarchand (1970: 138) for the period 1932-1954. The position had appreciably changed by 1959.

November 1959. As an arbitrary starting point in this first cycle, one might take the Hutu Manifesto (Nkundabagenzi, 1961: 20-29), issued under the signatures of a small group of Hutu intellectuals in March 1957, shortly before the arrival of a UN Trusteeship Visiting Mission. It declared that the crucial problem in the country was the monopoly of political power by one race, the Tutsi, the political monopoly being the basis of an economic, social and cultural monopoly; and it proposed a number of reforms, including redistribution of land, for the democratisation of the country. Lemarchand writes (1970: 152) that 'the issues raised in the *Manifesto* became a staple news item in the local press and a prime subject of discussion on the hills.' The Manifesto may seem to an external observer quite conciliatory in tone: it was menacing, nevertheless, to many Tutsi elite as a challenge to Tutsi privilege by a nascent Hutu political movement.

In May 1958, twelve Grand Bagaragu (Vassals) of the Mwami joined issue with the Hutu proponents of egalitarian ideologies. These Bagaragu represent the extremist Tutsi wing in the politics of polarisation. The core of their statement (Nkundabagenzi, 1961: 35-36) is an ideological polarisation. At the level of myth and early history, they rebut any Hutu pretensions to common ancestry, claiming that on the contrary, the Hutu were already in the country when the ancestors of the Tutsi arrived. Tutsi kings had conquered the Hutu, killed off their princelings, and reduced Hutu to serfs. By what right then could Hutu claim to be the brothers of Tutsi, and demand a share in a common patrimony to which only brothers have the right to lay claim? Clearly there was no basis for understanding between the forces represented by these Grand Bagaragu, and the new western educated democratically oriented Hutu leaders.

The second step in the polarisation cycle was the formation of ethnic organisations, beginning with the *Mouvement Social Muhutu* (MSM). Founded in June 1957 by Kayibanda, one of the signatories to the Hutu Manifesto, who later became President of the Republic of Rwanda, the movement was committed to a programme indistinguishable from that of the Manifesto (Lemarchand, 1970: 151). Differences in political perspectives led later to the formation of two national Hutu political parties. Gitera, another of the signatories of the Manifesto, left the *Mouvement Social Muhutu* in November 1957 to establish APROSOMA (*l'Association pour la Promotion Sociale de la Masse*). Though its objectives were to mobilise the common people, both Hutu and Tutsi, in a programme of social and political reform, it developed in practice as a Hutu party (Bushayija, 1960: 507), regionally based in the South. Kayibanda converted the MSM in October 1959 into a specifically Hutu party, the 'Parti du Mouvement de l'Emancipation des Bahutu' (PARMEHUTU) dedicated to a thoroughgoing social, economic and political democratisation of the country. PARMEHUTU also had a regional bias: it was national in scope and support throughout Rwanda, but its main strength lay in the North.

These two major Hutu parties confronted the Union Nationale Rwandaise (UNAR), founded in August 1959. 'Though ostensibly dedicated to "the union of all Rwandese for the purpose of achieving true progress in all spheres", and under the nominal presidency of a Hutu, Francois Rukeba, UNAR was clearly intended to serve as the instrument of Tutsi supremacy' (Lemarchand, 1970: 158). It included in its membership not only Tutsi notables, known for their nationalist tendencies, but also Hutu. Finally RADER (Rassemblement Démocratique Ruandais) was officially established in September 1959, under the patronage of the Catholic Church, and under the leadership of Tutsi and Hutu progressives, as a party of reconciliation (de Heusch, 1964c: 103-104). It was an attempt at national reconciliation which was to fail spectacularly, as de Heusch comments. In its very brief history, the party expressed the characteristic ambivalences of parties of reconciliation in sharply divided plural societies. APROSOMA also failed to make a significant impact, leaving the field to the two protagonists in the process of polarisation, UNAR and PARMEHUTU, respectively the parties of Tutsi dominance and of Hutu challenge.

An increasing ideological polarisation accompanied the formation of parties representing conflicting ethnic (or racial) interests. The party manifestos do not make this explicit.

PARMEHUTU declared in its manifesto that it had no hatred for the Tutsi: to raise up the Hutu who had been kept backward under feudalism implied no hatred for their brothers (the Tutsi). Hutu would combine their efforts to aid their racial brothers (Hutu), but they would be happy to collaborate with those Tutsi who loved Rwanda and recognised the injustices suffered not only by the Hutu, but also by the 'petits Tutsi' (Nkundabagenzi, 1961: 114). UNAR, as a party of national unity, appealed to all Banyarwanda, regardless of ethnic, social, or religious differences, to make common cause in seeking the political, economic, social and cultural emancipation of the country; it presented itself as sensitive to the problems of group relations, and as committed to the fight against all forms of provocation to racial hatred (Nkundabagenzi, 1961: 95-101).

Nevertheless, behind the blandishments of party manifestos, and the facade of tolerance and concern for other groups, lay the reality of ideological polarisation at different levels. First of all, at the level of general perspectives, there is a profound incompatibility. The PARMEHUTU manifesto is concerned with racial discrimination against Hutu and seeks the eradication of inequality and the establishment of a democratic, egalitarian society. The UNAR manifesto ignores the issues of discrimination against Hutu and of Tutsi hereditary privilege, concentrating on a wide series of reforms and measures for development. There is a commitment to democratic conceptions, and to universal suffrage. However, this does not easily accord with elitist reservations in its Foundation Charter, to the effect that Rwanda society is composed of individuals of very unequal value, that it is not equitable to give the same weight to the vulgar thought of the ordinary person as to the perspicacious judgment of the capable man, that universal suffrage will inevitably result in the subordination of the lettered minority by the uncultivated majority, a situation which would prolong slavery, but that it was nevertheless impossible to deny universal suffrage to the Hutu. Manifest opposition would provide the colonialists with more ammunition (Nkundabagenzi, 1961: 94).

In its discussion of human relations in its Manifesto, UNAR's real concern is with race relations between Black and White, and not with the issues of Hutu-Tutsi relations raised by PARMEHUTU.

There is a second level of ideological polarisation in terms of immediate major objectives. This is similar to the ideological conflict between the major parties in Zanzibar, the challengers of traditional power seeking democratisation before independence, and the incumbents immediate independence. Thus Munyangaju (1959: 7) distinguishes Rwanda from other African countries on the basis that in Rwanda the dominant preoccupation was the liberation of the people, not from European imperialism, but from feudal absolutism. The PARMEHUTU Manifesto argued the necessity for this, abolition of the colonisation of Black by Black being a necessary condition for true independence (Nkundabagenzi, 1961: 114). UNAR, on the other hand, committed to immediate independence, denounced the idea of internal autonomy as a ridiculous, destructive, divisive collaboration. These ideological differences were part of the struggle for power between traditional authorities hoping to maintain their present dominance in an independent Rwanda, and a new elite seeking radical change in the political structure under Belgian tutelage, as a preliminary condition to independence, in which they might hope to rule as representatives of the enfranchised majority.

The third level is that of mythical interpretation, centring on the belief in, or rejection of, common ancestry, and on the conception of a traditional ideal of harmonious group relations. I have commented on the use of the myth of common ancestry as a basis for reformist demands by Hutu, and the rejection of common ancestry by the Grand Bagaragu in an extremist assertion of the traditional Tutsi claim to domination by right of conquest. In contrast to the extremist Tutsi position, a conservative Tutsi ideology projected a mythical conception of harmonious adjustment between groups, without distinction in access to political functions, and with equality expressed in

membership of the same clans.[5] UNAR, in its appeal for national
unity, crystallised this conception in the slogan, *le peuple
tripartite*. In UNAR propaganda, the harmonious, egalitarian
peuple tripartite represented the reality in the past. For reformist
Hutu leaders, the conception of a golden past might serve as an
ideal, against which to attack prevailing discrimination (see
d'Hertefelt, 1964: 232). As to the revolutionary leaders, the
mythologies were simply mystifications, from which it was
necessary to liberate the people by the total destruction of the
institutions supporting inequality, and not by an attack on the
symbols themselves (*ibid.*).

III

The injection of terrorism, in a traditional idiom, and evoking, I
would suppose, fearful memories of the brutal ferocity of Tutsi
warriors in the field, carried polarisation to the point of violent
confrontation in the peasant jacqueries of November 1959. Tutsi
terrorism against their political opponents took the form of
traditional sanctions against traitors to the country and enemies of
the Mwami. This was accompanied by a measure of military
mobilisation, threatening savage reprisals.

An ideological polarisation, as we have seen, preceded these
events. The publication of the Hutu Manifesto, shortly before the
arrival of a United Nations Trusteeship Visiting Mission, served
as a focal point for ideological conflict. The manifesto was only
discussed by the Supreme Council of Rwanda fifteen months
after publication, in June 1958, when the Mwami declared that
there did not exist a Tutsi-Hutu question: the problem was only
one of wicked rumours propagated by a small group of enemies
of the country, acting under foreign influence; but they would
not succeed in sowing dissension; the whole territory was united
in the search for the bad tree producing the fruits of division; the

---

5. Munyangaju (1959: 33) offers an interesting discussion of the ideological uses of
common membership by Tutsi, Hutu and Twa in the same clans, the community in
clanship being invoked to demonstrate that the authorities actually derive from the
three races. Thus rebellious Hutu are in fact betraying clan fraternity.

tree would be found, cut down, uprooted and burnt; it would be totally extirpated (Nkundabagenzi, 1961: 37; d'Hertefelt, 1960c: 124). Here then was authority for extirpation of heretical ideas.

Following the visit of a Belgian Parliamentary Mission in April 1959 to investigate the conditions under which authority could be transferred, tensions mounted. Both Hutu and Tutsi gave evidence, which expressed the ideological conflict of perspectives between Hutu and Tutsi 'progressives' on the one hand, and the Tutsi traditional elite on the other. It was in this context that the *Guerriers-défenseurs*, a sort of traditional suicide squad for the protection of the country against invasion, issued their call to combat.

Children of Rwanda, Be Ready for Combat

APROSOMA who combat the Kalinga (sacred drum of kingship) will be conquered by the People Tripartite.

APROSOMA who hate Rwanda and its Mwami will be conquered.

APROSOMA who oppose independence for Rwanda will be conquered. .

APROSOMA who wish to condemn us to eternal slavery will perish.

Gitera chosen for his felony against Rwanda,

Gitera, bribed to oppose the independence of Rwanda will be garotted by Rwanda by means of the very same bonds he stretched out to enchain her.

Fathers and Mothers of Rwanda,

Children of Rwanda,

Young people of Rwanda,

Rise as one person.

Gitera and his paltry, ridiculous parties have sold Rwanda.

Let us all take the following oath in unison:

'O Rwanda our mother, we die for thee,
I swear total allegiance to thee.'

Here is the order: Be ready for combat.

Our rallying flag is Rwanda.

Our government is triumph.

(Nkundabagenzi, 1961: 75-76)

During a colloquium held in Brussels (30 May to 7 June, 1960), Anastase Makuza, a Hutu leader, who later became President of the National Assembly of Rwanda, gave a fuller account of this tract, which cited the names of leading Hutu collaborators of Gitera, and which, he declared, was immediately distributed among the population through the Chiefs and Sub-Chiefs, all 'fanatically attached to feudalism' (p. 37).

The sudden death of the Mwami in July 1959, and a dramatic coup attending the appointment of his successor, greatly raised the level of polarisation. The Mwami had taken ill in Usumbura, the administrative center for Rwanda-Burundi, and died, it seems, while receiving medical treatment. Rumours circulated, and were widely believed by the Tutsi, that the Belgians had poisoned the Mwami, in complicity with the political movements opposed to the traditional elite. The failure of the royal clan, and of the traditional authorities subordinated to the royal clan, to deny these rumours and calm the population,[6] was evidence of the growing antagonism of the Tutsi elite to the Belgian administration, whom they viewed, quite rightly, as supporting Hutu political demands. Tutsi were caught up in two processes of polarisation, involving the Belgians on the one hand and the Hutu on the other. The Tutsi traditional authorities, suspecting the motives of the Belgian administration, staged a *coup d'état* at the burial of the Mwami. Bands of Tutsi, Hutu and Twa, armed with lances, with machetes and with bows and arrows had been circulating in the area of Nyanza, site of the royal court (Nkundabagenzi, 1961: 89). According to one account (Atterbury, 1970: 54-55), some units of the traditional Tutsi army and armed squads of Twa were hidden round the burial field, and leapt into view when the Tutsi elite confronted the Belgian administrators with their choice of Mwami. There had been no prior consultation, and the Belgian administration had little choice but to accept the *fait‧accompli*. The result, however, was to identify the Mwami with Tutsi political interests, undermining his image as a unifying symbol, transcending sectional division.

With the growth of exclusive political organisation, the

6. According to Maus, a former member of the Council of the Vice-Governor General (Nkundabagenzi, 1961: 88).

sharpening of ideological differences, the heightened tension resulting from the mobilisation of armed units, and the appropriation of the Mwami by Tutsi political interests, the stage was set for terrorism against the enemies of king and country.[7] It must have seemed all the more necessary to some of the UNAR leaders because the report of the Belgian Parliamentary Working Group was expected shortly, and communal elections were to be held toward the end of the year.

The meeting of UNAR on 13 September 1959 could be considered as a declaration of war by the party and the Mwami against Hutu leaders (Makuza, Brussels Colloquium, May-June 1960). The President of UNAR emphasised in his speech the need for a single party, grounded in tradition, and declared that any person who did not become a member of UNAR would be regarded as an enemy of the Mwami and of Rwanda. The Secretary-General called for a war without mercy against all the traitors, that is to say all those who did not assist in the conquest of immediate independence, and he pledged the use of any means necessary, and in case of a definitive rupture, eternal hatred. There followed a conciliatory speech by another member of the UNAR committee, after which the President concluded the meeting with the injuction to fight all those Rwandese who were not members of the party, and hence against unity, against Rwanda, against the Mwami, and against tradition.

Now the terrorism began in earnest. The name APROSOMA, initially applied to educated Hutu seeking the emancipation of their people, and to members of the party, became identified with traitors, enemies of King and country (Bushayija, 1960: 507; d'Hertefelt, 1960: 128). The phrase, enemy of the Mwami, conveyed ominous traditional threat. It was a phrase going back to the beginning of time (according to one of the participants at the Brussels Colloquium), and the launching of the phrase was highly significant, an extremely grave incitement of the masses (Report of the Brussels Colloquium, 46-48). Gitera was an

7. I am following the account given by A. Makuza at the colloquium in Brussels in May-June 1960. This no doubt gives the Hutu perspective, but it seems consistent in its main aspects with accounts given by scholars and Belgian administrators.

obvious target, and he was attacked by armed pygmies when he
returned from a counter-demonstration of APROSOMA. Tracts
published the names of traitors. Bands formed in almost all the
regions, including a terrorist organisation (*équipe* des *hommes* de
main de l'*UNAR*), under the name *Union Nationale des Patriotes
Ruandais* (39, 43). UNAR had many supporters among the
Swahili, a small Islamic section of the population, who also
furnished *hommes de main*. Bands circulated, intimidating by
threats, blows and attacks on property, those who had not joined
UNAR. Makuza mentions the terrorising use of a song, '*orchestrée
par les enfants*', and intoned preparatory to acts of intimidation.
'Come to the rescue of Rwanda. Its enemies, who hate it, are
... worthy of death' (38). Rumours circulated of impending war.
There was the fearful expectation of deadly conflict.

One further element should be added to this account. In much
the same way that APROSOMA became a symbol of protest (of
'treachery'), so the Kalinga seems to have become a symbol of
traditional Tutsi domination, and the Hutu press directed violent
criticisms against it. In fact, the Kalinga was only a drum, but it
was a sacred drum identified with the Mwami. Other drums
were beaten in honour of the Kalinga, as they were beaten in
honour of the Mwami. If the Kalinga was a symbol of unity for
the Tutsi, it had quite other connotations for the Hutu, since it
was no ordinary drum, not even an ordinary sacred drum. It was
distinguished by the nature of its trappings, the genitals of
conquered Hutu rulers. Clearly castration was well within the
known repertoire of Tutsi sanctions against enemies of the King.
Inevitably in this social ferment, any incident could set off violent
confrontation.

IV

If it is indeed true that every revolution has its 14 July, then the
week of 3-11 November 1959, was the 14 July of Rwanda.
According to one analyst (Jean-R. Hubert, acting for the Belgian
prosecution in Rwanda, 1959-1961), a Christian atmosphere
bathed all the events of this week, 'astonishing as it may be'. 'The
first spark was on 1 November, when a Hutu sub-chief was

assaulted as he left the mission where he had attended mass. Two days later a Tutsi chief, forced by Hutu to leave his home, moved out carrying his most precious possession, a statue of the Virgin. In the course of the following days, the right of asylum in ecclesiastical premises revived quite naturally, and the White Fathers defended this right with their lives. At a hearing of the Council of War,[8] an Abbé of Rwanda declared that he considered himself the chaplain of the Mwami's troops' (Hubert, 1965: 7). Unfortunately Christian piety is no prophylactic against atrocity.

The *flambeau*, then, was an attack on a popular Hutu Subchief in the Gitarama region, Dominique Mbonyumutwa, spokesman for the Hutu Social Movement, and one of the few Hutu sub-chiefs in Rwanda. According to his own account (Brussels Colloquium, May-June 1960: 44-46), he had aroused the enmity of the Mwami's entourage by asking for promotion to a chiefdom. On 1 November, and without ado (*sans autre procédure*), a band of about a dozen unarmed young Tutsi attacked him. He seems to have made his escape quite easily, but the rumour spread that he had been wounded, and indeed killed. The same day, 'Swahili' molested the treasurer of the Hutu Social Movement in the commercial centre of Gitarama. On 3 November, Hutu, seeking news of Mbonyumutwa, confronted the local chief. Under the spur of the arrogant contempt of a visiting subchief who declared that the entire problem would be solved if these protegés of the whites, these administrative lackeys, were exterminated by the Twa and by the Swahili, Hutu killed two subchiefs and wounded several others.[9]

---

8. Belgian military jurisdiction, judging the crimes committed in these events.

9. There are numerous versions of all these events, and I have tried, as well as I can, to give a substantively accurate account. Of course, UNAR placed responsibility entirely on the Hutu, alleging, in a report on the disturbances, that the formation of UNAR was seen as a threat by those engaged in ethnic politics, and that, in this situation of political tension, PARMEHUTU had launched massacres of traditional authorities, and of members, and sympathisers, of UNAR. The main sources used are Lemarchand (1970), Hubert (1964), the Brussels Colloquium (1960), UN Commission (1960: T1551) and a variety of reports by the political parties and Belgian administrators included in the documents assembled by Nkundabagenzi (1961).

Now a movement of incendiarism, of the looting and sacking of Tutsi huts, spread outward from Gitarama to the North and West. It seems to have been quite spontaneous. The incendiaries moved in small bands, generally locally based. This was to be expected, given the dispersed nature of settlements, the disjunctive influence of hilly terrain, and the dyadic relations under the clientage system. But the events of the last few years, the elections, the founding of political parties, the sharpening ideological conflict, and the launching of terrorism, had effected some measure of mobilisation of Hutu, making them readily available. Makuza, at the Brussels Colloquium, insisted that the policy of the Hutu leaders was strictly defensive, but he added that the masses were sufficiently well organised to confront any eventuality (32).

This peasant jacquerie was directed primarily against property. The bands burned and pillaged thousands of huts, they plundered plantations, they killed livestock. They murdered though not greatly. However, Hubert's figure of 13 killed by Hutu must be well below the actual number of murders (Hubert, 1964: 40; Lemarchand, 1970: 167). But certainly their targets were not persons, and one can accept, with some qualification, the view expressed by the Belgian Special Resident that although there were victims in these confrontations, they were not numerous, and that clearly the intention of the Hutu was neither to kill nor to wound (Brussels Colloquium, 1960: 28).

Many Hutu believed that the attacks had been ordered by the Mwami, to whom there was still great loyalty and devotion. Lemarchand (1970: 164) draws a parallel with French peasant uprisings in the name of the King, and comments that in Rwanda, too, there were few signs of organised political insurrection in the disorders. A further parallel might be found in the belief of Muslim liberals in Algeria, in the period between the two wars, and prior to the Blum-Viollette proposals, that the abuses under which they suffered came from the settlers and the local administration, but not from the French Government, which was acting in ignorance of the true situation. In some areas in Rwanda, peasants believed that they were acting in accordance with the wishes of the Belgian administration (Nkundabagenzi, 1961: 150).

The jacquerie had a distinctive territorial distribution, reflecting structural and cultural differences between regions. De Heusch (1966: 136, 143-145) distinguishes between the central area, in which the Tutsi had consolidated their power, integrating Hutu and Tutsi into a caste society by means of the system of client relations (*ubuhake*), and regions in the north and west, with recent implantation of Tutsi authority, creating a structure purely and simply of domination and subordination, a structure characterised, according to Vansina, by frequent rebellions, or, in Lemarchand's phrase, by a 'climate of messianic unrest' (1970: 101). Lemarchand (1970: 98-99) draws on a distinction made by Max Weber to explain the differences between the centre as an area in which the ethnic groups had been integrated into a caste structure, with a functional division of labour, and the north as an area where ethnic coexistence was the rule rather than the exception. In contrast to the cultural homogeneity of the Tutsi, there was cultural variation among the Hutu (d'Hertefelt, 1960b: 452-453), the northern region representing 'a distinctive subculture, characterised by the survival of specific social, economic and political institutions ... and a remarkable popular awareness of the norms and traditions in existence prior to the Tutsi invasion' (Lemarchand, 1966a: 321). Demographic and socio-economic variables combined with these cultural and historical variables to increase regional differentiation, the pastoral areas being generally areas of greater Tutsi concentration and of ancient hegemony, the agrarian areas in the north and northwest being areas 'with a clear preponderance of Hutu culture' (d'Hertefelt, 1960a: 406-407 and 1960b: 451-453). Now the jacquerie erupted with special violence in areas of relatively recent Tutsi implantation: it was in these areas, too, that Hutu had made their greatest gains in the 1956 elections (de Heusch, 1964c: 108 and 1966: 145; d'Hertefelt, 1960a: 407).

The counteraction of the Tutsi authorities was on a much more massive scale, as they drew on the traditional apparatus. They sounded the drums in a time-honoured call to arms. They initiated terrorist type police action, as Hutu leaders were brought to the Mwami's palace for interrogation, torture, or summary judgment; they dispatched assassination squads, generally led by Twa and directed against leading Hutu; and they mounted military operations usually in formations of some hundreds, but at times involving thousands of men, as in the attack on the APROSOMA centre at Save (Hubert, 1965: 34-41; Lemarchand, 1970: 164-167; Brussels Colloquium, May-June 1960: 28-29; Nkundabagenzi, 1961: 152-156). There were the inevitable atrocities. The murder of the Secretary-Treasurer of APROSOMA, his body speared 53 times, hacked nine times with a machete, and knifed once, was among the most atrocious, recalling some recent murders in Northern Ireland. Hubert gives an account of this murder, but does not say whether it was bathed in the light of Christianity. Understandably it was rumoured among Hutu that the leaders had not only been murdered but also castrated, for the adornment and greater glory of the sacred Kalinga (see Makuza, Brussels Colloquium, May-June, 1960, 103, and Ndazaro in Nkundabagenzi, 1961: 254). It is impossible to gauge how the conflict might have developed at this stage, if Belgian military intervention had not succeeded in restoring order. Would there have been a full scale civil war, with Hutu increasingly consolidated against Tutsi or, since Tutsi leaders commanded an appreciable military force, would there have been large scale massacres of Hutu on the Burundi pattern?

The November jacquerie represented a high point, perhaps a point of no return, in the process of polarisation. It made the prospect of peaceful coexistence between Tutsi and Hutu all the more remote (Lemarchand, 1970: 169). It raised the social consciousness of Hutu, appreciably by violent means, but this change was effected with restraint on the taking of life and could have been effected without recourse to murder or grave physical injury.[10] In the north, this aroused social consciousness was

10. Only estimates of casualties are available. Hubert's figures of 37 killed by Tutsi is as much as underestimate as his estimate of 13 murdered by Hutu. Including those killed by the Belgians, the deaths would certainly have exceeded 200 (Lemarchand, 1970: 167).

expressed in the extreme form of a desire to expel Tutsi from the area (Report of Belgian Commission in Nkundabagenzi, 1961: 150-151), stimulated, too, one may be sure, by peasant hunger for land. There was the beginning of the erosion of the authority of the Mwami as he became identified with the Tutsi traditional authorities, thus undermining a significant force for national unity. Tutsi progressives who might also have given some impetus to unifying tendencies, were a special target for attack by the traditional authorities seeking to forge a united front against the Hutu political parties (see Makuza, Brussels Colloquium, May-June 1960, 44). Many Tutsi chiefs and subchiefs, members of UNAR, had been killed, arrested, dismissed, or they had fled or resigned, opening positions for Hutu replacements as an interim measure (Nkundabagenzi, 1961: 157; Lemarchand, 1970: 173ff). From the point of view of the Belgian administration, this would facilitate democratisation (Colonel Logiest, Brussels Colloquium, 52), thus obviating the problems the French metropolitan government faced in seeking to implement reforms through a hostile administration in Algeria. In the result, however, it also made available the necessary cadres for a revolutionary assumption of power in January 1961 and for genocidal type massacres in December 1963/January 1964. Meanwhile a series of confrontations kept the flames well-stoked.

V

The massacres were the climax of a struggle for power, in which violence and terror became the instruments of political change. The constitutional procedures established by the Belgian Government with continuous United Nations intervention, served as stimulus for this escalating violence.

As part of the process designed to transform by peaceful means a rigid centralised authoritarian plural society into an idyllic western type democracy, the Belgians instituted a provisional special Council, consisting of the major parties, to replace the Tutsi-dominated Superior Council. This provisional council proceeded to initiate policies for agrarian reform which were accepted by the Tutsi representatives on the provisional council but rejected by the Mwami (Maral, 1965: 9). Indeed, such were the relations between the political parties, and so far was the provisional council from reconciling their differences, that the Hutu parties and RADER, the party of conciliation, formed a common front against UNAR in April 1960, and UNAR was not represented in May/June 1960 at the Brussels Colloquium.

The visit of the United Nations Mission in March 1960 provided occasion for violence. Threatening rumours heightened tension as groups demonstrated for and against immediate independence. According to an account given by the Belgian Special President, who was committed to the Hutu cause, there was an outburst of popular anger in Biumba territory, during the time that the Mission was actually visiting the area. Thousands of Hutu mounted the hills where Tutsi lived, chased them away but without wounding them, and destroyed their huts. 'It was an act of independence, an act severing the bonds of the people to their lords.' In April 1960 there was similar action in the Astrida area, but more organised, with incendiarism in two chiefdoms (Mvejuru and Buhanga-Ndara). If Tutsi had not yet fled their homes, they were politely asked to leave, and allowed to take with them some personal possessions, before their huts were set alight. 'There was not one Tutsi wounded in the whole of this operation, showing the difference between UNAR and Hutu operations' (Brussels Colloquium, May/June 1960: 60-62).

The communal elections in June and July 1960 provided further occasion for violence. These elections introduced, in conception, a democratic procedure for election of local executive authorities, that is the burgomasters and the communal councillors, with many parties participating. (See discussion by Lemarchand, 1970: 177-183, and d'Hertefelt, 1960a: 403-438.) In fact, however, they were a struggle for ethnic (or racial) domination and released terrorism and counter-terrorism. Lemarchand writes that an all-pervasive climate of fear and suspicion gripped the country at the approach of the elections in a way reminiscent of 'la Grande Peur' which seized the French peasantry and caused them to engage in gratuitous acts of violence against the manorial lords. The initial challenge usually came from Tutsi extremists seeking to keep their opponents away from the polls through intimidation and terrorism. The Hutu response was to burn down countless Tutsi huts in retaliation. 'In some areas, committees of public safety and militia units were organised. Before long the whole southern half of the country was converted into a vast training ground for Hutu counter-terrorists, arsonists and criminal bands. As time went on the Hutu did not even wait for the challenge to occur. They simply went ahead and burned the huts of the Tutsi, as if it now were a mere routine of duty' (Lemarchand, 1970: 179-180). The result of the elections was a great victory for PARMEHUTU and the election in most communes of Hutu burgomasters, who proceeded to establish their power over the communes, in some areas instigating local disorders to provoke the exodus of Tutsi families, or arresting individual Tutsi on the flimsiest of grounds (Lemarchand, 1970: 180-185).

The next state in the constitutional development was the declaration of a Republic in January 1961 by communal councillors and burgomasters. This took a very similar form to the coup d'etat by Tutsi traditional leaders in July 1959. It seems almost to have been a replay, a similar type of 'scenario', for the rejection of the institution of monarchy. But this coup was effected with the complicity of a local Belgian administration, powerfully committed to the Hutu cause. The result in the words of the UN Commission for Rwanda-Urundi in March 1961, was that 'a racial dictatorship of one party has been set up in Rwanda, and the developments of the last eighteen months have consisted in the transition from one type of oppressive regime to another' (Lemarchand, 1970: 194).

The legislative elections and the referendum on the monarchy in September 1961 confirmed both PARMEHUTU dominance and the de facto Republic. In the course of these elections, Hutu, being in power, availed themselves of the same techniques of terrorism as the Tutsi had used two years earlier. 'In general, the troubles of the months of August and September were organised by these politicised functionaries (burgomasters, prefects, and ministers) with a view to disorganise their political opponents ... [These men] used their prerogatives to arrest, torture and incarcerate their political adversaries' (Chairman of the UN Commission for Rwanda-Urundi, quoted in Lemarchand, 1970: 195, who writes that 'to speak of electoral fraud is almost a euphemism. In view of the repeated threats, admonitions and brutalities committed by the burgomasters, it is a question whether the right to vote can be said to have any significance besides that of showing on which side coercion tended to predominate'). Manipulation had gone far beyond the notorious electoral frauds of the French in Algeria. Murder was now well established on both sides as a weapon in the political struggle.

With independence in July 1962, PARMEHUTU, as government in power, had committed itself, under pressure from the United Nations, to reserving for UNAR two ministerial posts, and some other key positions. The ministerial posts did not survive a year. The Government soon suppressed all opposition, including that of APROSOMA. It removed Tutsi from positions of power and eradicated UNAR, banning its newspaper, and executing its leaders.

Guerilla warfare, launched by Tutsi refugees, whose numbers mounted to some 130,000 by the end of 1963, fed into the conflagrations set off by the constitutional process. Raids from neighbouring territories established a pattern of reciprocal violence, leading ultimately to the massacres in December 1963. Tutsi violence escalated from isolated acts of terrorism in the settlement of personal scores with Hutu officials, to action by armed bands seeking to inflict maximum damage on Hutu officials, and finally to attempts at invasion. In the region of Biumba, in March 1962, the murder by Tutsi bands of two policemen in one raid, and of four Hutu (including one policeman and two civil servants) in another raid, led to massive indiscriminate reprisal, in which 'between 1,000 and 2,000 Tutsi men, women and children were massacred and buried on the spot, their huts burned and pillaged and their property divided among the Hutu population' (Lemarchand, 1970: 218-219). Here then was a paradigm for massacre.

VI

Well-defined processes are to be observed in this movement to polarisation and massive atrocity. There is first of all a geographical extension of violent confrontation to the entire country. Areas which had not experienced large scale Hutu uprisings in the initial conflagrations of November 1959 soon became engulfed in the general conflict. (See Hubert, 1965: 53, 59, and Annexure 2, Nos. 1-35 and 60-62 which gives brief detail of the violence in the form of incendiarism, assault, expulsion and murder. The massacre which Hubert locates in Kibungu territory seems to be the massacre in Biumba territory referred to above.)

The second process also involves an extension of violent confrontation, but not simply geographical. Increasingly all members of a particular section become categorised as enemies and targets for atrocity. It is a process of polarisation, in ideology and action, through the aggregation of members of the society into opposing camps. At the ideological level, de Heusch (1964a: 422) describes this process among Hutu officials, following Tutsi raids on the night of 4/5 July 1962, as an aggravation of the anti-Tutsi psychosis. 'From then on every Tutsi, in the interior as well the exterior, whether or not supportive of these military adventures, and whether or not he had broken ties with the Mwami in exile – every Tutsi ... will be considered an enemy of the country and a communist *en puissance*, an ally of the terrorists in the exterior.'

This process of aggregation is expressed in indiscriminate violence, or rather by a very limited discrimination, in the sense that there *is* a selection of targets, but by the sole criterion of membership in a different ethnic or racial group. It involves the imposition of collective responsibility. Tutsi targets seem to have been relatively selective, with violence directed primarily against Hutu leaders or officials. Hutu violence, on the other hand, after the first murder of Tutsi sub-chiefs in the Mbonyumutwa episode, rapidly became generalised, as shown in the widespread incendiarism, in the direction of retaliatory action against any Tutsi, regardless of responsibility, and later, even more emphatically, in the genocidal type massacres.[11]

The third process may be described as the routinisation of atrocity. Lemarchand refers to this process when he writes that as time went on, during the communal elections of 1960, Hutu burned the huts of Tutsi as if it were a mere routine of duty (p. 256 above). It must have been good fun as well. From my reading, I recall a comment that Hutu seemed to amuse themselves greatly, *beaucoup s'amusent*, when engaged in burning down Tutsi huts. I have not been able to trace the reference, but it seems likely that incendiarism would have been quite a sport, though not so deeply gratifying as the inflicting of torture, the engaging in murder or the perpetrating of massacre. In any event, incendiarism was an early idiom of polarisation.

The reciprocity of violence is a more general process underlying other processes. Where it takes the same form on both sides, as in incendiarism or arrest for interrogation and torture by both Tutsi and Hutu, it helps to establish routines of violence. Where it takes a different form, as for example, the massive retaliation of large scale incendiarism following an attack on a leader, or massacre by way of reprisal for murderous raids on officials, it escalates the general level of violent confrontation, unless the reprisals are so deadly as virtually to suppress resistance. In general, reciprocity of violence is a great multiplier of acts of violence, thereby contributing to the extension of atrocity in terms of locality and target.

The final process, then, is that by which violence escalates. Routinisation at a particular level encourages recourse to new and more terrifying violence, thus promoting escalation, but the major impetus derives from the reciprocity of violence and its generalisation, so that all become potential targets and a prey to fear and terror. The ultimate in escalation is represented by the

---

11. Lemarchand (1970: 113) presents a typology of protest movements which shows the target in the North (Rukiga) in 1960 to have been Tutsi chiefs and sub-chiefs as against Tutsi generally in the Central region.

genocidal touch, characteristically expressed in the slaughter of noncombatants, the aged, women and children, in a root and branch extermination of all accessible members of the hated group.

Before the November 1959 uprisings, Tutsi were in a position to mount massive military operations, relatively speaking, by drawing on traditional institutions, and they could perhaps have crushed their rivals; but their power was broken by a combination of mass resistance and Belgian intervention. In exile, they suffered many restraints as refugees, they were divided by ideological and personal differences, and they were cut off from the resources which had been available to them in Rwanda. Hutu had the power of numbers, armament in the way of agricultural implements and paraffin, easy accessibility of their enemies among whom they lived interspersed, and increasingly, Belgian support. Tutsi violence in exile moved, as we have seen, from personal vendetta to armed raids against localities and finally to invasion. Hutu violence at first took the form largely of attacks on property in reaction against Tutsi aggression. It moved to a new level as Hutu became increasingly aggressive, initiating violence, extending the area of operation and attacking persons as well as property. Then finally it reached the level of mass murder, attaining its ultimate expression in the massacres following the Bugesera invasion on 21 December 1963.

The strategy of the Tutsi invaders was to launch attacks simultaneously from different countries (Uganda, Tanzania, Congo, and Burundi).[12] Only the force from Burundi, however, succeeded in penetrating Rwanda to any depth, the raids from Tanzania failing to materialise, those from Uganda being intercepted by the Uganda authorities, or immediately repulsed by the Rwanda National Guard, and the small raids from the Congo quickly suppressed. The Burundi invading force numbered 'approximately 200 or 300 men (some say only 80) armed, for the most part, with bows and arrows and home-made rifles' (Lemarchand, 1970: 222), but the invaders seized arms and

12. I am following closely the account given by Lemarchand (1970: 216-227).

ammunition when they overran a military camp, and they drew
in recruits from a Tutsi refugee centre, where they received an
enthusiastic welcome. The force now numbered over a thousand,
but it was easily overwhelmed by units of the Rwanda National
Guard, armed with mortars and semi-automatic weapons and
under the command of Belgian officers.

Counteraction was massive and seemingly final. The Rwanda
authorities arrested, and summarily executed less than a week
later, some twenty leading local Tutsi politicians, including one
of the two UNAR members of the government, the President
and Secretary-General of the local UNAR, and the President and
Vice-President of RADER. De Heusch (1964a: 424) uses the
phrase 'selon la technique d'amalgame', to describe this process of
generalisation by which a legal and constitutional opposition in
the country was equated with monarchist and terrorist
organisations in exile. It would seem from this account that the
leaders were also tortured.

Steps were taken to organise civilian 'self-defence' groups
among the Hutu population through the burgomasters and
prefects, and under the supervision of ministers. In situations such
as these, as in the Algerian revolution during critical periods for
the settler population, only atrocity can be expected from civilian
militia. The national radio 'repeatedly beamed emergency
warnings, asking the population to be "constantly on the alert" for
Tutsi terrorists. In this atmosphere of intense fear, saturated with
rumour and suspicion, the worst was bound to happen. The
killings began on December 23, in the prefecture of Gikongoro,
at the instigation of the local prefect ...' (Lemarchand, 1970:
223). Gikongoro was a core area of Tutsi opposition, and here
the Hutu, armed with clubs, pangas and spears, methodically
began to exterminate all Tutsi in sight – men, women and
children. An estimated 5,000 Tutsi were massacred in Gikongoro
and perhaps another 5,000-9,000 in other areas. Lemarchand
(1970: 255) comments that the term Terror would seem to apply
more pertinently to Rwanda in terms of numbers killed than to
the Jacobin Terror of the French Revolution: 'in proportion to
the total population of Rwanda, the 10-12,000 people slain by the

Hutu convey an image of hysterical blood-lust infinitely more frightening than the 17,000 official executions carried out during the fourteen months of the French Terror.'

The massacres were accompanied by unspeakable brutality. But a Christian touch was not altogether wanting. Thus, Lemarchand (1970: 226) refers to the courageous action of Catholic Fathers in refusing to surrender Tutsi who had found asylum in their mission stations. In a bizarre episode on Christmas day (Roux, 1969: 57) a band of Hutu, armed with clubs, machetes and lances, screened a congregation at Christmas service, removing the Tutsi worshippers, whom they led to a rocky promontory above a river. The Tutsi asked the grace of a last prayer, whereupon both Hutu and Tutsi, in a similar reflex, fell upon their knees, praying loudly. Then, according to the narrator, the Hutu proceeded rapidly and with propriety (*proprement*) to the execution of the victims, consigning their bodies to the river.

BURUNDI

While these events were unfolding in Rwanda, the country of Burundi was moving at a much slower pace towards its own genocidal conflict. Indeed, polarisation in Rwanda and its fearful expression were intimately related to the process of polarisation in Burundi. Yet the social context, the infra-structure of group relations, was very different from Rwanda, and seemed to offer real possibilities for national integration in the new phase of decolonisation and political independence: but in the end, an even more massive holocaust overwhelmed the Hutu in Burundi.

I

Lemarchand, in his exceptionally fine scholarly study of *Rwanda and Burundi*, provides a detailed analysis of the process of polarisation in Burundi to 1969, completing the account in a report on *Selective Genocide in Burundi* (1974a) and in a paper on Ethnic Polarisation and Political Violence' which he presented at a colloquium he co-sponsored in Brussels in December 1974, in the hope of initiating dialogue in a movement for reconciliation. His analysis of the traditional bases for equilibrium supports his conclusion that though there was a genuine potential for a sharp polarisation of group loyalties and identifications, Hutu and Tutsi being readily recognisable categories, definable in cultural terms, the potential for ethnic violence in Burundi was small compared with Rwanda, and the revolutionary quotient of ethnic violence relatively low (1970: 43, 474, 45).

Lemarchand argues (1966a: 314-317, 1966c: 404-408 and ff, 1970: 23-46, 474, 1974a: 6-8, 1974b: 28) that many factors militated against ethnic conflict. We have discussed these in Chapter 5. In the first place, a complex differentiated structure provided a variety of social bases for interethnic relations. The dominant stratum consisted of dynastic families, viewed within the society as a distinctive ethnic group, but competing among themselves for power. The King was simply *primus inter pares*. The situation of rivalry and of fragmented power encouraged alliances across ethnic divisions. The King found in the Hutu his natural allies against rival dynastic families, and he relied greatly on Hutu for the administration of his crown lands. Similarly, competition drove the rival dynastic families to seek support from Hutu and Tutsi.

The subordinate groups, Hutu, Tutsi and Twa were themselves internally divided. Neither Hutu nor Tutsi could claim any degree of internal cohesion (Lemarchand, 1966c: 417). Differential social rankings attached to the various patrilineages, sometimes giving rise to greater social distance between patrilineages within an ethnic group than between the ethnic groups themselves, and providing, in any event, a multiplicity of reference group identifications. The Tutsi comprised two distinctive strata, a higher stratum of Tutsi-Banyaruguru and a lower of Tutsi-Hima. Regional differences, associated with differences in the distribution of ethnic units and sub-units, further complicated the pattern of group relations. And finally there were the differences, within each group, of power, wealth and status. Below the level of the dynastic families, 'no single line of cleavage could be said to govern the allocation of social status, wealth or power. Ethnic divisions were largely irrelevant to the distribution of social prestige, and of only marginal significance with regard to wealth' (Lemarchand, 1974a: 7).

A society so constituted, in which power, wealth and status were not superimposed on the ethnic identity of Hutu and of Tutsi, provides many bases, and the stimulus of varied interests, for the transcending of ethnic divisions. Moreover, a system of clientage, separate from and subsidiary to the political structure, linked Hutu and Tutsi in a web of interlocking relationships, while common beliefs in the divinity, in the sacred kingship and in the unity of the nation, provided a further basis for integration or at any rate for the containment of ethnic tensions.

II

The process by which Burundi society became sharply polarised along ethnic lines, may be most conveniently summarised by reference to key events, which constituted, as it were, a series of points of polarisation in the actual unfolding of the Burundi massacre. The context is one in which the Belgian mandatory power had already given an increased salience to ethnicity in its administration of the territory, and was now preparing the country for independence.

The first of the key events, the murder of Prince Rwagasore in October 1961, followed the overwhelming victory of his party, the *Parti de l'Unité et du Progrès National* (UPRONA) in the legislative elections preceding independence. A charismatic leader, son of the Mwami, with 'strong affective ties' to Hutu (Lemarchand, 1970: 328), he seemed ideally qualified to lead a party dedicated to national unity. Members of a rival dynastic family, leading the opposition party, the *Parti Démocrate Chrétien*, had instigated his murder. The Belgian administration seems to have had some responsibility in the matter (Lemarchand, 1970: 340-341). The elimination of Prince Rwagasore left a vacuum in which ethnic rivalries began to replace the dynastic conflict.

The next major polarising event was the Kamenge episode. It

may not have been specifically motivated by the desire to commit ethnic atrocity but it took that form. The protagonists were the Syndicats Chrétiens, a still embryonic trade union organisation founded under Belgian auspices and serving as a forcing ground for the nascent Hutu leadership, and the Jeunesses Nationalistes Rwagasore (JNR), a youth organisation inclined to terrorism which increasingly fulfilled the functions of Tutsi storm troopers. The Syndicats Chrétiens, at a congress in January 1962, condemned the JNR for propagating hatred and aggression, and made the charge that its organisation and actions were directed by militants of the Rwanda UNAR youth movement. The JNR reacted by launching in the capital a series of armed raids, accompanied by arson and murder, against Hutu personalities in the trade union movement and the Hutu *Parti du Peuple* (Lemarchand, 1970: 345, 348-349).

The Kamenge episode was seemingly a precipitant of ethnic conflict, the years which followed being marked by the growth of exclusive organisation, and by the sharpening of ideological opposition. Debates on the issue of responsibility for Kamenge contributed to the division of the parliamentary representatives into a Monrovian (Hutu) group and a Casablanca (Tutsi) group. Ethnic polarisation appears also in the distinction between UPRONA *populaire* (Hutu) and UPRONA *traditionaliste* (Tutsi) in the legislative elections of May 1965. In August 1962, an internal quarrel over leadership of UPRONA between a Hutu and a member of one of the princely families unleashed cycles of polarisation. Ethnic leaders brought pressure to bear on the gendarmerie, army, trade unions and student organisations (Lemarchand, 1970: 358-359). The small *Fédération des Travailleurs du Burundi* 'emerged as one of the most stridently pro-Tutsi and anti-Western pressure groups in Burundi' and senior students, for the most part 'already predisposed to become actively engaged in the politics of ethnicity', were stimulated to greater involvement (*ibid.*). Young Tutsi militants continued to provoke and terrorise Hutu trade union leaders and politicians. Tutsi elites sought to eliminate their opponents 'in a nightmarish sequence of plots and counterplots, accompanied by widespread terrorism and assassination', driving the opposition to counter-terrorism in a cycle of reciprocal hatreds and violence (*ibid.*). And Lemarchand (1970: 359-360) adds the comment that 'by 1964 the atmosphere was so heavily saturated with racial tension that one may indeed wonder why explosions of violence did not occur even more frequently, and on a wider scale'.

The explosions of violence were not long delayed. In October 1965, following the assassination of the Hutu prime minister by Tutsi refugees from Rwanda in January 1965, and the passing over of Hutu in the appointment of a new prime minister, notwithstanding their overwhelming victory in the legislative elections of May 1965, and following upon changes in local administration which 'raised the spectre of continued Tutsi hegemony at the grass-roots level' (Lemarchand, 1970: 415), a group of Hutu army and gendarmerie officers unsuccessfully attempted a coup. In all probability, some Hutu politicians and officials also participated. The coup was almost immediately suppressed in the capital. In the countryside, however, roving bands of Hutu terrorists began to attack Tutsi families and set fire to their huts. Members of a Hutu youth group went on the rampage in one province, slaughtering at least five hundred Tutsi. As usual in these situations, the reprisals were more massive, with an estimated 2,500 to 5,000 Hutu killed by the army, by civilian defence groups organised under the supervision of the army, and by the government acting through the refinement of a Counsel of War. The purge which extended to the army, the gendarmerie and the politicians, virtually liquidated Hutu leadership (Lemarchand, 1970: 416-421); and disclosure of a planned coup in 1969 provided pretext for a further purge of Hutu elites and soldiers.

The attempted coup, the massacre and the reprisals in 1965 were a point of no return. Weinstein and Schrire (1976: 17) describe the events of 1965 as marking the failure of peaceful ethnic conflict regulation. They certainly brought about a profound deterioration in ethnic relations, and they served in a way as a sort of trial run for the holocaust of 1972. I have given an account of these later massacres and counter-massacres from a variety of perspectives. But the atrocities of 1972 were not the final atrocities. In 1973, guerilla invasions by refugee Hutu in neighbouring territories led to particularly bloody repression (Wingert, 1974: ch. 10)[1]: and according to some witnesses, the army and police continue to liquidate Hutu suspected of involvement in the 1972 rising (Jean de la Guérivière, 'Après les tueries', *Le Monde*, 13-14, 15 January 1974). The result has been a profound transformation of Burundi society.

> ... a new society has in fact emerged, in which only Tutsi elements are qualified to gain access to power, influence and wealth: what is left of Hutu society is now systematically excluded from the army, the civil service, the university and secondary schools. The four Hutu holding ministerial positions are virtually impotent, their sole function being to mask the fact of Tutsi domination. Tasks formerly performed by Hutu are now the privilege of the Tutsi, as are virtually all other positions in the modern economic sector ... Hutu status has become synonymous with an inferior category of beings; only Tutsi are fit to rule, and among them none are presumably better qualified than the Banyabururi (Tutsi-Hima). (Lemarchand, 1974a: 18)

III

In seeking the causes of this extreme polarisation, the first question which arises is whether the social structure was not more highly conducive to ethnic conflict than appears from the analysis of the many crosscutting relationships. This was certainly the view of the student movement, MEPROBA, (See Chapter 5, Section 3). Its secretary, Charles Batungwanayo (1972: 19-20), in a statement on the causes of the genocide, rejects the conception that the ruling dynastic families, the Ganwa, constituted a section apart, subjecting Hutu and Tutsi equally to exploitation. He argues that the Ganwa were simply the Tutsi aristocracy, the remaining Tutsi acting as intermediaries of the feudal power, and reigning as a class of local squires over the great mass of Hutu: colonialism had not modified this basic structure, but on the

---

1. There were counter-reprisals by Hutu against Tutsi in Rwanda, indicative of the close involvement of these territories in each other's destiny.

contrary, it had reinforced Tutsi supremacy.

There is very little in the way of detailed quantitative information relevant to the question of inequality and discrimination between the ethnic groups. Lemarchand (1974a: 8-11, 1970: 82-83, 355) presents data on discrimination against Hutu in schooling at the elite Groupe Scolaire during the period 1946-1954, in membership of the highest counsels of the state in 1959, and in the top-ranking civil service positions in 1965. (See also Weinstein and Schrire, 1976: Tables I, II and III.) Clearly these data demonstrate appreciable ethnic discontinuity at the political level before independence, and at the administrative level three years after independence.

Moreover, ethnic identity almost immediately became a significant factor in the struggle for power. In 1959, the Hutu leader, Ngendadumwe, who held the position of prime minister twice before his assassination in 1965, wrote of the paradox that in spite of representing a minority, the near totality of offices of chief, sub-chief and judge were in the hands of the Tutsi (Lemarchand, 1970: 83). The polarising conflict between the youth movement (JNR) and Hutu trade union and political leaders had already erupted by January 1962. In the same year, the year of independence, ethnic solidarities expressed themselves in the division between the Monrovia and Casablanca groups. Ethnic arithmetic guided political strategy from the very first. Thus, before the first legislative elections, Prince Rwagasore balanced ethnic composition in the Central Committee of UPRONA: and ethnic representation became a guiding principle in the appointment of cabinet ministers.

If the salience of ethnic identity was marked in the whole process of political struggle, expressing a basic discontinuity in the social structure, there can nevertheless be no doubt that the ethnic continuities were highly significant. The principle of ethnic representation is not only a measure of *discontinuity*, it is also a measure of *continuity*. Its persistence, in the form of parity of representation between Hutu and Tutsi in the cabinet appointed in November 1967, that is after the abortive Hutu coup of 1965 and the successful Tutsi military coup against the monarchy in 1966, is evidence of the reality of these continuities as a political force. So too was the presence of Hutu officers in the National Revolutionary Council in 1968. On the other hand, the inclusion of four Hutu ministerial positions in the post-holocaust cabinet appears to be merely a token representation, dictated largely by the need to placate, in some measure, a subordinated and tragically repressed majority, rather than a political expression of the salience of relationships across ethnic barriers.

Quite apart from policies based on ethnic arithmetic, evidence of the significance of interethnic continuities may be found in the initial failure of the Hutu ethnic party, the *Parti du Peuple*, to gain electoral support. It is to be found also in the refusal of some members of parliament to identify with either the Monrovia or Casablanca factions, and in the deviations from the principle of ethnic affiliation in membership of these factions (Lemarchand, 1966c: 416). Moreover, other bases of affiliation, such as loyalty to region and ideological affinities, continued to be salient, providing opportunities for political solidarity across ethnic lines.

It does not seem possible to give anything more than qualitative impressions of the relationship of continuities to discontinuities in Burundi society. But even if detailed and quantitatively precise data were available for a comprehensive tabulation of continuities and discontinuities, for the evaluation of their salience in the different sectors, and for the striking of a balance sheet between them, this would hardly provide a clear basis for predicting the probability of ethnic violence. These situations are by no means determinant. They offer to the political actors a range of objectives and of means for attaining them. However, I think it is clear that the discontinuities have a greater charge of energy in them because they are linked to violence and destruction: and I assume then that it would need a great preponderance of continuities to counteract the potential for ethnic violence inherent in the discontinuities.

The situational context provided a major stimulus to the manipulation of ethnic discontinuities in the social structure. Since, in the context of the movement to independence and to a western type democracy, ethnic solidarities offered a basis for support in the struggle for power, it was inevitable that they should be activated. Ethnic politics would have particular appeal to the representatives of the majority group, denied the resources of the traditional elite. The result of electoral competition and of democratic procedures, unleashing mass politics in a society characterised by appreciable ethnic discontinuities, was an extreme ethnic polarisation.

In this process, the elite played a crucial role, as they struggled for positions of power, prestige and wealth, opened by liberation from colonial rule. Given the poverty of Burundi, it is not difficult to understand the desperation with which they waged this battle. Thus it comes as no surprise to read in Lemarchand (1970: 411) that feelings of ethnic repulsion were probably strongest among the new elites – the intelligentsia, youth leaders, bureaucrats, military and police officers. Bureaucratic ambitions no doubt also entered into the ferocious brutality with which Tutsi students at university and school battered their fellow Hutu students to death. I do not mean to suggest that this struggle was consciously directed to office or explicitly formulated in ideologies of bureaucratic competition: action would proceed under other ideologies, often masking, or rationalising, or subordinate to, the realities of the elite struggle for power.

Violence characterised the struggle from the outset, beginning with the assassination of Prince Rwagasore after the first legislative elections and continuing to the 'prophylactic violence' of the 1972 massacre. It not only expressed the deterioration in ethnic relations; it served also to polarise relations still further, effecting by these dramatic and fearful events, a qualitative transformation of the conflict into deadly enmity. Characteristically it moved from the occasional spectacular murders of selected politicians, through widespread terrorism and assassination, to the final holocaust of genocidal massacres.

The annihilating struggle in neighbouring Rwanda powerfully influenced the course of events in Burundi. Here were two countries, with similarities in origin, ethnic composition and colonial history, linked administratively and moving under the same mandatory power and through the same constitutional changes, to independence. To be sure, the structure of ethnic relations had evolved very differently in Burundi, but this did not stop events in Rwanda having their immediate repercussions in Burundi, nor did it prevent the deadly ethnic conflict of Rwanda serving as model and guide to action.

The history and destiny of the two countries were closely interwoven, as they arrived at the same solution of genocide, though at different tempos and with different ethnic victims and beneficiaries. The rapid revolutionary assumption of power by Hutu in Rwanda, following the coup of Gitarama in January 1961, raised expectations among Hutu elite, though initially only a small minority of hard-core Hutu politicians took their cue from the PARMEHUTU party in Rwanda (Lemarchand, 1970: 344-345). For the Tutsi in Burundi, the burning down of huts, the atrocities, the murders, the massacres in Rwanda presented the horrifying spectacle of the terrible fate which might await them at the hands of rampaging bands of terrorists. Understandably, many Tutsi would have viewed the alternatives in somewhat stark terms as a choice between Tutsi domination and Tutsi extermination (Melady, 1974: 72-87). Perhaps some of them might have been inspired to reenact, for the benefit of their own group, the Rwanda solution,[2] viewing the alternatives as to slaughter or to be slaughtered.

Thus Rwanda, as political paradigm, played its part in the polarisation of ethnic relations in Burundi, both at the level of ideology and action. Some Belgian administrators contributed to this process by importing perceptions of Rwanda society into their policies for Burundi. The influence of events in Rwanda, however, extended further to the direct impact of refugees on the

---

2. Lemarchand (1974a: 13-17) discusses the role of three Tutsi leaders in the struggle for power on behalf of the Tutsi Banyabururi group, directed against Hutu and against the Tutsi Banyaruguru, but he dismisses as implausible the suggestion that the Hutu rebellion was deliberately engineered by the Bururi 'lobby'. Weinstein and Schrire (1976: 33) suggest that some credence might be given to the view that members of the Bururi faction planned a coup against the Tutsi Banyaruguru, and used the Hutu threat as a cover.

internal politics of Burundi. The Bugesera invasion which precipitated the Rwanda massacres was after all launched from Burundi. When the matter was debated in the Burundi parliament, the Monrovia faction suggested the deportation to Rwanda of those who had taken part in the invasion, whilst the Casablanca faction argued, in the words of one of its deputies, that Burundi had indeed a moral obligation to assist the refugees and their brothers in Rwanda, 'victims of Kayibanda's genocide' (Lemarchand, 1970: 357-358). Tutsi refugees murdered the Hutu prime minister, with collaboration by Casablanca elites and the refugee leadership (Lemarchand, 1970: 387-388). By 1965, there were 52,000 refugees from Rwanda in Burundi, most of them Tutsi, deeply embittered by their violent expulsion from home and country, and by their grief for friends and relatives most atrociously massacred. Through their leaders, they maintained relations with the Tutsi elite of Burundi, for whom they constituted an important resource in the struggle against the Hutu.[3]

The influence of Rwanda was part of a much wider international involvement in the affairs of Burundi, both of neighbouring and of overseas powers. A number of analysts have described this involvement, which included support for the Tutsi in their annihilation of Hutu, either by direct assistance or by the complicity of silence or of indifference.[4]

It is a tragic story of military support in the massacres from Zaire and France, of endorsement by China and North Korea of the Burundi government's policies, of the muted reactions of the United Nations, of the failure of the United Nations Commission on Human Rights to openly cite Burundi for its violations under the Charter and under the Universal Declaration of Human Rights, and of moral support extended by the Organisation of African Unity to the Burundi Government

3. See Lemarchand, 1970: 384-390, for a discussion of the complexity of the relationship.

4. See Lemarchand, 1970: Chapter 15 and 1974a: 19-22; du Bois, 1972; Morris, 1974; Martin, 1974; Greenland, 1973; Bowen, Freeman and Miller, 1973, and reply by U.S. Department of State; Melady, 1974; Weinstein, 1975.

at its summit conference in Rabat in June 1972.[5]

From all these accounts, I want to extract one aspect for comment, the CIA factor. By this I mean the exploitation of internal divisions in a country by the agents of an outside power, acting surreptitiously, in pursuance of the global interests of that outside power, with almost total indifference to the consequences for the host country, employing almost any means regardless of their destructive potential, and ready for almost any alliance regardless of ideology and objectives. The CIA factor seems to be invariably present in countries where there are sharp internal divisions. It is like a great parasite, feeding on societies weakened by political strife. Now the term is normally linked to the USA, but I use it generically. In the case of Burundi it would include not only the secret interventions of Western powers, but also a Chinese alliance with segments of the Tutsi refugee leadership in Burundi, Chinese support in the arming and training of Tutsi refugee leadership in Burundi, Chinese support in the arming and training of Tutsi guerilla fighters, Chinese intrigues in Burundi, and possible Chinese complicity in the plot to murder the Hutu Prime Minister, Ngendadumwe. As the rivalries between East and West found scope in the conflict between Tutsi and Hutu, the CIA factor entered as a further element in the polarisation of ethnic relations in Burundi.

By all these processes, Burundi moved to genocidal massacre.

5. See Lemarchand, 1975: 15, Melady, 1974: 23-27 and Weinstein, 1975: 18, 20.

8

Eliminating the Middle Ground

I

By the middle ground, I refer to those relationships between people of different racial, religious, or ethnic background, and those ideologies, which might form the basis for movements of intergroup cooperation and of radical change, without resort to destructive violence. Where the carriers of these ideologies are significant in number or power, the process of polarisation requires that they be appreciably recruited or coerced into one or other of the warring camps, and that the irreducible minority is either silenced or eliminated, at the same time that its ideologies of conciliation are discredited.

Various theories are available as to the conditions conducive to a significant role for the mediators. One may borrow from theories of the structural roots of moderation in class structured societies. Thus the basis for moderation might be found in a diamond shaped structure, the centre greatly swollen with the middle classes, which would hardly seem to be a situation conducive to polarisation. The parallel in the case of societies which bring together people of different racial, or ethnic, or religious groups, would be such an intermingling as greatly to diminish the incidence of these distinctive statuses or affiliations.

Alternatively, where the distinctive identities are maintained, the basis for mediation might be sought in a network of cross-cutting relationships, including joint participation in associational activity. Clearly, in adapting this theory of the roots of moderation in class-structured societies to plural societies, the conception of cross-cutting relationships must imply something other than a series of interrelationships in which members of the

same group are always dominant. Such societies may be stable for
long periods of time, and the dependence of the subordinates on
these cross-cutting relations may inhibit protest. But the problem
I am posing is the very different one of the structural roots of
cooperation for radical change in intergroup relations in a
situation of conflict.

From this perspective, it is necessary that there should be an
appreciable range and volume of cross-cutting relationships,
extending beyond simple interdependence, to relations of
equality at many different levels. It would seem natural to
emphasise similarity of material interests as the basis for
cooperation, but the evidence from plural societies is that the
most intense conflict is often to be anticipated precisely where
there are similar material interests. This is specially true for the
relations between workers, traders, and farmers of different
groups, where it is the very similarity of their interests which
frequently sets them in sharp conflict. Probably the most likely
social basis for cooperation at the level of occupations, is among
professionals, though it is also at this level that extremes of
militant hostility may be found.

One would anticipate that the sharing of the same culture
should promote cooperative relations, and that this situation
would be the least conducive to polarisation. But the fate of
highly assimilated Jews in Germany shows that there is no
necessary relationship between cultural homogeneity and even
survival. Moreover, people of quite different cultures may be
dedicated to the same politically significant values.

Still, one may perhaps make a rough provisional assumption
that where there are extreme discontinuities in structure and
culture, the social situation is likely to discourage joint
participation in movements for significant political change, and
conversely that continuities in structure and culture provide a
more favourable milieu for cooperation, but that the relationship
is quite indeterminate.

II

In Algeria, before the revolution, extreme discontinuities characterised the relations between the indigenous people and the settlers. At a general level, the discontinuity was between a subjugated, impoverished people of Muslim religion and Islamic culture, with distinctive patterns of social organisation, and a ruling European Christian settler minority, economically privileged and politically dominant.

In more detail, the discontinuity was marked, at the economic level, in the different distribution of the populations in the sectors of the economy, with Muslims concentrated in the agricultural sector (87.8%) and Europeans in the secondary, industrial sector and in the tertiary sector of services (85.6%).[1] This in turn was associated with differential access to resources and differential rewards. Some two-thirds of agricultural production was in European hands (Nouschi: 1962: 116), the great majority of Muslim farmers being engaged in subsistence agriculture. Muslim holdings averaged 14 hectares as against an average of 109 hectares for Europeans, who also enjoyed most of the credit facilities, and cultivated the best land and the most remunerative products, the contrast in life chances being expressed in the gulf between an estimated individual average revenue of 22,000 francs per Muslim farmer in 1954 and a corresponding European average of 780,000 francs (following the source quoted by Aron, 1962: 227).[2] To this should be added the large numbers of the Muslim landless agricultural proletariat and of migrant labourers in metropolitan France. As to the industrial and service sectors, these constituted a European fief. Muslims directed few important industries: for the most part, they were engaged in relatively small artisan type ventures (Nouschi, 1962: 115).

1. Aron, 1962: 223. See Aron generally for discussion of the differentiation between the populations.
2. Nouschi (1962: 117) gives figures based on an analysis of the value of agricultural production in 1953 which show a greater discrepancy: 1,800,000 fr. per person for Europeans and a few rare large Muslim landholders, and 17,691 fr. per person among the peasants.

Europeans virtually monopolised wholesale trade, export and import trade, banking and finance. In Algiers, they were largely employed in office work, in a variety of middle class occupations, as skilled manual workers, civil servants, and professionals. By contrast, Muslims in Algiers were mainly manual workers, large numbers being employed on a daily basis or unable to find employment: some 10% of the work force engaged in petty trade, and some 6% followed the liberal professions (Nouschi, 1962: 115).

At the political level, the ancient wrongs of conquest, despoliation, atrocity, repression were crystallised in discontinuities in basic political rights. Europeans, as citizens, enjoyed a franchise and a privileged political status, which served as a trampoline for economic advance. Muslims remained disenfranchised, subject to special penal laws, politically impotent, vulnerable to economic exploitation. Inevitably this was a situation from which would develop exclusive political organisations with increasingly radical demands. And though at the time of the revolution, Muslims had been recognised as citizens on a basis of equality with European settlers, nevertheless the system remained heavily weighted against them. The franchise was in fact unequal. Executive power was vested in a French governor-general assisted by a Council. The key administrative positions were held by European settlers or French expatriates, and the representatives to the Algerian Assembly were chosen by two electoral colleges, continuing in effect, under a different form, the distinction between citizens of French civil status, and citizens of local status (though the first college did include certain categories of French citizens retaining their personal Muslim status).

Corresponding to these political and economic discontinuities were discontinuities in most aspects of life. Large Muslim sections lived in remote and isolated mountain areas — a predominantly rural population, in contrast to a largely urbanised settler population. In the towns, high levels of segregation maintained this basic discontinuity, expressed, too, in distinctive patterns of worship and family structure. Extreme discrimination in the opportunities for education had added the additional dimension of the contrast between a largely illiterate Muslim population and an essentially literate European population.

With such widely ramifying discontinuities, there would seem to be little objective basis for a middle ground between the warring groups. Yet the picture I have presented is quite stereotypic, following what seems to be the well-established convention of ignoring the differences within each of the racial sections and of attributing to individuals the general attributes of the groups to which they belong. One has only to compare the situation in Algeria on the eve of the revolution and in South Africa at the time of the revolutionary movement in the 1950's, to appreciate how much more room there was for mediation in Algeria. Under the South African constitution, Africans and other 'non-whites' had always been excluded from Parliament. Africans enjoyed a limited representation in the Cape Province, but even this minimum of representation was finally abolished in 1960. Many laws provided control over political expression. As Africans became more militant in the 1950s, the Government perfected its machinery for repression. In 1960, under the Unlawful Organisation Act, the major African political organisations were outlawed. In 1968, under the Prohibition of Political Interference Act, the Government introduced the new crime of engaging in 'mixed' politics, thereby prohibiting interracial political parties and interracial political cooperation.[3] In addition, over a period of settlement going back some 300 years, and under the stimulus of industrialisation and urbanisation, many ties had been established between members of different racial groups. Fearing that the intimacy of these relations was establishing a middle ground, and undermining racial domination, the Government proceeded systematically to prohibit and control a wide range of interracial contacts.

By contrast, in Algeria, at the time of the revolution, the

3. For a full discussion of these restrictions on the basic political freedoms, see A.S. Mathews, *Law, Order and Liberty in South Africa*, University of California Press, 1972, Part 2, and for controls over interracial association, see my discussion in *An African Bourgeoisie*, Yale University Press, 1965, ch. 4.

Algerian Assembly consisted of an equal number of members elected by the two electoral colleges. Each electoral college, moreover, returned the same number of deputies and senators to the French Parliament. Political parties contested the elections. The militant nationalist party had been suppressed from time to time, but it continuously reappeared. There were harassment and sabotage of nationalist leaders, and fraudulent elections to exclude nationalists from the Algerian Assembly, but this persecution was in no way comparable to the liquidation of militant African leadership in South Africa. There were no laws to prohibit interracial political organisation. Muslim Algerian workers in France joined the French trade unions. After 1936, following the abolition of the *Code de l'Indigenat*, Muslim workers in Algeria freely participated in the same trade unions as their European fellow workers. This continued until 1956, when Muslims established a separate trade union, protesting against the spirit of tutelage and elitism in the existing trade unions, and their abandonment of the goal of independence for Algeria. Yet, the new trade union still sought to maintain good relations with the French trade unions and opened its ranks to local European workers (see Weiss, 1970: Part I).

Even during the revolution, Algerian students continued to study in France, and in 1955-1956 there were some 1300 Algerian students in French universities (Moore and Hochschild, 1968: 27). A small French-educated Muslim intelligentsia in Algeria maintained cordial relations with French colleagues. It was from an association of Muslim and French intellectuals, in a committee to promote theatre in Arabic, that the proposal originated to invite Camus to launch an appeal for a truce on the killing of civilians (Lebjaoui, 1970: 38ff). To this stratum of French educated intellectuals belonged the great Algerian writer, Mouloud Feraoun, whose participation in the social centres initiated by the French anthropologist and author, Germaine Tillion, led tragically to his assassination and to the assassination of French and Muslim colleagues in the last period of OAS terrorism.

At a very general level of analysis, a clear dichotomy separated the rich market-oriented agrarian capitalism of the European farmers from the impoverished subsistence agriculture of the Algerian Muslims. But in fact there was an appreciable Muslim rural elite. The Constantine plan, which the French had begun to implement in 1958, estimated that there were some 25,000 substantial landed proprietors, owning 2,300,000 hectares (Chaliand and Minces, 1972: 11). The Constantine plan also gave an estimate of 90,000 Algerian owned small enterprises (industrial, artisan, and commercial), of which 7,000 to 8,000 employed salaried workers (*ibid.*). Conversely, if the great bulk of agricultural wealth was concentrated in the hands of Europeans, nevertheless the majority were small landowners (see Aron, 1962: 224). So, too, the great majority of the European nonagricultural work force fell into the category of *petits blancs*. According to figures available in July-August 1961 (Lentin, 1962: 1816-1817) almost half the European non-agricultural work force (147,500) belonged to the categories of artisans (19,000), petty traders (25,000), specialised workers (28,000), nonspecialised workers (66,000) and domestic servants (9,500). Almost 100,000 were employed in offices in commerce and in the lower administrative positions. The 'top' stratum numbered 74,340: it consisted of the higher level administrators (16,740), manufacturers (*industriels* 5,600), technicians (39,000), and professionals (13,000).[4]

Thus there would seem to have been many bases in the objective situation for a mediating role in the conflicts, and the strength of this base can be seen in such facts as we have previously mentioned, the fraternisation of 13 May 1958 (though some commentators view the Muslim participation as entirely forced and without significance), the large numbers serving in the French army, and the willingness of sections of the FLN to incorporate Europeans in an independent Algeria. But apparently similarity in occupation is no necessary basis for political cooperation. The more significant factor seems to have

---

4. These figures are almost the same as those given in the Census of 31 October, 1954, immediately before the launching of the revolution. See *Statistique générale de l'Algérie: Tableaux de l'économie algérienne (1960)*, 26-27.

been the nature of the occupation, with the liberals and progressives drawn from the 'top' stratum, and the workers and '*petits blancs*' generally contributing strong support to the extremist, settler ultras (see for example, Lentin, 1962: 1817). The situation was the very antithesis of working–class solidarity.

Other potentialities remained equally unrealised. The Communist Party was of course interracial in ideology, and in membership, though dominated by its European members. It was never, however, a major political force in Algeria: there was appreciable distrust of the party among Algerian nationalists;[5] the party was oriented towards France and the international proletarian movement; it was quite opposed for many years to the goal of Algerian independence; it was slow in identifying with the revolutionary movement, and its contribution, either as a party or by individual members, was quite modest. In any event, the ideological radicalism of a communist party challenges so many interests that it is difficult to see how it can perform a mediating role in a situation of sharp conflict between racial groups. It seems likely to suffer the same fate as a liberal party. Indeed, in South Africa the initial major targets of Government oppression under apartheid were communism and African nationalism, followed by liberalism. There was a tendency to equate liberalism with communism.

The trade unions in Algeria, because of large Muslim membership, might have seemed a more promising base for interracial cooperation in political change. But the Algerian trade union movement was a part of the French trade union movement and metropolitan perspectives and interests dominated its policies. In the relationship of its local members, Muslim and European, there was the basic opposition of privileged coloniser to underprivileged colonised, and a tension between Muslim demands for national independence and trade union reticence on this issue. While the new Algerian trade union, the *Union Générale des Travailleurs Algériens*, sought to establish links across

5. See Weiss, 1970: 24–25, 30; Ouzegane, 1962: chs. 3 and 6; Humbaraci, 1966: 170ff.

the racial divisions, it was essentially an arm of the Nationalist movement, and government persecution and terrorist attacks forced it underground.[6]

For many years there was a strong commitment among French-educated Muslims to policies of interracial conciliation and evolutionary change. But with the failure of their policies as a result of settler resistance to reforms and the brazen and contemptuous corruption of electoral procedures, they lost credibility with the mass of the people. Many were driven by despair to join the revolutionary movement.

The course of the struggle itself, as we have seen, further served to polarise the populations and to eliminate the middle ground. The imposition of collective responsibility, the increasing categorisation, the reduction of issues to stark alternatives in a sharpening of the ideological conflict, the random killings, the indiscriminate arrests, the accumulation of episodes of terrorism and of atrocity, drove Muslims and Europeans increasingly into enemy camps. But there remained many Muslims closely identified with France and the status quo. A minority held prestigious political and administrative positions, there being a convergence of the interests of conservative French administrators with the interests of the great landed proprietors. Others, among both settlers and Muslims, still sought interracial cooperation in a nonviolent struggle for political change. These liberals had to be silenced, or destroyed, and terrorism was directed to this end by both Muslims and settlers.

Courrière (1972: 132) quotes a comment by the French director of information in Algeria that the liberals were the half-breeds (*métis*) for both Muslims and settlers. This was very clearly shown in the reactions to the first Muslim prefect in Algeria, Mahdi Belhaddad, committed to a concept of a new Algeria

6. The trade union management moved to Tunis, establishing also in Paris an association, the *Amicale Générale des Travailleurs Algériens*. This was not a trade union, in competition with the French trade unions. In any event, the Amicale was also suppressed after some eighteen months but continued to operate clandestinely (Weiss, 1970: 34ff).

which would fuse the different communities, and remain linked to France. He became the *bête noire* for the European ultras, civil and military, while his popularity among Muslims equally disquieted the FLN extremists, who plotted to discredit him. Courrière (407-408) comments that for reasons diametrically opposed, the FLN extremists and the European ultras joined in the same political tactic – the annihilation of reason.

During the revolutionary struggle, there was a fierce intimidation of liberals. Nora (1961: 64) writes of jeeps touring the streets during the summer nights of 1958, broadcasting the summons to murder. 'French people, you are about to gain a great victory, not over the rebels, but over the enemies within, the traitors, the defeatists, the intellectuals, the Jews. Renew yourselves in their blood. Frenchmen, to arms!' Advocates were inundated with anonymous letters, professors received warning visits.

Assassination, a later phase in the terrorising of liberals, completed what intimidation, and warnings by plastic bomb, could not accomplish. Advocate Popie became the target of death threats after defending an FLN militant. He belonged to a small group of liberals, who had met on several occasions, and he was seeking to promote the liberal cause in a television interview. He declared that there already existed the cadres of a liberal party, whose task it would be to persuade the Europeans that *Algérie française* was dead, and that they should look to a future in which they would enjoy all the rights of fully integrated citizens in an Algerian Republic. This broadcast was his death warrant. Several days later, on 25 January 1961, he was stabbed to death in his chambers by two French specialists in close combat (Courrière, 1973: 229-231). Some months later it was the turn of M. Perrin, another member of the liberal group, who had reported to a police force, extensively impregnated with supporters of the OAS, the presence of OAS terrorists in a neighbouring building. Assassins coldly shot him down in front of his wife. 'In the minds of a large part of the European population, all these liberals who collaborated with the Arabs were even more detestable than the FLN or the communists' (Courrière, 1972: 398).

General Challe, when he arrived in Algeria to head the generals' revolt of April 1961, was reported to be carrying with him a document containing 'the names of fifty liberals who were to be arrested on sight, given a speedy trial for "treasonable contacts with the FLN" and presumably shot' (Hennisart, 1970: 79). The OAS now came out into the open, established itself officially, and liberated activist friends, including the assassins of Advocate Popie. They distributed arms, and moved off to hunt down all the enemies of the nation, 'the communists, that is to say the liberals, the Gaullists, all those who were so imprudent as to say that "perhaps it was necessary to come to an understanding with the Arabs, with whom one was going to live side by side in equality" ' (Courrière, 1972; 322). In Oran, in the last period of OAS terrorism, at the *Place des Armes*, corpses of murdered European liberals were publicly displayed (Hennisart, 1970: 459).

Ferhat Abbas (1962: 88), in *La Nuit coloniale*, comments that in the history of France, the party of liberals and intellectuals did not cease to make itself known, to condemn the colonial regime and to defend the oppressed; but the party always remained inefficacious and its interventions purely academic. I do not know why liberalism, between the two world wars and after the Second World War, should have been so weak a force in colonial affairs in France, as compared say, with liberalism in England. The reasons for the failure of liberalism in Algeria, however, are no mystery. The lack of strong support from France, and the commitment of so many of the French administrators in Algeria to conservative settler policies, were important factors. But above all, Algeria represented an extreme type of plural society, in which the initial differentiation between conquerors and conquered served as a foundation for a great superstructure of privilege. The discontinuities of colonisation were superimposed on the initially sharp contrasts of structure and culture. No common religion resulted from the contacts between coloniser and colonised: constitutional arrangements, for most of the period of colonisation, were such as to exclude Muslims from citizenship by reason of religious criteria, accession to citizenship calling for the renunciation of Muslim status. The great majority did not share a common educational background, though there was a small French-educated Muslim elite. Common political institutions developed over time, but they were deliberately rendered ineffective. The long history of brutal conquest and the gross and manifest injustices of colonisation fed into the ultimate irreconcilability of goals, between a settler population committed to integration with France, and a Muslim goal of independence in an era of worldwide decolonisation.

All this left small room for liberals. A liberal policy, oriented to conciliation and cooperation, is often unstable under conditions of increasing polarisation between hostile sections. The extremists have their firm rigidly fixed ideological positions. Liberals must of necessity be somewhat flexible in seeking to mediate. But the appeal to reason is hardly a viable appeal. There is no basis for discourse between visceral commitment and reasoned argument. And since the liberals in Algeria had only a small social base in the society, they were unable to survive, particularly since the government could not, or would not, provide protection. If liberals had turned to violence, they would have been no match for the terrorist groups. But violence was no alternative for the liberals. They were not specialists in violence, it was not in the liberal idiom, it was no instrument for conciliation.

The Barbouzes did attempt to meet terrorism by counter-terrorism. They were a small group of Gaullists, not liberals, committed to the concept of Muslim-French cooperation and community. They sought to propagate their ideas and to resist the tyranny of the OAS. Though well-versed in the means of violence, and men of the most remarkable courage, they were finally wiped out. Their leader, Lucien Bitterlin, who survived the massacre, gave an account of their crusade under the title *Des morts pour rien*. Are we also to say of the many liberals, French and Muslim, who died in the attempt to promote understanding, that they too died in vain?

III

In Algeria, the discontinuities in structure and culture raised almost insuperable obstacles to the development of a middle ground. In Zanzibar, by contrast, before the revolution in 1964, the situation seemed in some ways to offer possibilities for relatively peaceful integration. There were many continuities both in the structure and culture of the society. Yet the scale of the society was such that these continuities proved ultimately ineffective to prevent the country being overwhelmed by massive, destructive violence in the movement to independence. Sufficient power could be mustered for the massacre of Arabs without need of a thorough-going polarisation of the society; and the society was never in fact fully polarised. There were differences, too, in the geographical distribution of continuities and of discontinuities, Zanzibar Island, the seat of government and administration, being marked by great discontinuities between Arabs and Mainland Africans, while Pemba Island was characterised by considerable continuity between Arabs and Shirazi. And the discontinuities in Zanzibar Island prevailed in shaping the destiny of the country.

Ethnic demography provided the structural basis for mediation in the mixed identity and identifications of the Shirazi group.[7] The Shirazi were the oldest established group on the islands and the most numerous. They had arrived from the mainland of Africa very many centuries earlier, and they claimed to have intermingled with Persians. They also included ex-slaves, and the descendants of slaves. There was some intermarriage with Arabs, and some ethnic mobility by self-identification. Thus in terms of ethnic origins one might have anticipated that the Shirazi could have provided a bridge between the main antagonists, Arabs and Mainland Africans.

There were other continuities between the population groups. Swahili was the common language, and Islam the common

7. See my discussion of 'Continuities and discontinuities in race relations', and 'Theories of revolution and race relations', (1974: 113-139, and 175-202).

religion, there being only small numbers of Christians, mainly
Mainland African, and of Hindus. From the stereotypic points of
view of ethnic conflict, or of racism, each of the population
groups represented a distinct economic stratum. Arabs were
categorised as the ruling stratum, the senior bureaucrats, the large
plantation owners, Indians as merchants and financiers, and
Africans, both Shirazi and Mainland, as fishermen, cultivators,
and labourers. But these stereotypes characteristically neglected
the many continuities in economic situation (Kuper, 1974: 119ff).
These were most marked between Arabs and Shirazi on Pemba
Island, where there were always both Shirazi and Arab
plantation owners. The greatest discontinuity, by economic and
other indices, prevailed between Arabs and Mainland Africans on
Zanzibar Island in terms of level of occupation, economic
rewards, style of life, milieu and historical role. There were also
marked discontinuities on Zanzibar Island between the Hadimu
section of the Shirazis and the Arabs, the Hadimu having been
the most exposed to Arab domination and demands for labour, in
contrast to the Pemba Shirazi who believed that they had entered
into a voluntary relationship with Arabs and that they had not
been subjected to an enforced subordination.

Though in terms of structure, culture, numbers, and of historic
beliefs and race relations on Pemba Island, the Shirazi seemed
ideally placed to provide stability and to mediate between
Mainland Africans and Arabs, they themselves became involved
in ethnic or racial politics, but in a curiously vacillating and
ambivalent way, reflecting their intermediate situation in the
society. In the last chapter, I described the unstable character of
Shirazi alliances, moving between Mainland African and Arab.
Given the aggressive assertion of their interests by the two
antagonists, it was perhaps natural that Shirazi should form their
own political party, but this then introduced an ethnic party,
whereas an interethnic political party, offering a distinctive
national programme, might perhaps have become a significant
integrative force.

Moreover the alliances formed by the Shirazi had unfortunate
consequences. If the ZPPP had thrown in its weight with the

Afro-Shirazi Party or if there had been no breakaway, the party of Mainland Africans would have gained a legislative majority and perhaps there would have been no slaughter of Arabs, and Arabs (and Indians) would have been able to live peacefully in the country and contribute to its development. Or if the ZPPP had retained a distinctive identity, instead of throwing in its lot, and becoming identified, with the Zanzibar National Party, it might have been able to play a significant mediating role. Nevertheless, the Shirazi, by virtue of their intermediate situation in the society, and their distribution between the different political parties, still represented a potential force for conciliation and integration.

There were other forces within the society, contributing to the creation of political ties across social and ethnic divisions. The ideologies of each of the main parties were such as largely to exclude the main antagonist, but their appeals were based on the concept of multi-racial nationalism, though somewhat nominally in the case of the Afro-Shirazi Party. The Zanzibar National Party sought to foster a sense of non-African national identity. It emphasised its multi-racial composition, based on Zanzibar citizenship, thus allaying the fears of such immigrant minorities as the Asian, Arab and Comorian, and appealing to the cultural pride of the Shirazi as the first Zanzibari. Islam, too, provided a basis for a unifying multi-racial nationalism (Lofchie, 1965: 229-230). Moreover, the need to win over Shirazi, and indeed also mainland African voters, would have acted as some restraint on racist propaganda.

The Afro-Shirazi Party held itself out as the representative of the African majority, including under that term Mainland African and Shirazi. The official policy of multi-racial nationalism was subordinated to that divisive interest. But it was obliged to modify its anti-Arab racism in the electoral campaigns among the Shirazi on Pemba Island. This need of Mainland Africans, as a minority, to win over appreciable sections of a population of varied origins and political perspective might have acted over time to broaden its ideological appeal, perhaps by greater emphasis on economic inequalities, not only as affecting

Mainland Africans and Shirazi, but among members of *all*
sections.

Arabs did not constitute a totally unified political group.
There were differences of opinion regarding the electoral
strategies appropriate for implementing the ZNP's multi-racial
policies, and conflicting political perspectives between Marxists
and the religiously oriented. In 1963, before the July elections, a
section had broken off and established a Marxist party of the
masses, UMMA. It provided a meeting ground for
representatives of many different groups; it took steps to unify
the trade union movement, divided between the main parties,
and it succeeded in unifying the opposition press. All these moves
represented relationships across racial and ethnic barriers. There
is no way of estimating what significance these cross-cutting
relationships might have held for the political future. They might
have been the basis for a revolutionary seizure of power, but it is
inconceivable that a seizure of power by a movement consisting
mainly of Arabs and Comorians could have taken the form of a
genocidal attack on Arabs. On the other hand, if UMMA should
have decided against violent revolution, its policies would have
promoted a diversification of social and ethnic relationships, and
established new bases for political division, transcending the
racial cleavages, in a constitutional struggle for power.

The brief history of the political conflict between Arabs and
Mainland Africans in Zanzibar is marked by a number of missed
opportunities for policies of interracial and inter-ethnic
cooperation and conciliation. There was the involvement of
African civil servants in politics in 1951, and the beginning of
political communication between African and Arab leadership,
but this was suppressed by the Government in the interests of a
politically neutral bureaucracy (Lofchie, 1965: 157ff). The
Freedom Committee in late 1958 brought together the ASP and
ZNP: it only lasted, however, for some 15 months. If, at the
constitutional talks in 1962, the ASP had accepted an offer by the
ZNP/ZPPP coalition of three ministerial seats, or if the coalition
had been willing, after the July 1963 elections, to include the
ASP in a three-party government, the political basis might have

been laid for policies of national integration.

Though none of these opportunities were taken, there still remained the potentialities for integration in the continuities and cross-pressures discussed above. However, they were not allowed to develop. There were no liberal mediators to be assassinated. Okello's revolution cut short all possibilities of evolutionary change. But even if the opportunities had been seized and even if there had been the development of a middle ground, Okello might still have launched his genocidal holocaust.

IV

The general context of the massacres in Rwanda was the introduction of a western-type political democracy, preparatory to independence, in a society structured on diametrically opposed principles. Whatever the terms used to describe Rwanda society, whether feudal, totalitarian, caste, racial domination, the central conception was of inequality and rigidity. Yet a society of this type must suddenly be transformed into a western democracy, with a party in power and a parliamentary opposition, and an equality in voting and access to office. What a strange conception! To be sure, the Belgian government planned a more gradual evolutionary process than events allowed. It emphasised the need for economic development, as a condition of peace, order, and democracy, and it introduced a variety of reforms to restructure the society, the most crucial being the decree of April 1954 which defined procedures for the dissolution of *buhake*, the bond of vassalage linking the traditional social and political systems. But this change was still new and raw, and often disorienting or frustrating of the expectations it had aroused. (See discussion by Lemarchand, 1970: 127-133). Moreover, *buhake* proved so tenacious that it survived the revolution, becoming an instrument of patronage and power in the hands of the new political elite. The political reforms had the effect then, of introducing a political system profoundly at variance with the social structure of the society. There was little social basis for conciliation, for a middle ground of cooperative relations under the stimulus of mass politics offering the prize of a new racial domination to replace the old.

There are, however, a number of areas in which the analyst might have seen some social basis for political cooperation or mediation. In respect to the economy, I have argued (1974: 123-126, 183-189) that Rwanda was a society close to the subsistence level, experiencing periodic famine (it is indeed one of the poorest countries in the world), and that many Tutsi and Hutu must have shared a similar economic situation. I offered some evidence in support of this contention from a survey by Leurquin. d'Hertefelt (1960c: 114-115) refers to the pauperisation of an important segment of the Tutsi caste as a result of changes introduced by the Belgian administration. Munyangaju (1959: 35-36) writes of some levelling at the present time (1959), more the exception than the rule, arising partly through the social mobility of Hutu, but more often through the practical assimilation of impoverished Tutsi to the life style of Hutu. Of more significance, he shows that only a small number of clans and families enjoyed the prerogatives of power and privilege. Tutsi members of other clans and their corresponding families were as subject to discrimination as Hutu, save that the class of toiling Tutsi (*la classe laborieuse Tutsi*) might conserve the hope of eventually benefitting from an almost miraculous promotion, or from an opportunity for an administrative position, or from protection against vexatious exactions (pp. 21-22). Thus, if Rwanda society is viewed from the point of view of the distribution of Tutsi and Hutu in its economic structure, rather than from the point of view of the racial incumbency of important positions, then there is evidence for some similarity in economic situation between Tutsi and Hutu, more particularly at the lower levels, though it seems impossible to give any reliable estimate of its extent.

Common clan membership of Tutsi, Hutu, and Twa might have provided a basis for cooperative action. The Abbé Kagamé, scholarly protagonist of Tutsi interests, refers to what might be described as a mystic contact within the kinship group, heralding the fusion of the populations in a national unity (1957: 271).

Common religious affiliation would surely provide a bond. By the 1950s, more than 50% of the population of Rwanda was Catholic, and the predominant role of the Catholic Church in education greatly enhanced the significance of its religious teachings. Common participation in the cult of Kubandwa in central and southern Rwanda should similarly have drawn together the initiates of the different sections, in contrast to the Nyabingi cult in the North, which was a messianic type religion, contesting first Tutsi and then colonial domination.

Education, more particularly at the higher levels and in the same institutions, would presumably have shaped some common interests and perspectives and provided a common universe of discourse. Higher education in the past had been virtually a Tutsi monopoly, but this was beginning to change by the late 1950s. Already a small group of Western educated Hutu intellectuals had emerged, and appreciable numbers of Hutu students were enrolled in the elite Groupe Scolaire, Astrida (Lemarchand, 1970: 138).

One might add to this inventory, the possibilities for mutual understanding in the possession of a common culture and in opportunities for contact in non-segregated patterns of settlement. Whilst there were subcultural variations in the north, giving rise to a measure of cultural pluralism, the south and centre were relatively homogeneous culturally:[8] and though there were peripheral areas almost entirely Hutu, and though Tutsi infiltration and breaking up of the clusters of Hutu households in the northern region was rare, in other parts of the country Hutu, Tutsi, and sections of the Twa lived intermingled on the same hills, in the same geographic entities (see

8. Lemarchand (1970: 98) writes that central and southern Rwanda produced a relatively well-integrated society, a system of functional integration, legitimised by common values expressed in the traditional mythology. D'Hertefelt (1960: 450-453) draws attention to the marked heterogeneity underlying the linguistic unity, the relative cultural uniformity and the political centralisation. He distinguishes cultural variation between castes from cultural variation between regions. In the centre, acculturation had greatly reduced the differences between castes. In peripheral areas of Tutsi penetration, such as the north, there was an increase in cultural variation not only between castes but also between regions.

Munyangaju, 1959: 32 and Lemarchand, 1970: 267).

This may seem an impressive list of possible social and cultural bases for political conciliation. But many of these areas also had their negative potentialities, or seem not to have been of particular significance. At the level of the economy, the view presented here that many Tutsi and Hutu must have shared a similar economic or class situation is controversial. Some analysts argue that there was a sufficient agricultural surplus for redistribution in favour of the Tutsi, giving rise to differences in the standard of living, which might seem negligible to the outsider, but were significant for members of the society. Or they suggest that Tutsi opportunities for social mobility, however rare for the great majority of Tutsi, nevertheless represented a difference in life chances. However this may be, even if we accept the argument of appreciable similarity in class situation, there are many steps intervening between common class situation and joint action. Community of interest and of action are not an automatic consequence of similarity in occupation, standard of living, and prospects for advancement. On the contrary, they need to be taught, developed, cultivated, and seasoned in action. Even so, in plural societies, with long-standing ethnic or racial division, there is no certainty that these identifications of peasant or working class solidarity will be accepted. On the contrary, where there is a scarcity of resources, the probability is that the ethnic or racial identifications will prevail or be readily activated.

The mythic unity of the clan may have been more an item of Tutsi ideology than a significant social factor. Munyangaju (1959: 33-34) takes the view that the propagation of the idea of clan unity was an effective Tutsi strategem for securing the loyalty of naive Hutu and Twa: de Heusch (1966: 143) writes that the common clan membership did not in any way abolish the social barrier and he quotes Maquet to the effect that members of a clan belonging to different socio-racial groups did not show solidarity, and behaved as total strangers toward each other.

At the level of religious institutions, the cult of Kubandwa was practiced by both Hutu and Tutsi. It took the form of an initiation ceremony, organised within the lineage. Its significance for intercaste relations is quite controversial. De Heusch (1964b: 136ff) views it as a largely Hutu cult, which had revolutionary potentialities as a contestation of the caste structure, but resulted in practice in a flight from reality, providing psychosocial therapy for its participants. Vidal (1967: 153) interprets the cult as a ritual enactment of subjection to a royalty exercising power over the castes. However, both authorities and Maquet (1961: 149-150) are quite definite that separation of castes was maintained in the practice of the · cult. In any event, the Kubandwa cult was in retreat under the advance of Christianity, which was the major religious force in the revolutionary period.

Catholicism, in particular, exerted a powerful influence on political developments in Rwanda at many different levels. Initially the Catholic Church was committed to Tutsi supremacy in conformity with the Belgian policy of indirect rule. But this changed in the 1950s as European clergy gave their support to the movement for Hutu emancipation.[9] The Apostolic Vicar for Rwanda, Mgr. Perraudin, played a specially partisan role, his name evoking 'diametrically opposed, though equally emotional, reactions from Hutu and Tutsi, being viewed by the former as nothing short of a saviour, and by the latter as a hateful sycophant, guilty of spreading racial hatred and violence among the people of Rwanda' (Lemarchand, 1970: 107). A song circulating prior to the November 1959 uprising specifically named him an enemy of Rwanda (Makuza, Brussels Colloquium, 1960: 38).

Under these changing conditions of political commitment, Catholic teaching would have become a source of revolutionary sentiment, seminaries serving as nurseries for Hutu leaders. The authors of the Hutu Manifesto were a loose network of young people who had attended the same seminary (Lemarchand, 1970: 150). Gitera, founder of APROSOMA, and elected President of

9. 'Anglican missionaries continued to give unrelenting moral and material support to the Tutsi group' (Lemarchand, 1970: 133n).

the National Assembly in October 1960, combined traditional
appeal with Christian ethic and symbolism (d'Hertefelt, 1960c:
126-127). Kayibanda, another seminary student, founder and
president of PARMEHUTU, later Prime Minister, then
President, of Rwanda, served as personal secretary to the
Apostolic Vicar of Kabgayi, and edited the only really significant
newspaper in the vernacular, the Church-sponsored *Kimanyateka*,
which gave increasing coverage to Hutu grievances
(Lemarchand, 1970: 108). In general, the Catholic Church
greatly contributed to the stirring up of Hutu political
consciousness by allowing control over local channels of
communication to pass into the hands of Hutu politicians, and by
assisting them to articulate and propagate their demands (*ibid.*).

The influence of the Catholic Church would certainly have
been quite varied. Most of the local priests were Tutsi and strong
supporters of the monarchy. Some contributed to the
development of a Tutsi-oriented cultural nationalism, linked to
the movement for colonial independence. There must surely have
been attempts at mediation at different levels, as shown for
example in the letter of 11 October 1959 in which the Apostolic
Vicars of Nyundo and of Kabgayi warn against the 'non-
Christian spirit of racial hatred' in pronouncements of the Hutu
Social Party (Nkundabagenzi, 1961: 140). There must also have
been some influence of the Christian ethic on inter-personal
relations between Tutsi and Hutu. One can only suppose that at
times conflict was tempered with Christian charity, massacre
with mercy. There are accounts in the literature of individual acts
of heroism, of martyrdom almost joyfully embraced.[10] They
express the triumph of Christian faith over unspeakable cruelty
and atrocity. But it would seem that in general, the Christian
ethic was not a significant restraining influence, and that indeed
the Catholic Church contributed to the polarisation of race
relations.

As to the influence of education, a distinction must be drawn in

---

10. See the deeply moving account of Norman Wingert, *No Place to Stop Killing*
(Chicago: Moody Press, 1974).

terms of period, level of education and ethnic group. Lemarchand (1970: 134ff) describes the early Tutsi educated elite as representing 'an "upper crust" whose claims to superiority were based on a combination of caste privileges and educational qualifications'. The effect was to increase the rigidity of the system. Later generations of educated Tutsi from the Groupe Scolaire d'Astrida were 'progressive', recognising the need for social and political reform, but still attached to the values of their traditional culture, which they saw as sufficiently flexible for adaptation to the requirements of political modernisation. As to the Hutu educated elite, the 'radicals', the more intransigent, were those still at the seminary on the eve of revolution: 'lacking the necessary qualifications to gain entry into the administration through the normal channels, they saw little attraction in the prospect of social reform. Only by a total commitment to the cause of the revolution, to the creation of an entirely new society, could they hope to make their mark in life outside the Church' (140). The moderates were usually those who, after a brief stay at the seminary, studied at the Groupe Scolaire, hoping to secure a post in the administration. Lemarchand adds the comment that these divisions were held in check prior to the revolution by their common opposition to the privileges of the ruling caste, and 'their unanimous adherence to the Christian values of equality and freedom'. At the level of educated elite leadership, there would seem to have been some basis for conciliation between the more highly educated Tutsi of a later generation and the Hutu graduates of the Groupe Scolaire.

Cultural uniformity certainly influenced the course of the revolution (see Kuper, 1974: ch. 5). Patterns of voting in the areas of long-established Tutsi dominance showed the influence of loyalties across ethnic lines. Even in the communal elections of 1960 there still remained substantial pockets of resistance to the spread of revolutionary ideas. The incendiarism of the peasant jacquerie in November 1959 largely spared these areas. But in the end, they, too, were overtaken by genocidal violence, the massive massacres following the Bugesera invasion being launched in the prefecture of Gikongoro, which contained within its boundaries the former royal residence of Nyanza (see Lemarchand, 1970: 224fn.).

As to the effect of the intimacy of non-segregated residential patterns as a basis for cooperative relations, the only relevant information I have is that the incendiarism of the peasant jacquerie was generally the work of local groups, who would pass on the torch, like a relay team, to other local groups. I would suppose that, in time, vandalism and theft and finally slaughter must have become embedded in the pattern of interethnic neighbour relations.

Though the social basis was not very supportive, there were nevertheless attempts at the political level to bring the groups together. Hutu and Tutsi did not confront each other in the political arena as monolithic blocs. Regional and ideological differences introduced some variation in the forms of political action, and of polarisation, between Tutsi and Hutu.

I have already referred to Hutu political affiliation across ethnic lines. It was expressed in Hutu participation in Tutsi counteraction at the time of the November risings, and Hutu support for Tutsi in the 1956 elections and the communal elections of 1960. This electoral support was especially marked in areas of long established Tutsi domination, and is, of course, related to the regional differences between the plural society of the north and the *seemingly* integrated society of the centre and the south. In the north, the revolution took the form of a reversion to the political status quo of Hutu traditional structure, while in the central and southern regions, it had more the quality of a social revolution (see Lemarchand, 1966b: 609-610). Munyangaju (1959: 26) refers to ideological differences between Hutu politicians on the issue whether the campaign should be directed against all Tutsi indiscriminately, or against the high Tutsi aristocracy, or against the abuses committed by some of the representatives of the Tutsi race. APROSOMA took its stand initially as a party representative of the poor, Hutu and Tutsi, in a programme of democratic political and economic reform. Its reformist gradualist outlook attracted the professionally trained

among the Hutu. The target was not the Tutsi people, but rather
the abuses of the system; according to d'Hertefelt (1960c: 127), a
considerable proportion of impoverished Tutsi looked hopefully
to Gitera, the founder of APROSOMA. Munyangaju (1959: 29)
also emphasises the potential significance of APROSOMA as a
rallying point for the Tutsi and Hutu masses. But Gitera soon
moved to an identification with Hutu interests, thereby changing
'the stratification problem from a large social to a narrow caste
basis' (*ibid.*), and alienating potential supporters. In June 1960, in
a strange manifesto, Gitera declared that APROSOMA was
now to be known as UHURU, that is, Union of the Hutu of
Rwanda-Urundi, and that its new programme included a
commitment to the immediate and absolute independence of each
race from the other (Nkundabagenzi, 1961: 258-261). The party
proved unstable in other ways, entering into a common front
first with PARMEHUTU and RADER against UNAR, and
then later, in November 1960, moving into a common front with
RADER and UNAR against PARMEHUTU.

Ideological diversity also characterised the Tutsi movements
(see d'Hertefelt, 1960c: 132-133). Convinced, of their natural
right to rule by reason of conquest and divine ordinance, the
conservative (extremist) wing, such as the Grand Bagaragu,
sought the restoration of traditional institutions. The progressives
included leading Tutsi officials, among them Chief Bwanakweri,
who crystallised the opposition to the Mwami and founded
RADER as a middle-of-the-road party. RADER functioned as a
small party, with particular appeal to the educated, bringing
together Tutsi and Hutu, but primarily it seems Tutsi students, in
a programme of political democratisation and economic reform.
The main political force among the Tutsi was, however, that
which UNAR came to represent as a party committed to cultural
nationalism, immediate independence and social reform, and as
the embodiment of national unity. However, the ideological
expression of this national unity in the denial of the reality of
racial difference and of racial discrimination, in the belief in the
mythical community of common ancestry and in loyalty to the
Mwami as symbol of unity, became less persuasive when UNAR

launched terrorist attacks against Hutu leaders and the Mwami identified with Tutsi interests.

These ideological differences took a somewhat different form as Tutsi refugees poured into neighbouring countries. Lemarchand (1970: 198-206) describes the factionalism among the refugees, with shifting lines of cleavage between fanatical monarchists, conservatives and progressives, and between activists and politicians. He discusses the strategic divisions on the question whether to subvert the regime from within, or by force from without; and he analyses the great rift which developed between the internal leadership of the movement, based in Rwanda, and the leadership-in-exile. Since the cycle of raid and massive reprisal must have been obvious enough, the seemingly reckless disregard for the safety of Tutsi still living within Rwanda may have been, in some measure, a calculated punishment for accommodation with the PARMEHUTU regime. The activists who, implacable in their enmity, launched the raids, and the UNAR internal leaders who condemned the raids and pledged loyalty to the Rwanda government, represented the extremes of ideological divergence among the Tutsi.

In the gross process of polarisation, however, the conciliators, the mediators, were either physically wiped out or expelled or otherwise eliminated. The major antagonists in the process of polarisation were UNAR, committed to immediate independence, and PARMEHUTU, seeking democratisation prior to independence. The ideological polarisation, however, merely masked the reality of a struggle for power between Tutsi and Hutu; and both sides (and the dynamic of the conflict itself), eliminated the middle ground.

Tutsi progressives were already under attack prior to the events immediately preceding the November uprising. The Mwami had taken action against the progressive movement forming under Chief Bwanakweri, transferring him to a remote area, when he began to initiate reforms in his chiefdoms. At the first meeting of UNAR in September 1959, the president of the party called on the population to combat the administration, the leaders of the movement for the promotion of Hutu, and those Tutsi who were seeking democratic collaboration. According to Makuza (Brussels Colloquium 1960: 44, 50), UNAR launched the initial acts of intimidation and terrorism mainly against Tutsi progressives: and in November 1959, APROSOMA, RADER, and PARMEHUTU protested to the Trusteeship Council of the United Nations and to the Belgian Parliament against 'the repeated acts of rebellion, of defamation, of intimidation and of terrorism, directed principally against the Hutu leaders and the Tutsi progressives, from the time of the meeting (of UNAR) on 13 September to 2 November 1959, when the populace exploded in fury'. UNAR members applied the pejorative term APROSOMA also to Tutsi progressives (Bushayija, 1960: 507).

Inevitably, the middle-of-the-road party, RADER, proved unstable, caught between the pressures on both sides, and vulnerable to the influence of the Tutsi elite. Internal dissension also weakened the party. In July 1960, RADER withdrew from the common front, in disagreement with the Hutu parties on the issue of the monarchy and complaining of persecution by PARMEHUTU in the communal elections. Little more than a month earlier, the co-founder of RADER had expressed his satisfaction in the party's relationship with Hutu, explaining that members of the party were able to return to their lands, and were well received. 'This is to say that the Hutu revolt was not a racist revolt. They were protesting against the regime' (Nkunda-bagenzi, 1961: 254). In the end, however, it was the Hutu who delivered the final blows to the Tutsi progressives.

The assault came partly from the masses, acting, one supposes without particular animus against the progressives, but sweeping them into the general category of oppressor, Tutsi. Given the near monopoly of important positions by sections of the Tutsi, and the abuses of the system, there would have been some tendency for Hutu to identify all Tutsi with the regime. The political attacks launched by PARMEHUTU leaders against the Tutsi must certainly have assisted this process (Munyangaju, 1959: 29). Moreover, in the impetuous movement of mass incendiarism, it was hardly to be expected that the marauding

bands of peasants would draw nice distinctions between their
potential victims on the basis of their political convictions. On
the contrary, they would tend to see them all as appropriate
targets.

Makuza, in his comments at the Brussels Colloquium (1960:
64-65) provides some justification for this process in the
November rising.

In almost all the regions, those who launched false rumours and defended the
politics of UNAR, were Tutsi. The problem was therefore to identify the
supporters of UNAR among the Tutsi. Then one saw that individuals who
had previously shown themselves progressive and were defended by the Hutu
masses, now surrendered to the attacks of UNAR, reversing their position to
defend UNAR politics. The Hutu then said: You see that those we ourselves
defended against their own brothers, turn their arms against us. Are not the
others like them? It is in this way that the masses came to confuse the
progressives with others, declaring that if they were all killed, the Hutu
would be sure to remain. This was the basis for massive exclusions
(expulsions), because one said Tutsi + UNARIST = UNARIST = Devotee
of the Mwami and supporter of the Kalinga.

No doubt, this was a step in forming the polarising perspective of
Tutsi = UNARIST = Enemy. But the masses would not have
needed much justification to make the equation. It was no doubt
also arrived at quite spontaneously and pragmatically, rapidly
becoming established as a routine. In the region of Biumba, at the
time of the United Nations visiting mission in March 1960, Hutu,
in 'a veritable human tide drove out the Tutsi without distinction
as to their views', attacking Tutsi progressives in the same way as
Tutsi UNARISTS (Special Resident, Brussels Colloquium, 1960:
60-61). And when the period of genocidal attacks arrived, with
the slaughtering of whole families, women and children
included, the final point had been reached in the indiscriminate
attribution of collective responsibility and in the indiscriminate
subjection to the collective punishment of most horrible atrocity.

If there was an involuntary, spontaneous quality to the attacks
of the masses on the Tutsi of all political persuasion, the
elimination of the middle ground by the PARMEHUTU

politicians was quite deliberate. It was part of the attack on all political opposition, whether Hutu or Tutsi, by a new power elite. The PARMEHUTU Government imprisoned Gitera, leader of APROSOMA, in August 1962, for a period of five months, and it suppressed, in February 1963, the two ministries accorded to UNAR representatives under agreement with the United Nations (de Heusch, 1964a: 421). But it was the raids from the outside which provided the occasion for the liquidation of Tutsi leaders.

The invasion of July 1962 seems to have played an important part in polarising relations, hardening the attitudes of the officials against Tutsi. This is easy to understand since the officials had been a special target of attack in raids from neighbouring territories, which threatened their newly won power. In the July raids, the invaders were repulsed by the National Guard. Among the papers carried by the leader of the raid were found plans for the assassination of the president, information that some of the invaders had been trained in Morocco, and a photo of the leader in company with Russians at Cairo. 'This was enough to raise the spectre of communism. From that time onward, every Tutsi, in the interior as well as the exterior, and whether or not he had disavowed these military adventures, and whether or not he had broken with the Mwami in exile, every Tutsi ... will be considered as an enemy of the Republic and as a potential communist, an ally of the "terrorists" of the exterior. Such is the myth elaborated in official circles' (de Heusch, 1964a: 422).

The Bugesera invasion provided the final provocation, and the occasion for genocide. An ultimate form of settlement may perhaps already have been in preparation, since from 20 October, according to de Heusch (1964a: 424), the national police, guided by PARMEHUTU militants, were imprisoning and torturing UNAR militants in Nyanza. Following the invasion in December, the authorities not only slaughtered local UNAR leaders, who had condemned the raids and pledged support for the government, but also the President Bwanakweri and Vice-President Ndazaro of RADER, party of conciliation. The massacres provided the finishing touch. There were no longer parties to the conflict. There was no longer a conflict to mediate. There was no longer a role for mediators, and presumably there were no longer mediators. The Hutu of Rwanda had discovered for themselves, on a smaller scale, the Turkish solution to the Armenian problem.

Is it thus that history unfolds as the story of human freedom?

V

The problem of the elimination of the middle ground becomes significant in societies or situations of extreme pluralism, where sharp discontinuities in the structures of the society are superimposed on each other, and there is an accumulation of issues of conflict affecting the same parties. Burundi, at the time of the introduction of constitutional reforms, seemed quite remote from this state of pervasive cleavage. The major line of division was not ethnic, and many relationships bound members of different ethnic groups to each other in a complex system of alliances. The society appeared to offer a variety of bases for national integration under political independence. Yet the power of ethnic conflict swept all these aside, once competition for office began to be defined in ethnic terms, and violence became established as final arbiter.

UPRONA had made a promising start as a party of national integration, but with the murder of Prince Rwagasore, ethnic solidarities gave rise to ethnic factions within the party and the struggle for leadership became a source of ethnic polarisation. The Mwami seemed ideally placed to promote integration. In contrast to the situation in Rwanda, the institution of the monarchy was not associated with ethnic hegemony, nor integrated into the ethnic structures. Being somewhat detached from the ethnic competition, and a venerated symbol of national unity, the Mwami could act as arbiter, and for years he balanced the rival ethnic claims. But he did not bring about an accommodation between the parties. Nsanze (1970: 43-45, 64) charges that the Mwami exploited and manipulated the ethnic conflicts. Lemarchand (1970: 472-475 and 1966a: 326-335) comments that the Mwami played off the ethnic groups against each other in the building up of his own power, but eventually became identified with Tutsi interests; and that the dynastic families also lost their reputation for neutrality and became involved in propaganda and mob action.

Hutu had participated actively in the politics of the country, even holding the position of prime minister. They constituted a majority in the provisional government of 1960, and again in September 1965, when seven of the ten ministers were Hutu. But they were not able to translate their political participation into effective power, and Hutu frustration led to the abortive coup in 1965. Sections of the Tutsi had already injected violence into the conflict at a very early stage, and under the spur of events in Rwanda, violence and counter-violence, assaults, murders, massacres set in motion the process of polarisation which led to the Tutsi genocide against Hutu in 1972, and to the massacres of May 1973 in reprisal for raids launched by Hutu refugees in Tanzania.

Starting then with a social situation seemingly so favourable to conciliation, the conflict took such a violently destructive form as to leave no room for mediators or mediation; and today it is difficult to see a basis for reconciliation. It is not as if the genocidal massacres act, like vicarious participation in a stage tragedy, to induce a chastening catharsis. Between the groups there now lie the added horrors of genocidal massacre, of anguished mourning for family and friends, of exile and destitution. How then are Hutu and Tutsi to relate to each other in a society in which the basic reality seems to be defined as a choice between engaging in massacre or being the victims of massacre? And how can the executioners and the survivors find security and dignity, and a willingness to cooperate, in the social reconstruction of their society? Can one hope for a change of heart in the regime? That most dedicated Christian missionary, Norman Wingert, writes (1974: 118-119) of encouraging signs in Rwanda, where the new president had publicly called for Rwandans to 'love one another without regard to tribal or regional differences', and where Tutsi refugees feel sufficiently reassured by the change of government to return to their country. In Burundi, he finds cause for encouragement in information received from the U.S. Department of State that the Burundi government plans to include 'limited Hutu participation in public affairs'. He is encouraged also by reports that the government is reimbursing Hutu widows for houses damaged or destroyed during the reprisals, and that relief goods are getting through to some of the 50,000 Hutu widows and their children. The president, it seems, had remarked to a *Time* reporter with visible emotion: 'I am trying to consolidate the unity of my country, and would like to see our brothers outside our borders return and settle down to a guaranteed peace.' Yet the overall picture he presents is sombre, and he relies ultimately on divine intervention.

In the Burundi situation, then, let us put God where He belongs. There are the cycles of Tutsi-Hutu killings. *But there is a God!* Let us pray to God for an unforeseen, beyond-human intervention that will put an end to the fratricide. God may do the impossible and thus extend the opportunity for the preaching of the good news throughout the land (117).

Jeremy Greenland, a student of Burundi society, offers an even more sombre perspective on the possibility of reconciliation. He takes a different view from Wingert regarding the distribution of relief, commenting that 'the vast number of Hutu widows and fatherless children are classed as "rebels" and are ineligible for aid' (*Issue*, vol. V, no. 2, Summer 1975, 3). He argues that the campaigns to induce Hutu students to return to Burundi should be viewed with extreme suspicion, given the government's record of arresting and killing those Hutu who return home (*ibid.*). The reality for him is the determination of the government to maintain the *status quo* of Tutsi supremacy, but to put a more acceptable and human and benevolent face on this reality. Among the changes he lists, which I would describe as largely cosmetic, and this seems to be Greenland's conception, are an emphasis on national unity through the role of the president, the increased status of the UPRONA party, and propaganda; improvements in the relations between Burundi and Rwanda, suggesting that, with the Rwandese now '*un peuple frère*', Tutsi and Hutu should be able to cohabit in the same peaceful way;[11] reforms in the educational system; and finally the demotion of Tutsi considered to have been most active in organising the repression against Hutu, in a seeming attempt 'to efface the confrontation of 1972'. As an alternative to the policy of Tutsi domination, touched up in more acceptable guise, he suggests that the Tutsi voluntarily extend a share of their power to Hutu in a form which would convince Hutu exiles of the genuineness of the new policies; and he points to the catastrophes threatened by Hutu ‑ embitterment, and by the anticipated demographic expansion, with its attendant food crises.

I find it difficult to believe that the Burundi government can be persuaded by such arguments, no matter how cogent they may seem to the outside observer. Nor is the government likely to be more responsive to the appeals of the Catholic Church in Burundi after the massacres than it was before the massacres.[12] The government's possibilities of choice are limited by its own polarised definitions of the situation and by the reality of polarisation, which it carried to the extreme of massive genocidal massacres. Nor can I see how Hutu exiles can accept reassurances from the government, so that they will be willing to abandon guerilla action and risk their lives by returning home. The Burundi government is notoriously untrustworthy, treachery being well-established in the mores of the regime.[13] The

---

11. Lemarchand, in a paper on 'Les incidences extérieures de la crise' at the Brussels International Colloquium in December 1974, sees some possibility of a basis for movement to conciliation in the following circumstances: (i) Change of government in Rwanda and the more open policy of the new government; (ii) Some affinity between the elites in the two territories, both being drawn from intermediate groups, the Hima in Burundi and the Kiga in Rwanda; and (iii) More encouraging signs of the possibility of cooperation between Burundi, Rwanda and Zaíre.

12. See Weinstein and Schrire (1976: 27-28, 44, 53 and 61) for reference to protests by the Catholic Church.

13. Weinstein and Schrire (1976: 25) draws attention to a traditionally valued pattern of action in Burundi society known as Ubgenge, an art of intrigue and treachery. This is, of course, by no means unique to Burundi.

provisions of the new constitution of Burundi (July 1974), affirming adherence to the Universal Declaration of the Rights of Man, guaranteeing 'the inviolable and inalienable rights of man', extending equal rights to all Barundi and outlawing racial discrimination and ethnic propaganda, evoke memories of the chill and ominous laughter in a Grand Guignol spectacle. The only credibility in the constitution lies in the numerous provisions entrenching the powers of the president.

Even if the government should sincerely desire to cooperate with Hutu in restructuring Burundi society, and even if the government were willing to forego its strategies of culling Hutu elite or potential elite every few years, could it really control the processes of atrocity it has unleashed? There is a letter from ex-President Kayibanda of Rwanda to his dear friend President Micombero of Burundi at the time of the 1972 massacres, in which he writes of the murder of simple folk, the murder of schoolchildren, the burning of foreign automobiles as counterproductive, above all if Burundi were to pursue the path of butchery. Drawing on his own experience, he counsels President Micombero to halt the killing, which does neither Africa nor Burundi development any good; and he adds: 'We realise that that is very difficult, once the murderers have taken to the road' (Melady, 1974: 108-110). And who would know better than Kayibanda!

On the assumption that within Burundi, the sole basis for cooperation between Tutsi and Hutu is Hutu acquiescence in Tutsi domination, and indeed an almost total subordination, then the only possibility for initiating processes of conciliation and of joint endeavour for social change would seem to lie outside Burundi. There are now over 100,000 Hutu refugees in neighbouring territories, with little prospect of being absorbed into their host societies. The raids they launch in Burundi set off polarising cycles of atrocity and massacre. In a discussion of alternatives to violence, Weinstein (1975: 17-22) suggests that United Nations agencies and foreign powers, who provide assistance to Burundi, might devise programmes for a wider unit, inclusive of both Burundi and the refugee communities, and that international development programmes could also include refugee areas. The effect might be to reduce somewhat the threat of refugee raids, by improving the conditions of refugees and by providing a measure of employment. The cessation of raids would presumably lower the level of Tutsi insecurity in Burundi, and thus create conditions slightly less unfavourable to social change. At the same time, there would be opportunities for joint endeavour by Tutsi and Hutu in promoting the more inclusive programmes. A somewhat similar consequence would result from the development of regional projects, in which Hutu and Tutsi participate with representatives of neighbouring countries, thus transcending the narrow confines of their polarised prison.

In the absence of intervention, there would seem to be no possibility of escape from the interminable reciprocities of massive violence. With intervention, as by the United Nations, it might conceivably be possible to launch regional projects or to establish, and to maintain, a heavily policed separation: but given the policies the great powers pursue of battening on divided societies, the probability is that the great.powers will stoke the conflict, in the hope of securing some perhaps quite illusory gain. In the light of these threatened holocausts, the suggestions which are put forward for building some social basis for conciliation and change seem desperately slight. Perhaps the best hope for peaceful cooperation lies after all in the granting of Norman Wingert's prayer that God accomplish 'the impossible' by 'an unforeseen beyond-human intervention'.

Part Three

CONCLUSIONS AND REFLECTIONS

9

The Process of Polarisation

The process of polarisation of groups within a society implies the presence of both bonds and cleavages. Even in plural societies, dominated by minorities and characterised by extreme discontinuity between social, ethnic or religious groups, there are nevertheless many harmonious relationships which transcend the sectional divisions. The process of polarisation then is a process of the attenuation of the bonds linking together members of different groups, and the accentuation of the divisions between them.

Polarisation is a process which may be traced at the different levels of organisation, of ideology and of interaction.[1] For purposes of the study, I defined it in structural terms, as a process of the increasing aggregation of members of the society into exclusive and mutually hostile groups. It is a process associated with the growth of exclusive organisation and with a simplification of the social structure. There is a corresponding simplification of issues in ideologies, which portray the society as polarised into antagonistic groups with incompatible and irreconcilable interests, rendering inevitable the resort to violence: the ideologies justify revolutionary violence, and the counteraction of repressive violence. I excluded from the concept of polarisation situations of such disproportionate power between the different sections, that the weaker is simply the victim of genocidal massacre, and I emphasised reciprocity in aggressive

1. See the discussion by Bengt Höglund, *Concepts of Conflict*, Report No. 2, Department of Peace and Conflict Research, Uppsala University, 1970, ch. 2.

action and reaction. An intermeshing of violent interaction, an escalation of reciprocal violence (*l'engrenage de la violence*) usually accompanies extreme polarisation. In its course, the mediating relationships and the political ideologies, which might provide a basis for reform of the society, are swept aside as the society moves to cataclysmic violence.

The four case studies selected here are all of extreme violence. In Algeria, the process of decolonisation and of liberation from settler domination, set in motion a massive slaughter, mostly of the Arab-Berber population, and a vast uprooting of peasants from their traditional homes; it culminated in the flight of the European settlers. Following the Bugesera 'invasion' in December 1963, polarisation in Rwanda escalated to the genocidal massacre of Tutsi in parts of the country, accompanied by a great expulsion or flight of survivors. At about the same time, in Zanzibar, massacre and deportation and flight of Arabs completed the virtual elimination of an entire section of the plural society. In Burundi, the genocidal massacres of Hutu followed the increasingly violent struggle for power in the decade after independence. While in Algeria, Zanzibar and Rwanda, polarisation culminated in the expunging of the dominant minorities, in Burundi, Tutsi and Hutu remain locked in deadly embrace.

In my discussion of the course of the conflicts which overwhelmed these societies, I concentrated analysis on major aspects of the process of polarisation. These concern the relationship between social structure and polarisation, or the problem of the extent to which the structure of the society provided a context conducive to the accentuation of division; the expression of polarisation in ideology, bearing in mind the rather uncertain basis for assessing the actual role of ideology in the conflicts; the process of increasing aggregation into hostile groups; the escalation of conflict by reciprocal violence, with terrorism and atrocity; the accompanying contraction of the middle ground of contact, and of mediating relationships and ideologies; and the failure of attempts to restructure the society by peaceful means.

I. The structural factor

An extreme position on the relations between the social structure of the plural society and polarisation is to accord a deterministic significance to the structural factors. This is the approach taken by some of the writers on the Algerian revolution, in their assertions that decolonisation can only be effected by violence, or that there is no possibility of radical change in a colonial system by reform, or that the inevitable course of colonial history is to heighten the initial contradictions between coloniser and colonised. Structural determinism exaggerates, in the service of ideological interests, the constraints and pressures exercised by structural factors. I shall return to this problem later in the discussion of reformism.

The opposite extreme is to minimise the role of broad structural factors, placing the responsibility for polarisation on a struggle for power by elites. This was the conception expressed by the Bishops of Burundi in their pastoral letter when they rejected interpretations of the conflict in terms of nepotism, regionalism, racism or tribalism, and sought its root cause in the egoism of Hutu and Tutsi elites. In reacting to this interpretation, I accepted the significant role of Burundi elites in inflaming and manipulating ethnic hatreds, but I added the qualification that they must have been harnessing real social forces, embedded in the structure of the society, and in the perceptions of many of its members. I argued that the ethnic appeal would have little resonance, unless there was a marked structural basis of division and discrimination. The alternative is to view ordinary people as devoid of judgment and totally manipulable, as in this portrayal of Burundi peasants by one of their elites: 'The miserable masses on the hills ... have no understanding of what you ask them to do. You invite them to kill each other, they will kill each other. You offer them reforms, they applaud. One course of action does not exclude the other' (Bimazubuke, 1965; 22).

An intermediate position between these extremes seems to commend itself to good sense. But there are difficulties in establishing the relationship between the structure of the plural society and the process of polarisation. The relationship emerges with most clarity in Algeria. It hardly needs to be spelt out. The initial lines of division between coloniser and colonised, between conqueror and conquered, were substantially the final line of division in the revolutionary struggle. Algerians had been incorporated into the political system on a basis of inequality; emancipation from the political subordination of the individual called for renunciation of Muslim status; and conflict over these unequal conditions of political incorporation continued in one form or another until the revolution. Algerian nationalist movements and Algerian cultural and religious associations, drawing on a distinctive Algerian heritage, laid a basis for later mobilisation in revolutionary struggle. As to the settlers, they constituted a well-defined stratum, their privileged status arousing resistance to reforms, while their relatively small numbers encouraged affiliation to Metropolitan France in the commitment to the integration of Algérie française.

The role of structural factors is less clear in Zanzibar. The Commission on the 1961 riots praised the traditional racial harmony of Zanzibar before 1957, and this description seems to have been well accepted in evidence before the Commission. The elections of June 1957 proved most peaceful, yet by August 1958 the political conflict had created such tension that, in the words of the Commission, the Zanzibar administration considered that a mere spark would produce a conflagration; and the conflagration was in fact ignited by the 1961 election. The Commission concluded that the bombardment of words which followed the 1957 elections was a major cause of the rapid deterioration of race relations to conflagration point. This is perhaps a reasonable conclusion if one assumes that race relations were harmonious before 1957. But it is precisely this assumption that I think questionable, and I argue that on the contrary, the very rapidity of the polarisation is strong evidence of the significance of the structural factors, and of the reality of deep antagonisms between Mainland Africans and Arabs, though temporarily quiescent. There is objective evidence to support this view in the long history of racial associations and of communal separatism, in the immediate formation of a racially-based political party on the introduction of popular elections, and in the political exploitation of racial prejudice and religious. difference. It is supported further by the nationalist appeals of these two minorities, Mainland Africans appealing to African nationalism, and Arabs to Zanzibari nationalism, each seeking a majority base which would exclude the antagonist. There is also circumstantial evidence in the somewhat distinctive culture of Mainland Africans, and in their distinctive conditions of living on Zanzibar Island, mainly concentrated in the urban area and not forming part of either the traditional Shirazi communities or of Arab society. To these factors must be added the influence on Mainland Africans of the great movement for liberation from alien rule on the African continent.

In Rwanda, there was little to indicate in the council elections of 1953 and 1956, that the society was about to explode in violence. To be sure, the introduction of reforms, and changes in the structure of the society, with the growth of a small stratum of western-educated intellectuals, had stimulated expectations which the course of events frustrated. But the lines of battle were not drawn until the publication of the Hutu Manifesto. This served as a catalyst, by defining the issues in racial terms as a monopoly of political power, and in consequence of social and economic power, by the Tutsi race, and by expressing the aspirations of the Hutu elite and formulating the grievances of Hutu peasants. It was immediately disseminated, and widely discussed, in the settlements on the hills. At the same time, it was debated at meetings of the almost exclusively Tutsi Superior Council, which devised the strategy of a resolution to suppress reference in public documents to Tutsi, Hutu and Twa, as a means presumably of exorcising the phenomenon of ethnic division. Then followed the establishment of a Hutu movement, and the founding of polarising political parties, UNAR and PARMEHUTU, the former a party of Tutsi domination, seeking majority support in the conception ' of a unified Rwanda nationalism, and the latter explicitly dedicated to the promotion of Hutu interests. Generating extreme tension, heightened by terrorism, the conflict between the political parties almost immediately erupted into a Hutu peasant jacquerie against Tutsi.

Again I would argue that the explosive impact made by the Hutu Manifesto, and the rapidity of the mobilisation and escalation to violence, express the deep cleavage between Hutu and Tutsi in Rwanda society. Its structural basis is perfectly clear in the widespread differentiation between Tutsi and Hutu, and in the virtual monopoly by a Tutsi oligarchy of political power. The significance of the structural factor is also very clearly expressed in the different participation of Hutu in the relatively integrated central areas, and in the more divided northern region. It was in the North that the Hutu made their greatest electoral gains, and it was in the North that the jacquerie erupted with maximum force. This different structure of northern life has retained its significance in the internal struggles for power after independence, the northern Kiga now being the dominant section in both army and administration.[2]

The puzzling case is that of Burundi, given Lemarchand's description of the more fluid structure of Burundi society, with many ties between members of different sections, and a complex balance of social forces and political affiliations. It becomes difficult then to interpret the immediate salience of the ethnic cleavage on independence, and indeed in the political struggles preceding independence, and its rapidly increasing dominance as a basis for political division. The alternate view, as presented for example by the students' association MEPROBA, is that the society was characterised by a deep ethnic cleavage and by the oppressive domination of an ethnic minority, much along the lines of Rwanda society. The rapid movement to ethnic political mobilisation and to ethnic violence would then be entirely consistent with the basic structure of Burundi society. But this view fails to explain the significant involvement of Hutu in the government after independence and the policy pursued by the Mwami of balancing ethnic representation.

2. See Lemarchand, 'Les incidences extérieures de la crise,' in Lemarchand and Greenland, eds., *Les Problèmes du Burundi*, pp. 42-43.

Lemarchand emphasises the role of Rwanda as a model, and the influence of false definitions derived from Rwanda society, in creating similar conditions in Burundi, ethnic conflict taking on the quality of a self-fulfilling prophecy. I think this is plausible. I start from the premise that structural factors are by no means determinant, but act rather to restrain or encourage certain forms of political action, and to shape their consequences. It is impossible to gauge the strength of ethnic affiliation, compounded as it is of objective elements and subjective perceptions, and susceptible to rapid change. I am inclined to assume that ethnic identification may have been more salient in Burundi than would appear from the analysis of the many crosscutting relationships. In any event, it was of sufficient strength to be readily activated. Definitions derived from Rwanda society would have injected a powerful charge into ethnic conflict, raising the issue for the minority to the problem not merely of political power but of survival. Thus even if the ethnic division had not been a major cleavage in Burundi society on independence, it could readily be transformed into the dominating political reality, once ethnic membership became a matter of life and death.

II. *Ideology*

The theory that definitions derived from the conflict in Rwanda contributed appreciably to polarisation in Burundi accords considerable significance to the ideological factors. It is, however, very difficult to form any precise impression of the relationship between ideology and action in the present case studies, and this seems to be a general phenomenon in the study of ideology

In my own discussion of ideology, I sketched an ideal type, as it were, of polarising ideologies in plural societies, drawing on political party manifestos, and on statements by leaders and political analysts. I distinguished structurally between the ideologies of the revolutionary majority and those of the privileged minority. The former portray the society as characterised by an uncompromising dualism. This is often linked to a theory, which invests with authority the conception of an inevitably polarising society. The great variety and complexity of relations between members of the dominant and subordinate sections are transformed into a single dichotomy of polarised antagonisms. The issues which divide the sections similarly undergo simplification. There is an exorcising of the possibility of reform, based on characterisations of the social system, but responding also to the structural opportunity for converting numbers into dominating power, and theories of necessity and justification proclaim the inevitability of the resort to violence.

The ideologies of the dominant minority are more pragmatic. They may find supporting argument in theories of evolution, in myth, in conquest, or at the level of monstrous characterisations of the subordinate section. Repressive violence is justified in the name of law and order; it responds to the fear of minorities that the failure to react forcefully will be interpreted as a sign of weakness, and unleash vengeful hordes in murderous assaults. The possibilities of choice are presented in the form of stark alternatives, as in the choice between ruling and being ruled, or in extreme cases, as in Burundi, between engaging in massacre or being massacred, or as in the conception that Algerian independence would confront settlers with the choice between the valise and the coffin.

These ideologies may intermesh at different levels to produce an ideological escalation. Thus both parties may perceive the situation in terms of a dualism, characterised by an irreconcilable conflict of interests, as for example the OAS and extreme sections of the FLN in Algeria. They may both reject reforms, as purely illusory for the revolutionary majority, and as laden with doom for the dominant minority. In consequence, both parties may hold to the conviction that power cannot be shared. The same policy may have quite contrary connotations, as in the equating of assimilation with alienation. The same event may elicit diametrically opposed reactions, thus serving to stimulate further polarisation. Characterisations may ascribe similar qualities to the antagonists, as for example that they are impervious to moral appeal and respond only to violence, and these characterisations then justify violence. So, too, the violence of the one justifies the violence of the other.

The sort of elaborated ideologies I have sketched are only to be found, with varied selection of elements and emphasis, in the discussions of political leaders and theoreticians. Even in the case of these political leaders, it is difficult to gauge the significance of the ideology, whether it follows action in the form of rationalisation, or stimulates it, or is somewhat irrelevant, or indeed pure camouflage. With such leaders as Ferhat Abbas, one is in a better position to assess the role of ideology. There are his many published statements during the long period of his political career, his own autobiographical account, and the changing course of his political commitments as he came to abandon his dedication to liberalism, reform and non-violence, in favour of participation in revolutionary violence. But this is an unusually well-documented case. Generally, the role of ideology in the actions of the leaders is somewhat obscure and largely inferential.

As to the influence of ideology among the revolutionary masses, this is even more difficult to gauge. Moreover it would appear that there can be quite abrupt changes in the consciousness of the populace, as seemingly the case in Burundi. Lucien Goldmann[3] distinguishes between *conscience réelle* and *conscience possible*, suggesting by way of example, that a rigorous inquiry into the social consciousness of Russian peasants in January 1917 would probably have established that the great majority were loyal to the Czar, while at the end of the year this *conscience réelle* had radically changed: the overthrow of the Czar had been a form of possible consciousness at the time of the early survey. The distinction would seem to be relevant for the explanation of the abrupt change among many Hutu in Rwanda from quiescence to jacquerie or from reverence for the Mwami to republicanism.

Reviewing the case studies, Algeria experienced a long process of political crystallisation in nationalist and national cultural

---

3. See my discussion of this point in *Race, Class and Power*, 1974, 99ff.

movements, and one may suppose that the winning over of the Muslim masses to the revolutionary movement was accompanied by an assimilation of the basic political perspectives. In Rwanda, the Hutu Manifesto was a key declaration. It linked Hutu elite goals and the interests of Hutu peasants, and it identified the source of present misery in the Tutsi monopoly of power and privilege (though it could have laid the blame with perhaps greater cogency, but with less political promise for the future, on the Belgian colonial power). The Manifesto acted as a stormy petrel, and I think one can readily accept that it contributed greatly to the transformation of Hutu political consciousness. Probably the same might be said of the bombardment of words in Zanzibar, but this does not seem a persuasive view to me, and I interpret the bombardment of words as an expression of an already extreme antagonism. In Burundi, the massacres in Rwanda and the violence in Burundi, together with peasant economic grievances, would presumably have been the main source of ideologies of ethnic polarisation among the Hutu masses. In cases where ideology is indeed influential, there is no doubt a complex interplay between ideology and action, with action shaping ideology and ideology moulding action.

In general, the influence of ideologies among the masses is to be observed at the verbal level of slogans, phrases, labels, epithets, and at the level of symbols and symbolic events. The process of naming[4] is one of the means for rendering ideologies available for mass action. It is a process by which perspectives are identified or indeed created. Naming simplifies and concentrates an issue, it guides the expression of conflict, it selects targets for punitive reprisals, and it aggregates populations under mobilising slogans.

Thus, where a dominant minority feels vulnerable, and is confronted with a theory of democratic government or an electoral system which gives weight to numbers, it is driven to find majority support.[5] In Algeria this compulsion was

---

4. This discussion of naming derives largely from a talk given by Professor Neil Smelser on 'Psycho-determinants in social movements', at the University of California, Los Angeles, in November 1975.

5. In South Africa, the dominant white minority presumably feels sufficiently strong to resist the pressure for majority support: and the system is of course

crystallised in the commitment to *Algérie française*, in Rwanda it was expressed in the idea of *le peuple tripartite*, in Zanzibar in the polarising conception of *Zanzibari* nationalism. The use of terms, pejorative in themselves, or newly charged with pejorative meaning, canalises aggression. UNAR mobilised hostility against the political party APROSOMA by identifying the term APROSOMA with the traditional conception of enemy of the Mwami. The Swahili terms for African and Arab, with their charged racial connotations, became synonymous with the main political parties in Zanzibar. In Algeria, in the final stages of polarisation, the Muslim waving a green flag, or the anonymous Arab, was perceived as FLN and the Europeans, signalling *Algérie française*, were identified with the OAS. Such emblems as the Kalinga, or the nationalist flag, and commemoration of historic events, as of the French repression at Sétif, symbolise and activate the divided loyalties of the polarising societies. By these means, ideologies are translated into emotive cues eliciting conditioned responses.

III. *Aggregation into hostile groups*

The central process in polarisation is the increasing aggregation of a population into exclusive groups. At the subjective level, aggregation is associated with heightened salience of sectional identity, and with increasing perception in terms of antagonistic racial or ethnic interests. At the objective level, it is expressed in the growth of exclusive organisations, in the superimposition of lines of cleavage, and in the rapid escalation of local and specific disturbances to the level of general, nationwide intersectional conflict.

The development among the subordinates of exclusive

---

profoundly undemocratic. Apartheid policy has sought the answer to the potential threat of numbers by a policy of fragmenting Africans, and by heavy armaments and an increasing reliance on repression. In Northern Ireland, both Protestants and Catholics seek a majority base, Protestants in integration with Great Britain, and Catholics in integration with the Irish Republic, though whenever the British connection threatens their domination, some Protestants have turned to the concept of an independent Ulster where Catholics would still be outnumbered.

organisation, with a crystallising of ideological divergence, took somewhat different forms in the four case studies. In Algeria, it was a long and complex process, through varied and changing political organisations, and through trade union and religious and cultural associations. With the launching of the revolution and the need for mass support against a powerful enemy, Muslim leaders pursued a policy of militant aggregation, sanctioned increasingly by terrifying violence. In Rwanda, the Hutu Manifesto served as catalyst for a Hutu Social Movement, and for the founding of the political parties, APROSOMA, which became exclusively Hutu, and PARMEHUTU, established as an explicitly Hutu party. PARMEHUTU rapidly gained a mass following and conquered the political kingdom, as a result of peasant violence, electoral victories and Belgian support. Starting from the pervasive communalism of Zanzibar society, Mainland Africans organised politically in the Afro-Shirazi party, a *de facto* African party, with variable participation by Shirazi. Political aggregation, and the ensuing conflict, so thoroughly penetrated all aspects of social life that no dimension of social behaviour remained politically (which is to say, racially) neutral. Electoral politics had rapidly raised polarisation to conflagration point. In Burundi, the process of aggregation through political organisation followed an entirely different course. It took some years before a Hutu party gained appreciable electoral strength, and the dominant party UPRONA was a party of national integration, though sharply divided into ethnic factions following the Kamenge episode in which the *Jeunesses Nationalistes Rwagasore* attacked Hutu political and trade union leaders.

In the ordinary course, in independent countries, the dominant minority is already appreciably aggregated in exclusive organisations, and in control of state machinery and institutions to maintain its domination. In a situation of colonial rule, the dominant domestic minority might well be under pressure to organise for decolonisation on terms favourable to the maintenance of its privileged status. The formation of exclusive organisations by members of the subordinate section to promote their special interests, as in Rwanda, would act as an additional spur. The Zanzibar Nationalist Party became the political party of Arab dominance in Zanzibar, taking the form of a national integrating party, exclusive, however, of Mainland Africans. The *Union Nationale Rwandaise* (UNAR) served Tutsi interests in Rwanda, but as a party of national integration, though extremist Tutsi sections, such as the Grand Bagaragu, espoused exclusive political goals. In Burundi, the party of national integration, *Parti de l'Unité et du Progrès National* (UPRONA) was associated, in its inception, with the interests of the ruling dynastic family, and brought together both Tutsi and Hutu.

The position in Algeria was quite different. The French government was not committed to decolonisation. It still conceived of Algeria as incorporated within metropolitan France. The settlers found their security in French dominion over Algeria and in their status as French citizens. Both the metropolis and the local administration served their interests. They had no need to aggregate in new exclusive political organisations. When reforms were imposed under the Statute of Algeria, they were able to emasculate them, in complicity with the administration, by electoral fraud and by the coopting of politically moderate Muslims.

All this changed under the impact of the revolution, as the policies of the French government and the aspirations of the settler leaders began increasingly to diverge, and as the settlers were obliged to confront the reality of Algerian independence. In reaction, settler leaders sought to impose their policies on the French government by forceful means in association with the army. Then, increasingly threatened by the revolution and the fear of impending negotiations with the FLN, and later in response to General de Gaulle's promise of an *Algérie algérienne*, they moved to a policy of integration, but sought Muslim support for the goal of *Algérie française*. The 'miracle' of the fraternisation of May 1958, and the establishment of the *Front de l'Algérie Française* belong to this phase. Finally when the policies of settler domination in an Algeria integrated into France were obviously foundering on the French government's determination to grant independence, settler activists, with strong settler support, moved to the final desperate measure of a terrorist movement, the *Organisation Armée Secrète*. This was an exclusive settler organisation, though initially it seems there was some slight Muslim participation (Henissart, 1970: 162n).

As we have seen, the almost idiomatic response of a dominant minority in a plural society to militant organisation of the subordinates is repression. In Algeria, this took the form of the periodic banning of nationalist organisations and the harrassment of nationalist leaders. In Rwanda, Tutsi elite resorted to the traditional technique of naming their opponents traitors to the country and launching terrorism against them. This is, of course, the same technique used by the South African Government, when it names African nationalist leaders as communists under the Suppression of Communism Act, and then subjects them to the terrorising sanctions of the laws. It is presumably a standard device of repression. There was no direct attempt at repression of the political opposition in Zanzibar, but the leader of the Zanzibar Nationalist Party repeatedly urged the Government to make it an election offence to campaign on racial grounds, and this was clearly directed against the opposition Afro-Shirazi Party, whose basis of organisation and major appeal were racial. Moreover, after the first peaceful communal elections, and the catastrophic defeat of the ZNP, there was some eviction of squatters who refused to support the ZNP, and there was pressure by the party to secure the replacement of Afro-Shirazi labour at the docks. In Burundi, political repression took the form of the systematic culling of leaders and potential leaders, going back to the time of the Kamenge episode in 1961, and extending to the genocidal massacres of 1972 and 1973.

Repression may be of such dimensions as to eliminate opposition entirely or for a considerable period of time. Thus in South Africa, successive governments have kept the challenge of African nationalism at bay for some two generations; and in Burundi, the Tutsi have effectively crushed Hutu opposition for the time being. But repression may be counterproductive for the dominant minority, destroying the possibility of an accommodation of interests, heightening the solidarity of the subordinates, and polarising the society even further as groups begin to organise in desperation for violent confrontation.

Aggregation then may proceed not only by the action of each of the parties, as they consolidate their own support, but as a reaction to the measures taken by the antagonist. The actions of the antagonist, that is to say, may promote the aggregation of one's own population, as in the case of the idiomatic reaction of repression, and particularly of repressive violence, by the dominant section. In polarising societies, and especially under conditions where large sections of the subordinate population are an anonymous mass to the rulers, repressive violence often takes the form of the imposition of collective responsibility, and this has a high potential for aggregating the subordinates. In Algeria, the government imposed collective responsibility as a matter of deliberate policy, penalising whole communities and uprooting vast numbers in massive resettlement schemes. The imposition of collective responsibility also took the form of arrest, interrogation and torture in the search for information on terrorism, with disregard for personal responsibility. Government troops imposed their own forms of collective responsibility in reprisals against whole villages, as did settler vigilante groups and mobs in indiscriminate terrorism and race riots. In Burundi, the government carried the imposition of collective responsibility to its ultimate expression in genocidal massacres, presumably effecting a most extreme polarisation.

Subordinate groups, too, act on the principle of collective responsibility, when their terrorists engage in indiscriminate violence, in the sense that the target is any member of the dominant section, regardless of responsibility, as in the bombing of a cinema or milk bar. The effect is to deny members of the dominant section any choice in affiliation: they are enemies to the death by virtue of origin. What could be a more powerful weapon for the consolidation of their ranks!

IV. *L'engrenage de la violence*

Extreme polarisation may result from non-violent conflicts, but the process is likely to accelerate to much higher levels under the stimulus of violence, particularly when acts of violence so intermesh in reciprocal action as to generate cycles of polarisation. It is as if the whole process moves into high gear.

The initiating of cycles of polarisation may be deliberate or unpremeditated. The subordinates are likely to set cycles of polarisation deliberately in motion, as a means of gaining and consolidating support when they are weak and divided, and as a stimulus to militant struggle. They may make use of the dialectical relationship between provocation and order, when they provoke by their initiating violence the reaction of repressive violence and collective responsibility. Or they may incite the reprisals of extreme counter-atrocity, again on a collective basis, as in the Constantine area of Algeria in August 1955. The manifest injustice of outrageously punitive action against the collectivity is likely to raise the level of revolutionary consciousness and support, and may constitute a point of no return in the process of polarisation. Of course, the strategy may fail if potential supporters reject the methods used by the revolutionaries, or if the authorities react with restraint, or if the repression is powerfully effective.

Many of these cycles of polarisation, however, are not deliberately set in motion, and their consequences are quite unpremeditated. It is inconceivable that the Hutu in Burundi who initiated the violence in 1965 and again in 1972 envisaged the deadly repression and massive reprisals which would follow the failure of their plans. No doubt in most cases, there is a general awareness that reciprocal violence will be set in motion, but the initial provoking acts of violence are committed in the course of the struggle or in a gamble for power, or under the pressure of traumatic events, with reckless disregard for the consequences.

A dominant minority is not likely to engineer these cycles of violence for the sake of polarising its relations with the subordinate majority. They may, of course, provoke violence by the subordinates so as to justify an extreme repressive violence. The authorities are often accused of having deliberately incited the masses. Thus Ferhat Abbas made the charge that the French settlers and administrators in Algeria engineered the Sétif riots as part of a conspiracy to annul the liberalising measures of the French government and to suppress his new political movement, *Les Amis du Manifeste et de la Liberté*. So, too, the student movement MEPROBA charged that the course of events in Burundi seemed to indicate that the peasant jacquerie which served as the pretext for genocide was the result of deliberate provocation, part of a plan conceived years earlier. But the objective in the use of *agents provocateurs* in such situations as these is to suppress the challenge to domination, and not to promote polarisation. The cycles of polarisation arise largely in an unplanned way as a consequence of idiomatic responses based on conceptions of the primacy of law and order, and of the appropriate means for their maintenance. The OAS in Algeria *did* seek to polarise relations between the French government, the French army and the settlers on the one hand, and the Muslims on the other, in an attempt to destroy the possibility of a negotiated peace. The situation had, however, changed profoundly, the settlers no longer being in the position of a dominant minority, but confronted with the imminent reality of Algerian independence and Muslim rule.

The basic process underlying these cycles of polarisation is the reciprocity of violence, corresponding almost to a *lex talionis*. I described it as a great multiplier of acts of violence. It establishes routines of violence and of atrocity. Routinisation raises the level of violence by encouraging the resort to more extreme violence, as the routines become commonplace. The tendency of the more powerful party, usually the dominant section, to react with greater violence has the same consequence. The effect in plural societies is to generalise the conflict, by geographical extension of the arena, and more thorough polarisation of the plural sections. With the generalising of the conflict, there develops an increasing indiscrimination in violence, so that any member of the opposing group becomes a target for atrocity. As the level and scope of violence rise, the stakes are raised, and survival itself may be in issue.[6] The conflict consequently attains its most deadly expression.

We can trace this process of the escalation of conflict by mounting reciprocal violence in three of the case studies. In Rwanda, Hutu responded to the terrorism against their leaders by attacks on property. As the reciprocal violence continued, they moved to attacks on persons, and this prepared the way for the massacres, triggered by the miniscule invasions of refugees. In Algeria, we can trace the escalation of violence in the actions taken by the OAS against its own potential following, and also against Muslims in the process of reciprocal terrorism. At first the OAS used plastic bombs to intimidate, then came the assassination of selected victims, and finally indiscriminate murder of Muslims, provoking retaliation in like form by FLN terrorists, and generating an extreme polarisation. In Burundi, there is almost a direct line of escalating violence, starting with the assassination of Prince Rwagasore, and the attacks of Tutsi youth on Hutu leaders in the Kamenge episode; then follow a period of terrorism and counter-terrorism, and an attempted coup by Hutu with massacres in the countryside and massive reprisals by Tutsi in 1965, leading to the climax of massacre by Hutu and genocide by Tutsi in 1972.

Within this process of escalating violence, we may perhaps identify a point of no return. In Burundi, the Kamenge episode might be viewed as a precipitant of ethnic violence, and the attempted coup and massacres of 1965 as the point of no return. In Rwanda, we might select the peasant jacquerie as the crucial turning point in the rapidly escalating conflict. For Algeria, I suggested OAS terrorism as the point of no return, but this was a culminating phase of the conflict, and I think the term is more usefully applied to an early or intermediate state in the violent encounter between the sections. In any event, I find difficulty with the concept. Its connotation is that the conflict has reached a

6. See discussion by Weinstein and Schrire (1976: 56-58).

point at which the process of polarisation is irreversible, and the final violent confrontations fully determined. I can readily accept the view that if one follows the course of a particular conflict as it actually developed, it may be possible to identify a point of extreme violence, which is followed by the increasing rejection of other possibilities of action than trial by violence, and by the intensification of conflict in escalating cycles of polarisation. The episodes of extreme violence would constitute in the given context of the historically unfolding events a point of no return. I do question, however, any assumption that these 'points of no return' necessarily excluded strategies other than those pursued by the parties, or that they rendered inescapable the continuing resort to more murderous and massive violence.

Reciprocity in violence is by no means an inevitable process. Overwhelming violence may exclude the possibility of reciprocal violence, or the society may provide institutionalised procedures for containing the violence, or leaders may restrain the violent response, as exemplified in the political philosophy of Gandhi, or for that matter, in the discipline exercised by the FLN in the last stages of the Algerian war to frustrate the OAS strategy of provoking Muslim massacres of settlers. The history of Protestant Catholic conflict in Belfast in the nineteenth and twentieth centuries is a reminder that even where the reciprocity of violence has become established as tradition, it need not result in an extreme escalation of the level of violence, though no doubt the British presence may be the crucial restraining factor. However, in societies with a long history of violence along racial or ethnic lines, some equivalence in the capacity for violence of the warring sections, and appreciable discontinuities in structure and culture, the reciprocities of violence are readily set in motion, and easily overwhelm attempts at mediation.

V. *Elimination of the middle ground*

I have assumed that networks of cross-cutting relations between members of the different racial or ethnic sections favour policies of conciliation and mediation. This is, of course, controversial.

Some analysts argue that in plural societies with a differential political incorporation of the racial or ethnic groups, the individual interracial relationships are of little significance. Along similar lines, in a paper on 'conflict regulation in divided societies'. Nordlinger concludes that cross-cutting divisions affecting a significant proportion of non-elites are not generally related to conflict regulation. But Nordlinger is dealing with situations of severe conflict, and not with the processes leading to the severe conflicts, and he has confined his analysis to deeply divided societies, with democratic or, more broadly, open regimes, not a category into which any of our case studies fall. A series of comparative studies of societies, varying in the nature and extent of their cross-cutting relationships and superimposed cleavages, and under different conditions of economic development and political structure, is needed to test the significance of the assumption I make. In the meantime, it seems to me reasonable enough to maintain the position that a social basis for mediation may be found in the intersectional relationships. This is an assumption that the leaders of the polarised groups also make when they select as targets for intimidation or assassination those who seek to bridge the racial or ethnic cleavages in their social relationships or political affiliations.

Many circumstances militated against policies of conciliation and of mediation in Algeria, Rwanda and Zanzibar. Appreciable discontinuities characterised the relations between settlers and indigenes in Algeria, between Arabs and Mainland Africans in Zanzibar, and between Tutsi and Hutu in Rwanda. The small numbers of the dominant sections, both in relative and absolute terms, left them highly vulnerable, and conditions of rapid worldwide change favouring the rule of the majority, rendered the disparity in numbers even more threatening. The antagonists had not been under any pressure to institutionalise procedures for conflict regulation and conciliation, since responsibility for these functions rested largely in the colonial power. Great poverty, limited opportunity and the imminence of radical constitutional change, lent urgency and desperation to the political struggle. In

Zanzibar, there was the additional factor that Mainland Africans were not integrated into the local society, and that many of them must have been anchored in the continent-wide movements for national liberation.

But the societies were not totally devoid of a middle ground. It is difficult, however, to estimate its significance. The presence of continuities in these plural societies raises the quite intractable problem of striking a balance between continuities and discontinuities, between converging and diverging currents, in terms of their potential political contribution. In the Algerian conflict, the French parliament, the Algerian Assembly, trade unions and French educated Muslims all provided an institutional and social basis for cooperative political change. The Shirazi in Zanzibar, as a population intermediate between Arabs and Mainland Africans, seemed ideally placed to mediate between the warring sections, and the sharing of a common language and religion should have eased the task of conciliation. In Rwanda, integration of the sections in the central area, loyalty to the Mwami, the appreciable sharing of a common culture with common religious institutions and non-segregated patterns of settlement in much of the country, might have been the basis for movements of political cooperation. In all three territories, many members of the plural sections shared the same or similar economic conditions.

Yet these potential bases for peaceful change proved to be of little significance. Even in Burundi, the participation of Hutu and Tutsi in the same ruling political party and in government, and in a range of more egalitarian social relationships, failed to arrest the process of ethnic polarisation. In Zanzibar, the Shirazi party proved vacillating and unstable; it could not function as a third force, resistant to the racial antagonisms of the main parties. The Marxist party, UMMA, established in 1963, brought together representatives of many different groups, but it was overtaken by the revolution. In Rwanda, the middle-of-the-road party RADER was caught between the pressures of the main antagonists. Liberals seeking a policy of conciliation in Algeria came under violent attack, as did their counterparts in Rwanda and Burundi. In all four territories, the dynamic process of polarisation increasingly narrowed the middle ground of intersectional relationships, contracting the social basis for mediation, and sweeping aside both the potential mediators and their policies. There is perhaps a Gresham's Law of Conflict, by which 'the harmful and dangerous elements drive out those which would keep the conflict within bounds'.[7]

The elimination of the middle ground signified the failure of attempts to reform the societies by legal means. But there was a different relationship between reformism and polarisation in the four case studies. In Rwanda, Burundi and Zanzibar, the reforms themselves acted as catalysts for polarisation. In Algeria, on the contrary, it was the failure to initiate reforms, or to implement reforms passed by the French parliament, which added fuel to the conflict between the racial groups.

In Burundi, Rwanda and Zanzibar, the political reforms set in motion a fierce struggle for power under the most inauspicious conditions conceivable. In the first place, the accelerated tempo of political change allowed the parties no time to acquire experience in the new political procedures imposed by the colonial powers along the lines of their own metropolitan political systems: nor did they have the time to establish practices of controlled competition in the cooperative relations of a parliamentary system. The colonial rulers had not intended so rapid a process of change, but they were overtaken by the power and urgency of the continental movement for decolonisation. The effect of rapid change was all the more threatening, given the radical nature of the political reforms, totally at variance with both the colonial and traditional systems of rule.

Moreover, the hierarchical nature of social relationships within the societies was similarly at variance with the egalitarian basis of the political reforms. The introduction of greater equality in the society would thus have to be effected from the political structure downwards, so that the political innovations were in fact loaded with revolutionary charge. In addition, discrimination had

7. James S. Coleman, *Community Conflict*, New York, Free Press, 1957, p. 14.

denied the subordinate groups the trained cadres which would have enabled them to compete politically on more equal terms; and fear of an unequal contest, expressed in the plea for democratisation before independence, lent a desperate urgency to the electoral conflicts in Rwanda and Zanzibar.[8] The effect then of the plural structure was to encourage transformation of the radical innovation of representative parliamentary government into a racial (or ethnic) struggle for domination.

Under such adverse conditions of precipitate radical change, it seems quite inappropriate to talk of the failure of reformism. There was hardly a fair test of the possibility of a radical restructuring of the societies by peaceful progressive change. In Algeria, however, political reforms extended over a long period, from the first conferring, in 1919, of citizenship rights on some categories of Muslims, though with renunciation of Muslim status, to the declarations by General de Gaulle in 1958, after almost four years of revolutionary struggle, that Muslims would now enjoy full citizenship rights, as well as greater opportunity for social and economic advance.

The history of constitutional change in Algeria was characterised by the hesitant and compromised and belated legislation of the French government, and by settler resistance to both the passage and the implementation of reforms in Muslim rights until well into the period of revolutionary struggle. It included such major episodes as the defeat of the 1936 Blum-Viollette proposals for extension of the franchise, and the sabotage of the 1947 Statute of Algeria, through electoral fraud and nonimplementation of projected reforms. The term, failure of reformism, is most appropriately applied to this constitutional history, in the sense of the failure to legislate timely and

8. See Lofchie, 1965: 174, 213ff, Lemarchand, 1968: 34-35. In Burundi, the plea for democratisation before independence was made by the opposition party, under the leadership of the rival dynastic house (Lemarchand, 1970: 335-336). Batungwanayo (1972: 20), secretary of MEPROBA, in an analysis of the causes of the genocide in Burundi, comments on Belgian responsibility in precipitously conferring independence, without training sufficient cadres of Hutu, though knowing the social injustices of the country.

substantial reform, the failure to implement effectively the reforms actually introduced, and the failure of the reforms, as belatedly introduced and fraudulently implemented, to arrest the process of polarisation.

VI. *The failure of reformism*

The significance of the failure of reformism in Algeria, for the present discussion, lies not so much in the particular course of events, but in the problem of their inevitability. Was the failure of reformism inescapable under the conditions of the plural structure of Algerian society? Are there general laws governing societies of this type, which make it impossible to transform them by peaceful means? In Chapter 3, I presented some of the arguments in support of the contention that there are in fact such general laws, applicable to the Algerian case. These 'laws' emphasise colonialism as a major restraint, and they derive from the nature of colonialism, argument for the necessity of violence in the process of decolonisation. The argument is clearly untenable.[9] Many colonial societies gained their independence by peaceful evolution. But Algeria constituted a special type of colonial society, combining colonial status with settler domination; and the laws postulated with reference to Algeria can be reformulated in terms of independent societies under the racial or ethnic domination of a minority.

The general laws discussed in Chapter 3 may be stated as follows:

1. Regimes of minority racial or ethnic domination are established and maintained by violence, and they can only be radically changed by violence. (The law may be reformulated to state simply that regimes of minority racial or ethnic domination, which are maintained by violence, can only be radically changed by violence. This would allow for

9. See my discussion of this issue in 'Ideologies of violence among subordinate groups', (1969: 153-167).

cases of minority domination established by means other than violence.)

2. The laws in these societies, and the procedures for making these laws, were designed to establish and maintain an exploitative domination, and there is no possibility of reforming the system of domination by its very own laws and lawmaking procedures.

3. A privileged group will not voluntarily renounce its privileges. Hence reforms will only be introduced under pressure, and the response of the ruling group is to resist this pressure for as long as possible, and to concede the very minimum. In consequence, if reforms are introduced, they are invariably too late to be acceptable, and too modest to be significant.

4. Minority domination constitutes a system. In consequence, harmonious relationships between individuals of the dominant and subordinate sections have little or no significance for political change. The system itself must be overthrown.

5. Inherent in minority racial (ethnic) domination are contradictions, which heighten the antagonisms between the groups, and render inevitable the resort to violence. The deprivations of economic exploitation foster revolutionary challenge; social exclusion and inferior status create bonds of solidarity among the subordinates; cultural repression and denigration stimulate a cultural renaissance; political domination by an alien group engenders the antithetical reaction of nationalism.

These laws are certainly persuasive, when applied to societies with extreme pluralism, where minority domination has been established by conquest, and there are great discontinuities in culture and structure between the dominant and subordinate sections. With pacification, the violence of conquest is transformed into the state and its laws. The government becomes the executive of the dominant race, the laws the instrument of its domination. On the basis of political inequality, there arises a great superstructure of privilege, with dehumanising stereotypes of the subordinate group and other ideologies to justify domination. It is no doubt exaggerated to describe the settler leaders, in the terms used by Ferhat Abbas, as having only a digestive tube, or to say of their regimes that they cannot be humanised, that the human is alien to them. But certainly belief in a common humanity is appreciably alien. Public morality on human rights reflects the distribution of power. It is quite illusory to suppose that an appeal to moral values will be effective. Reforms have to be extracted, painfully: they are often interminably delayed, or derisory, or indeed fraudulent. Challenge to the system of domination is met by the culling of leaders, and the outlawing of their organisations. The violence hidden in the due process of law now becomes quite explicit.

South Africa is just such a society of extreme pluralism, where domination was established by violence, and the violence of conquest translated into law. On the basis of domination by conquest, and of political inequality, there has arisen such a superstructure of oppression that Africans are denied the most elementary human rights in the country of their birth. In an era of worldwide decolonisation, Africans are subordinated to the 'pass' system; pass laws, curfew laws, influx control laws narrowly restrict the times and areas in which they are free to move; their freedom of association is severely curtailed; they have been stripped of political rights in the main institutions of government; they are exposed to arbitrary arrest, and they are prosecuted annually in their hundreds of thousands under the 'pass laws'. In the greater part of South Africa, and above all in the industrial areas, they are virtually denied ownership of the means of production. Discrimination greatly limits their opportunities for employment, and their earnings are a small fraction of the earnings of white workers; the ratio of white to African per capita income was approximately 18:1 in 1973.[10] A vast armory of laws represses African initiatives for political change, destroys their organisations, emasculates their leaders as

10. See *Africa Bureau Fact Sheet*, No. 43, September/October 1975.

'communists', 'saboteurs', 'terrorists' and 'traitors', and generally perfects the instruments of oppression. The rule of law is more appropriately described as rule by law. In seeming confirmation of the thesis that societies of this type are characterised by a heightening of their inherent contradictions in the course of their development, there is an increasing disparity in political power and in absolute real income. To be sure, I have left out of account the satellite African states now being established in undeveloped and fragmented pockets of South Africa, with few resources and limited potentialities; and they do effect some modification of the political structure and perhaps offer a basis for more radical change.

In societies of this type, it seems to me that the leaders of a subordinated group must make a number of pessimistic assumptions, which may perhaps be more extreme than the situation warrants. They must assume that petitions, representations and appeals to moral values will be of no avail. They must banish hope that the regime will make significant concessions under its own initiative. They must reject the possibility of revolutionary change through normal constitutional processes, when they are denied effective political participation, and when the laws themselves legitimate domination. Their strategy should be guided by the conviction that only those changes will be made which the power of their organisation commands; and in mobilising their own resources, they must expect violent repression through the legal machinery of courts, police and army, and the extra-legal violence of citizen groups. But this does not mean a commitment to reciprocal violence or revolutionary violence as the necessary instrument for change. There is neither a logical nor an empirical basis for the conclusion that regimes based on violence can only be overthrown by violence. Nor is there any guarantee that violence will be effective in bringing about radical change, but only the certainty of high costs in human suffering. Yet the possibilities of change by non-violent means are not very encouraging in these societies.

The political history of Ferhat Abbas in Algeria is particularly illuminating. Here was a man totally dedicated to reform and non-violence, and clearly an effective leader. His policy was to seek transformation of social relations within the society, rather than the conquest of political power. Hence his immediate objectives were the social promotion of the masses and the attainment of equal rights. He saw in the politics of equality a basis for integration and the sharing of power and he argued that 'the politics of equality would have had the advantage of drawing together all the inhabitants, of whatever origin, of interweaving their interests, of making them live in symbiosis. This could not have failed to create a community of interests, to weaken racism, and to speed up by peaceful means, the advent of a fraternal Algerian Republic.' In the pursuit of his objectives over many years, he suffered the suppression of his political party, he was subjected to arbitrary arrest and imprisonment, he saw the rejection of initiatives for moderate reforms, and he was exposed to the humiliating spectacle of the cynical sabotage of reforms passed by the metropolitan government. Almost inevitably, he came finally to the conviction that revolutionary violence offered the only hope for liberation from oppression.

If the subordinate group is to organise effectively for non-violent change, there must certainly be a social basis for mustering power. This appears to be quite lacking, at the present time, in the situation of Hutu in Burundi, in contrast to the position in South Africa, where Africans may find leverage in the dependence of Europeans on their participation in industry and in the administration of their own oppression, and where the outside world increasingly exerts pressure for radical change. But given the potentiality for effective mobilisation, there still remains the difficult problem of maintaining the non-violent character of the movement. The relationship between the groups is likely to come quickly to conflagration point, in consequence of the violence of conquest and domination; and movements designed to be non-violent may readily erupt into violence under the provocation of extreme repression.

Perhaps the most crucial condition for the effectiveness of a non-violent movement for radical change is a cooperative response from the dominant group. Precisely this condition was absent in the Algerian case, the French government being hesitant in passing and implementing reforms, and the settler leaders adamant in resisting Algerian initiatives for reform. Where appreciable sections of the dominant group respond favourably, the power of the movement is enhanced, and at the same time, the expression of racial or ethnic hostility is restrained. If, on the other hand, only small numbers of the dominant group participate in the movement for equality, they are immediate targets for suppression. The movement retains an exclusive character, and the situation becomes highly conducive to the processes of polarisation and escalating violence, which have been the subject of this study.[11]

11. An interesting discussion of terrorism, providing comparative material on aggregation, escalation of violence and elimination of the middle ground is to be found in A.R. Molnar et al., *Human Factors Considerations of Undergrounds in Insurgencies*, ch. 11.

10

Reflections:
Reform or Genocide

This states the choices in too stark a form, even in the extreme conflicts of sharply divided plural societies. Reform and violence are often intermingled, indeed violence may serve as midwife to reform. Perhaps it is true that violence or the imminent likelihood of violence is always present in significant social, economic or political reform.[1] And reforms may themselves be the catalyst of violence, depending on the structure of the society, the nature of the reforms, the manner of their introduction, the power available to control their consequences, and the policies pursued by the leaders.

But the alternatives are also much too stark from a different perspective, that of the nature of the violence. There are many restraints on the committing of genocide – the unwillingness of the parties to engage in so fearful a crime, the capacity of potential victims to defend themselves, and pressures from the outside world. After all, though violence is ubiquitous, genocide is still somewhat rare. Yet this volume deals with three conflicts which culminated in genocide, in the short span of a single decade, in three different societies (Rwanda, Zanzibar, Burundi) though under the same conditions of radical change initiated by decolonisation; and the Algerian struggle was not without

1. See the discussion of 'Reform and political change' in Samuel P. Huntington, *Political Order in Changing Societies*, 1968, ch. 6, and at p. 357. See also A.O. Hirschman (1963: ch. 5).

genocidal episodes. Fanon wrote in 1959 of 'the genocide that is rife in Algeria'.[2] Sartre, though more extreme than Fanon in his incitement to violence, and in some ways dehumanised by his passionate, but partisan, concern for humanity, is more cautious on this point. In a speech in which he charged the United States with genocide in Vietnam, he described colonialism as established by perpetual massacres of genocidal character, and as being by its very nature an act of cultural genocide, but he introduced the qualification that the settlers could not carry massacre to the point of physical genocide, because of their need to exploit the native peoples; by exterminating the sub-proletariat in Algeria, they would have exterminated themselves as settlers.[3] I have also used the phrase 'genocidal massacre' to describe such episodes in the Algerian conflict as the massive and indiscriminate reprisals of Sétif, or the wiping out of Muslim villages, or the annihilation of a European mining community, and I think this use can be defended.

All four case studies are of extreme plural societies, and these societies are specially vulnerable to genocidal conflicts. But the annihilation of Communists in Indonesia, and of tens of millions of ordinary citizens in Soviet Russia, is a reminder that massive slaughter in societies is not confined to the conflicts between racial, ethnic or religious groups in plural societies.

Genocide is somewhat ambiguously defined, and it is rather loosely applied in service to ideological interests. Some analysts argue the need for a highly restrictive definition, and for careful discrimination in charges of genocide, so as to preserve the term for the ultimate abomination. Too general a use of the term would weaken its sanctioning power. But this implies that genocide strikes horror, whilst on the contrary there must be many circles of powerholders for whom genocide is by no means horrifying, or not sufficiently horrifying to override considerations of political expedience. Certainly the United

2. See the preface to *A Dying Colonialism*, 1965, 29.

3. This argument was presented by Sartre in his charge before the International War Crimes Tribunal, convened by him and Bertrand Russell, that the USA was waging war in Vietnam with genocidal intent (*Ramparts*, Feb. 1968, pp. 37-43).

Nations, the Organisation of African Unity, and the Commission on Human Rights, the international organ of the United Nations, specially sensitised, in conception, to violations of human freedom, seem highly accommodating to genocide: at any rate, they have taken no action on the genocide in Burundi. Moreover, there are many disturbing indications of an increasingly callous public opinion, as in the reaction to the slaughter of innocent hostages by terrorists;[4] and public opinion does not seem to be specially outraged by genocide.

A more convincing argument can be made for an inclusive definition. This would be based on the assumption that in defining a crime, there is an implication that any action falling short of the commission of the crime is quite permissible. Hence to define genocide very restrictively, would seem to be license and encouragement for all manner of atrocity not constituting this extreme crime. But if there is accommodation to genocide in international circles and in public opinion, then the problem of a more restrictive or more inclusive definition ceases to be significant.

The Convention on Genocide, approved by the General Assembly of the United Nations in December 1948 defines genocide as

any of the following acts committed with intent to destroy, in whole or in part, a national, ethnical, racial or religious group, as such:

(a) Killing members of the group;
(b) Causing serious bodily or mental harm to members of the group;
(c) Deliberately inflicting on the group conditions of life calculated to bring about its physical destruction in whole or in part;
(d) Imposing measures intended to prevent births within the group;
(e) Forcibly transferring children of the group to another group.

The definition is vague on a number of aspects. An essential

---

4. The terrorists gamble that their inhumanity will prevail over the humanity of the authorities. If the authorities refuse to submit, then they too become party to the slaughter of innocents, and share in the indifference to atrocity. But if they do submit, then they encourage further atrocity.

element in the crime is the intent to destroy a group 'as such'. A distinction must be made between intent and motive, so that it would be no defence presumably to claim that the motive for the deliberate annihilation of a group was to create a new world order, or to bring a highly destructive war to a rapid end, as in the obliteration of Hiroshima by the United States, or to draw attention to the grievances of the murderers. Yet in the debate on the framing of the clause, there was divergence of opinion as to whether the phrase 'as such' implied genocidal motive.[5]

There is uncertainty also in the use of the words to destroy *in part*. Many atrocities have a genocidal quality to them, such as the wiping out of whole settlements, the indiscriminate killing in race riot and reprisal, the bombing of bars, cinemas, underground stations and airports, the random taking and slaughter of hostages. But the aim of the Genocide Convention was to deal with destructive violence against large numbers. How many must be massacred to constitute the crime of genocide, and from what perspective is this magnitude defined?

A most notable omission from the definition is the slaughter of political groups. The initial resolution of the General Assembly of the United Nations (Resolution 9611, Dec. 1946) specifically mentions the destruction, entirely or in part, of racial, religious, political and other groups. The definition in the Convention includes national and ethnical groups, but excludes 'political and other groups'. Hence, the massacre of Communists in Indonesia lies outside the purview of the genocide convention. So, too, in Soviet Russia, the destruction of millions of peasants (men, women and children), the slaughter of members of non-Bolshevik political parties, and of 'enemies of the people' and 'rightist opportunists', and the vast numbers killed in political and administrative purges of the regime, and the murder of many members of such professional categories as engineers, would not fall within the present definition of genocide, but presumably simply constitute 'social prophylaxis'. Only the partial destruction by the Soviet regime of religious groups and certain

5. See N. Robinson, *The Genocide Convention*, Part II, 16-17.

national groups would be included in the crime of genocide.

Among the main arguments for the omission of political groups was the contention that they did not have sufficient stability, that many states would not ratify the Convention if the destruction of political groups was retained in the definition of genocide, and that the inclusion of political groups might result in United Nations intervention in domestic political struggles (Robinson, 1949: 15). This conception of the inviolability of the domestic affairs of a state has been a cover for all manner of violations of human rights, comparable to the role of military necessity as a justification for actions which would otherwise constitute heinous war crimes.[6] It serves as a shield also against responsibility for genocide, since the measures taken may be presented as a matter of domestic concern, a domestic necessity in the interests of law and order, and the preservation of the integrity of the nation state. Externally there may be protection, too, as the leaders of other countries hesitate to condemn the genocide, and thus compromise, not only political alliances, but also their own freedom of domestic action.

The basis of genocide is the categorising of racial, ethnic or religious groups as targets for eradication. Collective responsibility, collective guilt attach to the group as such. By reason solely of membership in the group, men, women and children share an equal guilt to the death. The question of their personal responsibility or personal guilt becomes totally irrelevant. They fall outside the bounds of a common humanity, and hence outside the restraints on cruelty, atrocity and slaughter.

In the sharply divided plural society, under minority domination, many aspects of the social structure contribute to the probability of genocidal conflict. There is already an emphasis on collectivities, with differentiation in their rights and obligations. Similar patterns of discrimination in many sectors of the society

6. See the discussion by Richard Wasserstrom of 'The responsibility of the individual for war crimes' in Virginia Held, Sidney Morgenbesser and Thomas Nagel, *Philosophy, Morality and International Affairs*, Oxford University Press, 1974, 47-70.

give rise to generalised statuses of domination and subordination. Often a heavy component of violence is embedded in the laws of the society and in the structure of its relationships. Usually there is a past history of violence and perceptions of the antagonist as responsive only to violence.

Once the conflict is engaged, with acts of terrorism and repression, it readily generalises and escalates. Under challenge, the defence of privilege by the dominant group is likely to take on an extreme ferocity. The distinction made by Erich Fromm between defensive and malignant aggression hardly seems crucial at this stage; the defensive violence is not to be distinguished from malignant violence in its manifestations. The violent conflict moves rapidly between sectors, since these tend to have the same basic pattern of dominant and subordinate relationships, and since the specific issues of confrontation are the expression of a more deep-seated and general division within the society. In consequence, polarisation spreads throughout the whole society, particularly under the outrage of indiscriminate terrorism against members of the dominant group, and collective reprisals against the subordinates in contemptuous disregard of individual responsibility. Denigrating stereotypes, which served to justify the domination or the hatred, dehumanise the antagonist and prepare the ground for collective slaughter.

Under these circumstances, a heavy responsibility rests on those who initiate violence. They set in motion cycles of polarisation with no predictable outcome, apart from the certainty of more violence. Yet there are situations in which the leaders of subordinate groups are driven to conclude that they have no other means for freeing their people from the burden of their misery and oppression.

In most cases, a greater responsibility must surely attach to members of the dominant group. I have described the 'general laws' relating to regimes of minority racial or ethnic domination as persuasive. There is certainly a high probability that members of the dominant group will resist transformation of the society, that they will withhold or delay or sabotage reforms, and that they will resort to repression and violence in defence of their privileges. But they are not obliged to do so: the situation is not fully determined. They have a freedom of choice and it is usually their unwillingness to share power and wealth, and to respond to approaches from the subordinates, which finally provokes the desperate violence.[7] But there may be no wealth to share, and power is not merely power to achieve common objectives; it is also power over others. The leaders of the subordinate group, if unwilling to share power, may reject reforms in a bid for domination. And changes brought about by the reforms may in fact spark the conflagration they are designed to prevent.

The South African Government now confronts the dilemma of political choice in a particularly acute form. For a generation, and indeed to some extent for almost two generations, successive governments have been persecuting militant political opponents of racial domination under the pretext of a communist menace. Suddenly, and most ironically, following the liberation of Mozambique and Angola from Portuguese rule, this mythical menace has become quite concrete in neighbouring countries, armed with communist ideology and military technology, and this at a time when the South African policy of apartheid is regarded with almost universal loathing.

7. In commenting on my manuscript, Pierre van den Berghe writes: I fear I can offer nothing to relieve your experimental experienced pessimism and your humanistic despair, but perhaps sociobiology can take us a little further step toward comprehension of irrational violence, and toward its practical prevention. We know that human groups have a propensity to draw social as well as physical boundaries, and to defend these boundaries with unlimited ferocity. We also know that race and ethnicity are among the most explosive of these boundaries, very possibly because they are so readily interpreted in the most fundamental human (and, generally, animal) idiom of social boundary drawing, namely *kinship*. Ethnic and racial groups are quasi- or pseudo-descent groups. (The rhetoric of 'brotherhood' is not accidental.) There is also an element of quantity as well as of quality in the explosiveness of cleavages. The more macro-divisive (to use Schermerhorn's phrase) these cleavages are, the more volatile and dangerous. The policy implications are clear: the best state is that which most studiously refrains from recognising in any shape or form, and for whatever motive, these macro-divisive cleavages of ethnicity and race. I realise, of course, that there is an enormous element of wishful thinking in seeing the state in the position of neutral arbiter when it so frequently is nothing of the sort. So my prescription has little meaning for colonial societies; but perhaps it does for 'consociational democracies'.

Looking back over the history of South Africa, it is agonising to reflect how many opportunities were missed to promote greater equality of participation. There was a long period during which the society might readily have been transformed. Indeed the first of these missed opportunities goes back to the very founding of the Union of South Africa in 1910, when the British Government sacrificed African rights to the racism of many white settlers. But there remained an appreciable Coloured and African vote in the Cape Province, which had some political significance and might have been the basis for a progressive sharing of political power. In the 1930s South Africa entered a period of vast economic growth. The new wealth might have been distributed more equitably to reduce the quite extreme inequalities between the racial groups. An increase in African purchasing power would also have stimulated the economy, as was argued by a government commission of that period, the Social and Economic Planning Council. At the same time, the extensive industrialisation of the country could have provided Africans, Indians and Coloureds the opportunity to acquire ownership of the means of production. The pass laws are the very cornerstone of the whole system of racial oppression, denying elementary human rights and providing the basic machinery for a totalitarian control of African life. At the end of the Second World War, they might have been abolished in recognition of African military service and support of the war effort, as briefly mooted by the then Prime Minister, Field Marshall Smuts. The non-violent resistance campaign in 1952, directed primarily against the pass laws, offered a further occasion for liberating the society from the oppressive weight and brutality of the pass laws. In the great urban expansion, which attended economic growth, there must surely have been room for racially integrated neighbourhoods. And the appreciable sharing of a common religion, and innumerable ties across racial divisions, might have been the basis for cooperation in the restructuring of the society. So much misery, suffering, injustice, and humiliation could have been spared, with a great and liberating release of creative energy, and a readiness now to take the final steps in the movement to equality of participation and the full sharing of a common humanity.

Instead, successive regimes have systematised discrimination and perfected oppression in a whole series of laws, governing every aspect of social life and life chances. Under apartheid, the denial of a common humanity has been a cornerstone of policy, with the society computerised through the totalitarian regulation of racial identity. Far from extending political rights, the government in 1936 took a major step toward eliminating parliamentary representation, thereby demonstrating that the only effective guarantee for the protection of constitutional rights in South Africa is the power to resist infringement. Whites largely monopolised the new wealth and productive resources. Though there has been a rise in African standards of living, discriminatory wage and industrial laws still maintain the earnings of many African workers below a decent subsistence level, with an increased disparity in the per capita income of Africans and Whites. Ownership of the means of production remains a white prerogative, with only negligible rights for members of other racial groups. The pass laws were made even more rigorous and oppressive under the Abolition of Passes Act, and related legislation. They now provide machinery for the total control, and for the ruthless canalising, of African labour in the service of industry. Over the years, these laws have taken their criminal toll of millions and millions of Africans. The response to the non-violent campaign against the pass laws was an extreme repression, accelerating the movement to a police state. As to the many relationships across racial barriers, the South African apartheid government proceeded to restructure the entire society on a tribalistic basis, adopting the almost inconceivable strategy of systematically regulating, under penal sanctions, virtually the whole range of interracial relationships, so as to extirpate contacts on a basis of equality, and to create the maximum segregation compatible with the thoroughgoing exploitation of subject peoples.

By way of compensation for this total repression, the South African Government offers Africans the fraudulent policy of potentially 'independent' Bantustans. It is a fraudulent policy in the sense that it denies Africans basic human rights in their own land and in the wealth they helped create, and it forcibly imposes on them the acceptance of fragmented ruritanias, most not economically viable and presently little more than satellite reserves, though their changed status may offer the possibility of exerting pressure on the South African regime. Now, as the challenge to white domination becomes more threatening, will the government remain cemented into its policies of racial oppression, which seems to hold the status in its thinking of a sacred article of faith? And will it thereby take the responsibility for much suffering and destruction of life? Or will it now be ready to open the society to the peoples it has oppressed for so long, and to affirm their common humanity? And if it seeks a peaceful transformation, will outside powers extend assistance, or will they seize the opportunity to batten on internal division under the strain of political change?

Bibliography

A.M. 'Regards sur l'enseignement des Musulmans en Algerie', *Confluent*, serie 2, June-July 1963, 596-645.

Abbas, Ferhat. *La Nuit coloniale*. Paris: Julliard, 1962.

Africa Bureau. *Black/White Income Distribution in South Africa*. London: The Africa Bureau, Fact Sheet no. 43, September/October 1975.

Ageron, Charles-Robert. 'Les Algériens musulmanes et la France (1871-1919)', *Revue Historique*, 494, April-June 1970, 355-365.

Ageron, Charles-Robert. 'Brève histoire de la politique d'assimilation en Algérie', *La Revue Socialiste*, Nouvelle Série, no. 95 (March 1956, 225-236).

Ageron, Charles-Robert. *Histoire de l'Algérie contemporaine*. Paris: Presses Universitaires de France, 1969.

Arnault, Jacques. 'Note sur la nation algérienne', *Procès du Colonialisme: Les essais de la N. C. 1958*, 6, 269-276.

Aron, Robert. *Les Origines de la guerre d'Algérie*. Paris: Fayard, 1962.

Atterbury, M.C. *Revolution in Rwanda*. Madison: African Studies Programme, University of Wisconsin, 1970.

Batungwanayo, Charles. 'Burundi, le pourquoi d'un génocide', *Remarques Africaines*, no. 407 (1-15 Oct, 1972), 19-21.

Berque, Jacques. *Le Maghreb entre deux guerres*. Paris: Editions du Seuil, 1962.

Bimazubuke, Gilles. 'Une guerre civile au Burundi?', *Remarques Africaines*, no. 246 (July 1965), 21-24.

Bitterlin, Lucien. 'Des morts pour rien', *Esprit*, no. 354, Nov. 1966, 648-667.

Bourdieu, Pierre et al. *Travail et travailleurs en Algérie*. Paris: Mouton, 1963.

Bourdieu, Pierre (with Abdelmalek Sayad). *Le Déracinement: La Crise de l'agriculture traditionnelle en Algérie*. Paris: Les Editions de Minuit, 1964.

Bowen, M., G. Freeman and K. Miller. 'No Samaritan: the U.S. and Burundi', *Africa Report*, July-August 1973, 32-38.

Bowen, M., G. Freeman and Kay Miller. *Passing By: The United States and Genocide in Burundi, 1972*. New York: Carnegie Endowment for International Peace, 1973.

Bragard, Lucie. *Génocide au Burundi*. Brussels: Dossier Pax Christi, December 1972.

Bushayija, Stanislas. 'Plaidoyer pour la democratisation', *La Revue Nouvelle*, XXI, 5 (15 May 1960), 503-513.

Camus, Albert. *Actuelles, III. Chroniques Algériennes, 1939-1958*. Paris: Gallimard, 1958.

Centre d'information sur le Tiers-Monde. *Dossier Burundi*. Leuven: March 1973.

Chaliand, Gerard and Juliette Minces. 'L'Algerie algérienne', *Le Monde Diplomatique*, July 1972, 11-16.

Chevallier, Jacques. *Nous algeriéns*. Paris: Calmann-Lévy, 1958.

Cohen, Jean. 'Colonialisme et racisme én Algérie', *Les Temps Modernes*, vol. 11, no. 119 (Nov. 1955), 580-589.

Coleman, J.S. *Community Conflict*. New York: Free Press, 1957.

Confer, Vincent. *France and Algeria: The Problem of Civil and Political Reform, 1870-1920*. Syracuse University Press, 1966.

Constitution of Burundi, 11 July, 1974. *Issue*, vol. V, no. 2 (Summer 1975), 24-28.

Courriére, Yves. *Les Fils de la Toussaint*. Paris: Fayard, 1968.

Courrière, Yves. *Le Temps des léopards*. Paris: Fayard, 1969.

Courrière, Yves. *L'Heure des colonels*. Paris: Fayard, 1970.

Courrière, Yves. *Les Feux du désespoir*. Paris: Fayard, 1971.

Davidson, Basil. *In the Eye of the Storm: Angola's People*. New York: Doubleday, 1973.

de Heusch, Luc. 'Massacres collectif au Rwanda?', *Synthèses* (Bruxelles), vol. 19, no. 221 (Oct. 1964a), 416-426.

de Heusch, Luc. 'Mythe et société féodale – le culte du

Kubwanda dans le Rwanda traditionnel', *Archives de Sociologie des Religions*, vol. 9, no. 18 (July-Dec. 1964b), 133-146.

de Heusch, Luc. 'Nationalisme et lutte des classes au Rwanda', In W. Fröhlich (ed.) *Afrika im wandel seiner Gesellschaftsformen*. Leiden: E.J. Brill, 1964c, 96-108.

de Heusch, Luc. *Le Rwanda et la civilisation interlacustre*. Brussels: Institute of Sociology of the Free University of Brussels, 1966.

d'Hertefelt, Marcel. 'Les élections communales et le consensus politique au Rwanda', *Zaire*, vol. XIV, 5-6 (1960a), 403-438.

d'Hertefelt, Marcel. 'Stratification sociale et structure politique', *La Revue Nouvelle*, vol. XXXI, no. 5 (June 1960b), 449-462.

d'Hertefelt, Marcel. 'Myth and political acculturation in Rwanda', in Allie Dubb, ed., *Myth in Modern Africa*. Proceedings of the 14th Conference, the Rhodes-Livingstone Institute for Social Research. Lusaka: 1960c, 114-135.

d'Hertefelt, Marcel. 'Mythes et idéologies dans le Rwanda ancien et contemporain', in Vansina, Jan, Raymond Mauny and L.V. Thomas, eds., *The Historian in Tropical Africa* (London: Oxford University Press, 1964).

de la Guérivière, Jean. 'Après les tueries', *Le Monde*, 13-14, 15 January, 1974.

dos Santos, Marcelino. 'Interview on Mozambique Liberation Struggle', *Southern Africa*, vol. VII, no. 5, May 1974, 15-17.

du Bois, Victor D. *To Die in Burundi*. Part II: Foreign Reactions. American Universities Field Staff Reports, Central and Southern African Series, vol. XVI, no. 4, New York, September 1972.

Dunn, John. *Modern Revolutions: An Introduction to the Analysis of a Political Phenomenon*. Cambridge University Press, 1972.

Ellul, Jacques. *Autopsie de la révolution*. Paris, Calmann-Lévy: 1969.

Ellul, Jacques. *Violence*. London: S.C.M. Press, 1970.

Fanon, Frantz. *A Dying Colonialism*. Grove Press: New York, 1965 (first published in France in 1959).

Favrod, Charles-Henri. *La Révolution algérienne*. Paris: Librairie Plon, 1959.

Fromm, Erich. *The Anatomy of Human Destructiveness.* New York: Holt, Rinehart and Winston, 1973.

Gordon, David C. *The Passing of French Algeria.* Oxford University Press, 1966.

Great Britain: *Commission of Inquiry into Disturbances in Zanzibar during June 1961.* Report. London: Her Majesty's Stationery Office, 1961. Colonial paper no. 353.

Greenland, Jeremy. 'Black racism in Burundi', *New Blackfriars*, London. October 1973, 443-451.

Greenland, Jeremy. 'The two options now facing Burundi', *Issue*, vol. V, no. 2 (Summer 1975a), 3-5.

Greenland, Jeremy. *Human Rights in Burundi: The Government's Response to Criticism.* Paper presented at the 18th Annual Meeting of the African Studies Association, San Francisco, October 29-November 1, 1975b.

Heggoy, A.A. 'Arab education in colonial Algeria', *Journal of African Studies*, vol. 2, no. 2 (Summer 1975), 149-160.

Heggoy, A.A. *Insurgency and Counterinsurgency in Algeria.* Bloomington: Indiana University Press, 1972.

Held, Virginia, Sidney Morgenbesser and Thomas Nagel. *Philosophy, Morality and International Affairs.* London: Oxford University Press, 1974.

Henissart, Paul. *Wolves in the City. The Death of French Algeria.* New York: Simon and Schuster, 1970.

Hirschman, Albert O. *Journeys Toward Progress: studies of economic policy-making in Latin America.* New York: Twentieth Century Fund, 1963.

Höglund, Bengt. *Concepts of Conflict.* Uppsala University: Dept. of Peace and Conflict Research, Report no. 2, 1970.

Hourdin, Georges. 'Ce que fut l'attitude des chrétiens francais', *La Nef*, vol. 19, cahiers 12-13 (Oct. 1962-Jan 1963), 66-84.

Hubert, Jean-R. *La Toussaint rwandaise et sa repression.* Brussels: Academie Royale des Sciences d'Outremer, 1965.

Humbaraci, Arslan. *Algeria: A Revolution that Failed.* New York: Praeger, 1968.

Huntington, Samuel P. *Political Order in Changing Societies.* New

Haven: Yale University Press, 1968.

Julien, Charles-André. *L'Afrique du nord en marche*. Paris: Julliard, 1953.

Julien, Charles-André. *Introduction* to Pierre Nora. *Les Francais d'Algerie*. Paris: Julliard, 1961.

Kagamé, Abbé Alexis. 'Le pluralisme ethnique et culturel dans le Rwanda-Urundi', International Institute of Differing Civilizations, *Ethnic and Cultural Pluralism in Inter-tropical Communities*. Brussels, 1957: 268-293.

Kharusi, A.S. *Zanzibar — Africa's First Cuba*. Richmond: Foreign Affairs Publishing, 1967.

Kuper, Leo. 'Ideologies of violence among subordinate groups', in Kuper and Smith, eds., *Pluralism in Africa*, University of California Press: 1969, 153-167.

Kuper, Leo and M.G. Smith. *Pluralism in Africa*. Los Angeles: University of California Press, 1969.

Lacheraf, Mostefa. *L'Algérie: Nation et société*. Paris: Maspero, 1965.

Lacouture, Jean. *Cinq hommes et la France*. Paris: Editions du Seuil, 1961.

Lambert, Jacques. *Manuel de législation algérienne*. Algiers, Librairie des Facultés: 1952.

Le Secrétariat Permanent du Clergé. *Dossier Burundi*. Bujumbura, Dec. 1972.

Le Tourneau, Roger. *Evolution politique de l'Afrique du nord musulmane — 1920-1961*. Paris: Armand Colim, 1962.

Lebjaoui, M. *Vérités sur la révolution algérienne*. Paris: Gallimard, 1970.

Lemarchand, René. 'Political instability in Africa: the case of Rwanda and Burundi', *Civilisations*, vol. XVI, 3 (1966a), 307-337.

Lemarchand, René. 'Power and stratification in Rwanda — a reconsideration', *Cahiers d'Etudes Africaines*, vol. VI, 4 (1966b), 592-610.

Lemarchand, René. 'Social change and political modernisation in Burundi', *Journal of Modern African Studies*, 4, 4 (1966c), 401-433.

Lemarchand, René. 'Revolutionary phenomena in stratified societies: Rwanda and Zanzibar', *Civilisations*, vol. 18 (1968), no. 1, 16-51.

Lemarchand, René. *Rwanda and Burundi*. New York: Praeger, 1970.

Lemarchand, René and Jeremy Greenland. *Les Problèmes du Burundi*. Brussels: Colloque International, 27-28 December 1974.

Lemarchand, René. *Selective Genocide in Burundi*. London: Minority Rights Group, 1974a.

Lemarchand, René. 'Polarisation ethnique et violence politique', in Lemarchand, René and Jeremy Greenland, eds. *Les Problèmes du Burundi*. Brussels: Colloque International, 27-28 December, 1974b.

Lemarchand, René. 'Les incidences extérieurs de la crise', in Lemarchand, René and Jeremy Greenland, eds., *Les Problèmes du Burundi*. Brussels: Colloque International, 27-28 December 1974c.

Lemarchand, René. 'Ethnic genocide', *Issue*, vol. V, no. 2 (Summer 1975), 9-16.

Lemarchand, René and David Martin. *Selective Genocide in Burundi* (Part I by Lemarchand, Part II by Martin). London: Minority Rights Group, 1974.

Lentin, Albert-Paul. 'Pied noir', *Les Temps Modernes*, vol. 17, no. 193 (June 1962), 1781-1845.

Lettre Pastorale des Evêques du Burundi ('La justice est possible et la paix aussi'), Bujumbura, January 1973.

Lodhi, Abdulaziz Y. *The Institution of Slavery in Zanzibar and Pemba*. Uppsala: The Scandinavian Institute of African Studies, 1973.

Lofchie, Michael. 'The plural society in Zanzibar', in Kuper, Leo and M.G. Smith, eds., *Pluralism in Africa*. Berkeley: University of California Press, 1969, 283-328.

Lofchie, Michael. 'Was Okello's revolution a conspiracy?' *Transition*, vol. 7 (Oct./Nov. 1967) 36-42.

Machel, Samora. 'Sowing the seeds of liberation', *Mozambique Revolution* (Dar es Salaam), no. 49, Oct.-Dec. 1971.

Maquet, Jacques. *The Premise of Inequality in Rwanda*. London: Oxford University Press, 1961.

Maquet, Jacques. 'Rwanda-Urundi: the introduction of an electoral system for councils in a caste society', in Raymond Apthorpe, ed., *From Tribal Rule to Modern Government*. Lusaka: Rhodes-Livingstone Institute, 1959, 57-67. Proceedings of the 13th Conference.

Maral, Paul. 'La revolution bantoue au Rwanda', in *l'Afrique et l'Asie*, no. 69 (1965), 3-13.

Marsh, Ngaio. *Death at the Bar*. London: Collins, 1966.

Martin, David. *Selective Genocide in Burundi*. Part Two. London: Minority Rights Group, 1974.

Mathews, A.S. *Law, Order and Liberty in South Africa*. Los Angeles: University of California Press, 1972.

Mejer, Jan. *The May Events: A Theory of Disruptive Crisis*. Dissertation, University of California, Los Angeles, 1976.

Melady, Thomas Patrick. *Burundi: The Tragic Years*. Maryknoll, New York: Orbis Books, 1974.

Middleton, John and Jane Campbell. *Zanzibar: Its Society and Politics*. London: Oxford University Press, 1965.

Molnar, Andrew R. *Human Factors Considerations of Undergrounds in Insurgencies*. Washington, D.C.: American University, 1966.

Moore, Clement and Arlie Hochschild. 'Student unions in North African politics', *Daedalus*, Winter 1968.

Morris, Roger. 'The United States and Burundi: genocide, nickel, and "normalization"', *The Progressive*, April 1974, 27-29.

Mouvement des Etudiants Progressistes Barundi (MEPROBA). *Génocide au Burundi*. Brussels, May 1972. *Génocide séculaire*. Brussels, February 1973.

Mpozagara, Gabriel. *La République du Burundi*. Paris: Berger-Levrault, 1971.

Munyangaju, Aloys. *L'Actualité politique au Rwanda*. Brussels, 1959.

Murray, R. and Wengraf, T. 'The Algerian revolution', *New Left Review*, 22 (December), 14-65.

Nkundabagenzi, F. *Rwanda politique*. Brussels: Centre de Recherche et d'Information Socio-Politiques, 1961.

Nora, Pierre. *Les Francais d'Algérie*. Paris: Julliard, 1961.

Nordlinger, Eric A. *Conflict Resolution in Divided Societies*. Cambridge, Mass.: Harvard University, Center for International Affairs, 1972.

Nsanze, Terence. *L'Edification de la Republique du Burundi au carrefour de l'Afrique*. Brussels: Editions Remarques Africaines, 1970.

Okello, John. *Revolution in Zanzibar*. Nairobi: East African Publishing House, 1967.

Ouzegane, A. *Le Meilleur Combat*. Paris: Julliard, 1962.

Parsons, Talcott. 'The problem of polarization on the axis of color', in John Hope Franklin, ed., *Color and Race*. Boston: Beacon Press, 1968, 349-369.

Quandt, W.B. *Revolution and Political Leadership: Algeria, 1954-1968*. Cambridge: M.I.T. Press, 1969.

République du Burundi, Ministère d'Information. *Livre blanc sur les événements survenus aux mois d'avril et mai 1972*. Bujumbura, 1972.

Robinson, Nehemiah. *The Genocide Convention*. New York: Institute of Jewish Affairs, 1960.

Rose, Richard. *Governing Without Consensus*. Boston: Beacon Press, 1971.

Roux, J.P. 'Les troubles du Rwanda et du Burundi', *Revue française d'études politiques africaines*, 39, March 1969, 48-62.

Sahli, Mohamed-Chérif. 'De l' "assimilation" a l' "intégration": une mystification politique', *Les Temps Modernes*, vol. 11, no. 119 (Nov. 1955), 591-615.

Sartre, Jean-Paul. 'Le colonialisme est un système', *Les Temps Modernes*, vol. 11, no. 123 (March-April 1956), 1371-1386.

Sartre, Jean-Paul. 'On genocide', *Ramparts*, Feb. 1968, 37-43.

Servan-Schreiber, J.J. *Lieutenant en Algérie*. Paris: Julliard, 1958.

Sorel, Georges. *Reflections on Violence*. New York, Collier Books: 1967.

Soustelle, Jacques. *Aimée et souffrante Algérie*. Paris: Librairie Plon, 1956.

Statistique Général de l'Algerie. *Tableaux de l'économie algérienne*. Algiers: 1960.

Tillion, Germaine. *France and Algeria: Complementary Enemies*. New York: Knopf, 1961.

United States Department of State. 'Reply to Bowen, Freeman and Miller', *Africa Report*, July-August 1973, 38-39.

Van den Berghe, Pierre L. 'Bringing beasts back in', *American Sociological Review*, vol. 39, no. 6, 777-788

Vidal, Claudine. 'Anthropologie et histoire: le cas du Rwanda', *Cahiers internationaux de sociologie*, XLIII (July-Dec. 1967), 143-149.

Weinstein, Warren. 'Burundi: alternatives to violence', *Issue*, vol. V, no. 2 (Summer 1975), 17-22.

Weinstein, Warren. 'Conflict and confrontation in Central Africa: the revolt in Burundi, 1972', *Africa Today*, 19 (Fall 1972), 17-37.

Weinstein, Warren and Robert Schrire. *Political Conflict and Ethnic Strategies: A Case Study of Burundi*. Syracuse: The Programme of Eastern African Studies, Syracuse University, 1976.

Weinstein, Warren and Robert Schrire. 'Burundi: The politics of survival', *International Journal of Sociology*, forthcoming.

Weiss, Francois. *Doctrine et action syndicales en Algérie*. Paris: Editions Cujas, 1970.

Wingert, Norman. *No Place to Stop Killing*. Chicago: Moody Press, 1974.

Yacono, X. 'La France et les Algériens musulmans (1871-1919)', *Revue Historique*, 493, January-March 1970, 121-135.

Zanzibar Government. *Evidence presented to the Commission of Inquiry into Civil Distrubances on 1st June, 1961, and Succeeding Days*. Notes of Proceedings Taken by Treasury Reporter, mimeograph.

Zanzibar Legislative Council. *Report of the Select Committee Appointed to Enquire into the Public Order Bill. Sessional Paper no. 7 of 1959*. Papers laid before the Legislative Council during the year 1959, pp. 33-44.

INDEX

Abbas, Ferhat, 16-17, 25, 29, 31-32, 35, 41-46, 50-52, 60, 63-64, 69, 113, 133, 219, 255, 263, 273-274
Afro-Shirazi Party, 153ff., 223, 260
Ageron, Charles-Robert, 56, 60, 68, 72
Algeria; agrarian systems, 17, 211, 215; ambiguities, 57; assimilation, 19ff.; celebration of centenary, 16-17, 20; Constantine plan, 215; Délégations Financières, 22-23; economic differentiation, 17-18, 23, 25, 211, 215; education, 19, 212-214, 220; electoral fraud, 36, 49, 214, 217; employment, 18-19, 211-212; European Minority, 55; exclusive political organisation, 212, 258-260; failure of liberalism, 219; failure of middle ground, 265-270; failure of reformism, 15-40, 52ff., 266ff.; fraternisation at Forum of Algiers, 37, 53; French constitutional policy, 15-16; ideological polarisation, 255-256; inequality in educational opportunity, 20; *Manifesto of the Algerian People*, 31-32; *Organisation Spéciale*, 49; polarisation, 128-145; political inequality, 21, 212-214; political movements: *Association des Amis du Manifeste*, 32, 43, 263. *Association des Oulémas d'Algérie*, 24, 28, 30, 32. Barbouzes, 220. Communist Party, 25, 216. Etoile Nord-Africaine, 23, 28. *Fédération des élus indigènes d'Algérie*, 24, 44. FLN (*Front de Libération Nationale*), 38, 40, 51, 59, 215, 218. *Front de l'Algérie francaise*, 74. *L'Union Populaire Algérienne pour la Conquête des Droits de l'Homme et du Citoyen*, 29. *Mouvement National Algérien*, 130. *Mouvement pour le triomphe des libertés démocratiques*, 34, 49. OAS, 60, 75-83, 143-145, 214, 218-220, 254, 264-265. *Parti du Peuple Algérien*, 30, 32. Popular Front government, 16, 25, 28. *Union démocratique du Manifeste algérien*,

34, 43; reformism, 15-40, 52ff., 113-114, 122-123, 266ff., 277-286; relations with France, 16ff., 46ff., 269-275; revolution, 26, 55, 129, 139, 213; settlers and *indigènes*, 15-40, 63-64; settlers and the metropolitan government, 19, 28, 37, 56-61, 259-260, 269-270; Socialist-Radicals, 25; Socialists, 25; structural, cultural discontinuities, 211-221; structure, 10, 250
Algerian Muslim Congress, 25, 29
A.M., 20-21
APROSOMA (*l'Association pour la Promotion Sociale de la Masse*), 177, 183-184, 188, 229, 232ff.
Arabs; and Europeans, 73; and Mainland Africans, 146-147, 151, 221, 250; dominate ZNP, 152; founding of Arab League, 69; in Algeria, 17; Manga Arabs, 146-147, 158, 162-163; Omani Arabs, 146; in Zanzibar, 248
Arnault, Jacques, 58
Aron, Robert, 18, 29, 35, 63, 125, 211, 214
assimilation (Algeria); ambiguous policies, 19, 57; Blum-Viollette proposals, 16, 25; Ordinance of March 1944, 31, 33, 50; renunciation of Muslim status, 19, 22-23, 26, 30, 32, 60; settlers opposed to, 20; Statute of Algeria, 29, 33-35, 43, 48-50, 57, 59-60, 259, 269
Association des Amis du Manifeste, 32, 43
Association des Oulémas d'Algérie, 24, 28, 30
atrocities; cultural differences in definition and form, 132-133; in Algeria, 67, 130-131; in Burundi, 88-95, 97-99; in Rwanda, 236; reciprocity, 72-73, 139, 144; routinisation, 194; see also genocide, violence
Atterbury, M.C., 182

Batungwanayo, Charles, 202
Belhaddad, Mahdi, 217